TICKET
TO THE
MOON

ASTON VILLA: THE RISE AND FALL
OF A EUROPEAN CHAMPION

TICKET
TO THE
MOON

ASTON VILLA: THE RISE AND FALL
OF A EUROPEAN CHAMPION

RICHARD SYDENHAM

deCoubertin
B O O K S

First published as a hardback by deCoubertin Books Ltd in 2018.
This updated paperback version was published in 2019.

deCoubertin Books, 46B Jamaica Street, Baltic Triangle, Liverpool, L1 0AF

www.decoubertin.co.uk

ISBN: 978-1909245-97-6

Cover design by Thomas Regan/Milkyone. Typeset by Leslie Priestley.

*Every effort has been made to contact copyright holders
for photographs used in this book. If we have overlooked you in any way,
please get in touch so that we can rectify this in future editions.*

For my Dad, Derek;

my late grandad, Bill; and my little boy, Isaac,

four generations of Villains.

Contents

Introduction

I ONLY HAVE VAGUE RECOLLECTIONS OF ATTENDING THE FIRST professional football match in my life. It was Aston Villa against Crystal Palace at Villa Park on Saturday, 21 February 1981. Only the help of modern-day technology in the shape of web archives allow me to be so exact. I have better memories of another game in that momentous season when Villa swept aside John Neal's Middlesbrough 3–0. Apart from it being drizzly and Villa dominating, I have a more unusual recollection. I was sat in the front row of the Trinity Road Stand close to the managers' dugout and with only the advertising hoardings separating me from the gravel path that joined the muddied playing surface. I felt that close to the pitch I could almost tug on the shirt of Villa's flying winger Tony Morley. It was there on that day I shared a most important revelation to my father. 'Dad,' I said, 'I need a wee-wee.' Dad took one look at the congested front row we would have had to negotiate and replied: 'Do it here,' as he stood me up and encouraged me to wee into the short wall housing an advertising hoarding.

Aston Villa played a significant role in my development as a child. But I was not forced into my Villa upbringing; it felt natural and was actually a third generation evolving. My grandfather Bill, an asphalter, was a Villa supporter and his favourite player was the prolific Villa and England striker from the 1920s, Billy Walker. My dad Derek's favourite was rampaging frontman Gerry Hitchens. My older brother Jeff, who played for the county, was likened to Andy Gray because of his blond curly locks – and maybe his goalscoring too. So Villa was in the blood. Naturally, my son Isaac is now a fourth-generation Villa fan.

My early exposure to Villa Park gave me a more advanced insight into the workings of Aston Villa and football in general than many of my school-friends, who were likely playing *Star Wars* in their back gardens instead. Not that I wasn't immune to outside interests, but there was usually a link to Villa somewhere, such as the quest to complete my Panini football sticker album. Aston Villa players were always the most hotly sought after, obviously, with Villa's Gordon Cowans proving the most elusive. If I wasn't pestering Mum and Dad for another packet of stickers I would have been listening to a Duran Duran seven-inch vinyl. When I heard Duran Duran were predominantly Villa fans, it only added to the attraction of their catchy tunes.

The basic facts are known of Villa's progress during this period, in terms of conquering Europe, and then a decline so swift they were relegated just five years later. When I became a sports journalist in later years, that sudden rise-and-fall journey and the mostly untold events behind the scenes fascinated me. The question of what happened to cause such a fall from grace strengthened in my consciousness when I hosted low-key question and answer evenings with the likes of Gary Shaw, Tony Morley, Ken McNaught, Gordon Cowans and Jimmy Rimmer. The overriding message from those league championship and European Cup-winning players who I grew up idolising was that their team's success would have continued had it not been for the return of Doug Ellis as chairman in November 1982. I was tempted to side with the majority view but felt this was a subject that warranted greater investigation.

I set myself the challenge of writing my latest book on a subject close to my heart. I have not just aimed to glorify my childhood heroes but have attempted to expose a narrative that has never really been studied in the detail required to understand Villa's climb from the cusp of bankruptcy in 1968 to glory in the 1970s and early 80s. And then their painful fall thereafter. Despite brief seasonal highs, Aston Villa has never been the same since. I have tried to avoid taking sides and aimed to present the history of events in a transparent way that tells its own tale. Readers no doubt will develop their own opinions from the contents of these pages – adding to what some may know already.

My own view is that the controversial departure of manager Ron Saunders in February 1982 had a more damaging impact on Aston Villa's prospects of extended glory than Ellis buying back into Villa later that year, which tends to be the common belief. I feel Ellis receives much unwarranted criticism around this transition, as

ASTON VILLA: THE RISE AND FALL OF A EUROPEAN CHAMPION

some people not so close to events blame Ellis for Saunders' departure, when he was not even part of Villa then. The exodus of players from that team had begun prior to Ellis's return when Kenny Swain moved to Nottingham Forest in September 1982. Allan Evans submitted a written transfer request before Ellis returned, so things were not all rosy at Villa prior to his reclaiming of power.

Ellis, however, is far from blameless in Villa's subsequent decline. While his diligence at ensuring the club avoided financial problems before and after the Millennium, he was often overcautious and wrongfully placed more emphasis on cost-cutting and banking half-decent transfer fees than investing in the team. The Graham Turner years crystallised this failure. He allowed quality players like Gordon Cowans, Steve McMahon and Dennis Mortimer to leave, often without replenishing the stocks with similar quality. Too often, Ellis was happy for rookies, either from the reserves or another club, to step into the breach. There will always be players who demand that opportunity through their own ability such as Mark Walters, Tony Daley and Tony Dorigo, or Martin Keown from outside, but too many inadequate players were entrusted for too long in the first team. That policy cost the club eventually and led to what became an inevitable relegation in 1987. In fairness to Turner, this book will detail how he identified several quality players who were gettable, but Ellis traditionally refused to pay the market rate to buy in these higher-profile players – and he and the club paid the price. Fast forward to recent times, it was during moments of reflection on a bizarre period in the club's history, when a golden era quickly descended into chaos, anarchy and failure, that I knew I had to write this book to discover what the hell happened: why was a gradual and then sharp rise followed by such a sudden, humbling fall?

So where did I start with this book, other than the idea itself?

I wrote a list of more than fifty names I wanted to speak to who I felt would have important views on this period, and thankfully I attained the vast majority of those interviews. At the very top of that list were Ron Saunders, Doug Ellis, Graham Turner, Allan Evans, Tony Barton's family, and Steve Stride, who began at Villa as assistant secretary before he was made secretary in 1979. They were my top six targets, easily explained. Ellis and Saunders are clearly the two chief protagonists through the book. Ellis controlled the club twice and was twice ousted, once in 1975 when he was stood down as chairman and reduced to the rank of mere board director, and again in 1979 when his position on the board became virtually untenable and he was bought out by Ronald Bendall. Saunders managed Villa from 1974 to 1982; his stewardship was significant in the club's success but also led to several personality clashes that greatly affected Villa's internal workings. Barton and Turner were the managers after Saunders and it was important to ascertain their roles in the departure of many of the European Cup-winning players and how much influence they had on transfers in and out of Villa, as Ellis has generally taken the brunt of criticism over the years for most things that went awry. Evans was a player who was there from 1977, through to Graham Taylor's successful promotion campaign out of the Second Division in 1988; similarly Stride's longevity at Villa from the early 1970s into the new millennium meant he was also a key voice in observing all significant events at Villa Park.

The many interviews I conducted during the creation of this book were executed in a variety of ways, whether over the telephone with people like Kenny Swain, Jimmy Rimmer, Charlie Aitken and others, via email and the phone with Ron Saunders Jr on behalf of his father, or in person. All were greatly appreciated and the memories of those key conversations will stay in the memory.

At the time, I was writing weekly 'Lunch with a Football Legend' columns for the *Daily Star Sunday* and while meeting some of those guests who had relevant Villa links, I was able to use the meeting as an opportunity to go into more detail about their time at the club outside of what would be relevant to the paper. These players included Allan Evans, Paul Elliott over an orange juice at the Holiday Inn, Central London, Kenny Swain at the Hilton Hotel, St George's Park, when he was still coaching England age-group teams for the FA, Ken McNaught at the Rose and Crown near Redditch, Gary Shaw at The Plough in Harborne, Garry Thompson at a pub in Marston Green, near Birmingham Airport, Des Bremner Horse and Jockey in Sutton Coldfield, Colin Gibson at his lovely house in Sutton Coldfield, Gordon Cowans in Sam's Clubhouse Sports Bar at The Belfry and many more.

Allan Evans' interview took place at the St Mellion Hotel and Golf Resort near to his home in Saltash, Cornwall. I was only too pleased to pay for dinner as both his honesty and the detail of his memories were excellent. Evans, a long-time teetotaller, also introduced me to a refreshing summer drink of ginger beer and lime with ice.

I was delighted to accept an invitation from Doug Ellis to interview him at his magnificent house in Four Oaks, one of the more salubrious areas of Birmingham. My Land Rover looked quite lonely on the sizeable loose-stone driveway. His co-operative and long-term personal assistant Marion sat in with us in a rear dining room that looked out onto his back garden. He informed me it was the garden he had walked round with tears in his eyes when having to tell Graham Turner he was sacked. I felt Mr Ellis was impressed by the depth of my research and knowledge of proceedings at the club during the era discussed. But I also felt he was relieved when he showed me to his front door afterwards, for during the two hours we spoke I never held back with any difficult questions that had to be asked. Ultimately, he has been criticised for many things and it was only fair he had an opportunity to explain his side of the story.

I was slightly frustrated not to come away with more detail on certain topics like the sale of players in the early 1980s, but he did maintain he never once ordered a manager to sell a particular player. This goes against the grain of common perception. However, Graham Turner, who has rarely spoken in detail of his Villa days, gave me a very honest interview in which he maintained he was in total control of player transfers in and out of the club. After thirty years have passed, why would he do anything other than say it as it was? So I genuinely feel Ellis was not as responsible for some controversial player sales as we have been led to believe over the years. There is no doubt, though, Ellis put managers under great pressure to bring in money before he would sanction reinvestment on new players.

Due to illness, Ron Saunders' quotes and experiences from his time at Villa were derived via the assistance of his son, Ronnie. The detail surrounding his exit from Villa Park is, in my opinion, extraordinary. This has always been a key development at the club that has been shrouded in mystery and I was very pleased to be able to clear up this matter more than I feel has ever been done in the past. This is not a failing of any other writers but just that Saunders has been such a private and introverted character since his retirement from football in 1987. My book presented an opportunity for him to set the record straight once and for all and also to respond to some comments that were not so complimentary. I was very grateful that the Saunders family kindly assisted me on these themes. On trips up to the West Midlands from his Essex home, Ronnie Jr discussed the topics I had raised by email with his father and mother, Breda, and I remain indebted to them for their time answering my questions and approving what I had written on certain sensitive subjects.

So many ex-player interviews were also wonderfully candid and insightful. Former right-back and Holte End hero John Gidman met me along with his friends over a pint of lager – and a bottle or two of red in his case – in The Plough, situated in the pretty Staffordshire village of Shenstone. His dislike for Saunders was still clear so many years after. And Andy Gray's comments were recorded over two phone interviews, such was the importance of what he had to say of his two spells with Villa as a player. He was speaking from Doha, Qatar, where he now works as a pundit for sports television network beIN Sports.

One final but not insignificant detail I would like to mention was how I managed to obtain secret boardroom minutes from the years that this book covers. Officials at the club, when Tom Fox was chief executive, allowed me to spend two full days in a cosy, book-cluttered, broom cupboard-like room above the ticket office in Aston Villa's main car park, where I leafed through thousands of pages of club documents that related to the time I was writing about. They covered topics such as player sales, transfer targets, financial information and general club developments. It felt like I had stumbled upon artefacts that were being hidden from the public domain, as private club documents usually are, but which were begging to be written up to assist with the telling of this story. I am extremely grateful to Aston Villa Football Club for opening up this archive and enabling me to tell this story with much more accuracy than might otherwise have been possible.

Richard Sydenham, October 2018

Foreword by Andy Gray

MY RELATIONSHIP WITH THE HOLTE END WAS ONE OF THE MOST awesome things to happen to me as a footballer. I remember lots of games but one of the most vivid memories I have was a game I didn't play in. I signed for Villa on Friday, 26 September 1975, and on the Saturday it was the Birmingham derby at Villa Park – which Villa won 2–1. I hadn't a clue what to expect and had not even heard about the rivalry before. Remember, I was a Glasgow boy brought up watching Rangers and the big games I was accustomed to were the Rangers–Celtic clashes. So here I was, aged nineteen and with no idea what was about to hit me on that day. I came out of the tunnel and saw the old Witton Lane Stand but as I turned right to face the Holte End and walk up the touchline, this wall of claret and blue greeted me and the noise was incredible. There were more than 53,000 supporters present that day; the atmosphere was amazing and my eyes were popping out of my head. I thought, 'I can't wait to get into the team and play in front of this.'

I scored a header against Pat Jennings in the Tottenham goal in my first league game at home. From that point onwards there was a bond between me and the supporters. I always felt that what the Villa fans saw in me was themselves. They knew, even if I didn't play well, that I wouldn't have left that pitch without having given everything I had to the club. We both admired each other. I never worried about getting hurt or getting kicked in the face if I thought I could score a goal. It's a pity more players today don't feel the same. Players today are more frightened of getting hurt; I wasn't. I used to joke, 'Where there's no sense, there's no feeling!' That's why I put my head in where others wouldn't. My job was to win games, to score goals and make the fans happy. That's what I went out every Saturday or every Wednesday to try and do.

This book details the club's incredible rollercoaster journey through the 1970s and 1980s, including the part I played in it. I left Villa acrimoniously to join Wolves in 1979 because I fell out with the manager Ron Saunders, but before we had those problems I learned so much at the club and loved my time there. The training was great and even when Ron wanted to leave the strikers out of his drills to organise his defence and midfield, I understood what he was trying to do. It is part of being young and learning your profession. I got all that at a very early age. I was happy to train every day with the coach Roy McLaren, Brian Little, John Deehan and maybe the reserve goalkeeper. You did sometimes feel out of it, but I understood the bigger picture. Ron was all about the team ethic and I bought into that 'all for one and one for all' mentality. We had some great times and I am sure you will enjoy reading in here about the glory days again, such as our 5–1 win over Liverpool when they were European champions, the League Cup wins in 1975 and 1977 and obviously the league championship and European Cup wins after I left.

People have asked me over the years whether I was envious about missing those successes. The answer: not at all. Villa did brilliantly. There were a lot of players there that I got on well with and who are still friends of mine. People like Gary Shaw, Peter Withe, Gordon Cowans. They deserved their success and worked hard for it. I wish it had been Wolves winning what they won, but it wasn't to be.

That team was a good side that achieved amazing things – probably overachieved if I'm being honest. I think they would have found it really difficult to have emulated what they did that year. They had two fantastic seasons where things could barely have gone any better. Teams need a bit of luck to win big trophies and Villa had that – they never suffered many injuries and used only fourteen players when they won the league, which was a quite extraordinary feat. Even with Tony Barton as manager in the following season, after Ron Saunders' departure, they won the European Cup, which was equally extraordinary.

The players that went should not have been irreplaceable. Gordon Cowans was a magnificent player – I love Sid – and Tony Morley was a huge part of that team, but I don't think it was a case that they lost players. I think it was the case that they overachieved in the first place. Maybe that was the pinnacle. We were a bit like that at Everton in the mid-80s when we won the FA Cup, the league, the European Cup Winners' Cup, then finished second in the league, then won the league again. So, Everton had a run of about four or five years – maybe twice as long as Villa – when they were very, very good and not too many players left and few came in. It's not easy to recruit at Aston Villa and that has always been the case, while competing against the big boys. Villa maybe let it slip at a time when they shouldn't have done.

I would expect anyone who was part of that team to believe that they could have had prolonged success if they had stayed together – but we will never know. I loved Shawsy and Sid Cowans, there's no doubt they were exceptional players. Maybe they would have gone on and won a league again, but they never really got close again after that great season of 1980/81.

It's just a shame that Villa haven't been able to move on to that level again since, which is what this book will detail: how the club managed to rise to be European champions and then slip so suddenly from those heights.

I suppose the million-dollar question is this: can Villa ever return to those glory days of the early 1980s? Well, the summer of 2015 was a good measuring stick whereby over £50 million was spent on twelve players or more, but they lost their two best players, Christian Benteke and Fabian Delph. Was that ever going to make them a better team? No, and of course they were sadly relegated to the Championship. If Villa are ever to return to their glory days of challenging at home and in Europe it is going to take an astronomical investment to the tune of around £300 million on player recruitment over a number of seasons. To ever replicate their title-winning feats of 1980/81 would take years, huge investment and management skills that we haven't seen for a long time.

Ultimately, Villa Park, in the middle of England with its great support – that place should be jumping every week. Villa fans like to see a certain brand of football: fast, attacking football and not frightened to have a go, which is how we tried to play under Saunders. Yes, you have to back off and defend, but when you get the ball, explode forward with pace and a cutting edge. The glory days have been away for too long but there's always hope for the future. For now, you'll have to make do with reading about them in here instead.

Andy Gray 210 Villa appearances, 78 goals

Doug Ellis and His Villa Revolution

'It was an absolute disgrace what was going on – there was no money anywhere. There was very little to get excited about at Aston Villa other than representing the club and being part of its history.' – **Charlie Aitken**

IT WAS JULY 2006 AND DOUG ELLIS WAS A CHAIRMAN ATTEMPTING to deal with a mutiny, two months before he sold Aston Villa for £62.6 million.

Dissatisfied players under the management of David O'Leary took the unusual step of leaking a statement to the media. They complained of a growing culture of frugality that was harming the club's growth and limiting ambition. They listed cutbacks from significant ones like investment in the team and the scrapping of an £8 million renovation of their training facilities to smaller albeit just as frustrating examples, such as how the club had ceased paying for the team's masseur, refusing to pay the £300 fee for watering the training pitch and even rejecting an expenses claim for a cup of coffee that the physiotherapist had purchased at an airport café en route to meeting a first-team player. Ellis, known in his early Villa days to tour the ground switching off lights before he left for home, was renowned for his keen eye towards the balance sheet, but these savings were clearly taking austerity to the extreme.

It must be said Ellis's affection for and attachment to the club could rarely be questioned, irrespective of the thoughts of his detractors. His subsequent sale to American tycoon Randy Lerner would indicate that further investment in the club then would have been foolhardy on his part, even if this cost-cutting logic was seemingly taken too literally. Many fans were grateful for his ability to keep Villa in the black at times when other clubs were facing liquidation through overspending but, equally, fans were frustrated by his overly careful approach to ambition. Fans, staff and the players felt the club should have tried harder to compete with the traditional powerhouses of the domestic game.

So why is this unflattering farewell relevant at the start of this story? Quite simply: irony. It is ironic how journeys start, how they progress along the way and how they end. Ellis's journey demonstrates the fickleness of football, when his initial positive influence is analysed, devoid of hindsight. However, his desire for control over or at least influence on the player transfers that contributed towards the club's slide after winning the European Cup scarred his legacy. Ellis was instrumental in dragging the club up from the edge of oblivion in the late 1960s and early 70s, helping to set it on its way to being a European power. Yet, appreciation seemingly eroded over time, as Ellis's time as either chairman or board member at Aston Villa Football Club would eventually number 36 years, after his first involvement in 1968.

So, what do we know of Herbert Douglas Ellis?

He was born on 3 January 1924, in the village of Hooton, Wirral. He lost his father when he was just three years old, due to pleurisy and pneumonia brought on by gas attacks sustained in the trenches during the First World War. He and his younger sister were then raised by his mother and this tough upbringing instilled in him a will to succeed in life through hard work. Ellis was a keen footballer in his youth but schoolboy trials with Tranmere Rovers were as far as his limited ability would take him – on the pitch. The closest he would ever come in those days to rubbing shoulders with the legends of the game he was so passionate about were occasional impromptu meetings with England great Tom Finney at a bus stop.

This was after Ellis's work at the travel agency for Frame's. It says much about the mentality of football stars of that generation that Ellis returned home after work one day to be told by his first wife that Finney – nicknamed 'The Preston Plumber' – had been atop their third-floor flat and fixed the leaking roof free of charge, after Ellis had casually spoken of it at the bus stop. His work at the travel agency impressed his boss Wallace Frame enough for him to be sent to Birmingham to manage a fresh enterprise at New Street Station. He arrived in 1948 and the city became his adopted home. Ellis outgrew Frame's and he started his own operation, identifying the growth areas in the travel industry, exploiting the package holiday boom in the 1950s and 60s. Once settled in

England's second city, he started watching Aston Villa and Birmingham City matches to fuel his appetite for live football. By 1952 he was able to buy season tickets at both clubs, soon becoming a shareholder at Villa. In 1955 he secured shares in Birmingham City also. His association with City jumped to board member status by November 1965 courtesy of his flourishing business reputation locally and the contacts he was making. Curiously, Ellis had first been invited onto the Villa board earlier that year only to be blackballed by other directors who he felt were envious of his wealth and success. Instead, he lent his support to their fierce rivals.

'You won't experience any blackballing at this club, Doug,' director Jack Wiseman told him. 'We will be happy to have you.' And his money, more to the point. Ellis would subsequently join Villa. He later considered his three-and-a-half years at Birmingham City an education in how not to run a football club.

'Ever since I came down from the northwest in 1949, I was an Aston Villa man,' Ellis insisted. 'I had two season tickets and would watch Villa one week and Birmingham the next, or whoever was playing at home out of the two. I would work until twenty past one and then leave for the match. Even when I was on the board at Birmingham my thoughts and loyalty were always with Aston Villa. At Birmingham City, there was a general lack of energy, organisation and leadership, which was a reason why I left and also a huge lesson for when I joined the Villa board.'

In 1968, Manchester United, with the much-lauded talents of Bobby Charlton, George Best and Denis Law, became the first English club to win the European Cup, beating Portuguese heavyweights Benfica in the final. It was also the year Villa's neighbours West Bromwich Albion won the FA Cup through a Jeff Astle goal and finished as the Midlands' leading club in eighth place of the top tier. Events at Aston Villa at this time were far less auspicious. The team finished sixteenth in the old Second Division in the 1967/68 season, twelve places and fifteen points behind their bitter city rivals Birmingham. The next season followed a similar pattern.

If the team was struggling to be competitive on the pitch, the club was failing on a much greater scale off it. Villa Park was in total disrepair and the board did nothing. The supporters' ire peaked on 9 November 1968 when they staged a protest against the board at Villa Park and in Birmingham's city centre after Villa lost 1–0 at home to Preston North End, sending the team crashing to the foot of the table. Just 13,374 attended the match, comparing poorly to the 50,067 that had watched the Birmingham derby a year earlier. The fans had had enough and they railed against chairman Norman Smith, a director since 1939, and the board. The local *Sunday Mercury* newspaper reported the next day that one thousand supporters had entered the playing area after the game and gestured angrily towards the directors' box. A police chief superintendent was quoted describing the events as the most violent protest of its type he had witnessed at the ground. The club had reached its nadir, certainly off the pitch.

Businessman Smith was once a local football referee and he cared about Aston Villa. His love for the club during his two years as chairman, though, was more like that of a passive custodian, bereft of any financial powers to make a difference in the improvement of the club on and off the park.

Enter self-made millionaire Ellis and his business associate and London merchant banker Pat Matthews, who would become club president while spearheading Villa's renaissance by structuring the new board – though he was happy for Ellis to be the new face of Villa on a day-to-day basis.

Villa were desperately in need of a cash injection and new ideas to move forward. Unlike three years earlier, Ellis's intervention and business acumen were now desired. And the role of Matthews, whose brainchild was a then-unprecedented share issue in the spring of 1969 that raised £205,835, should not be underestimated. That financial influx wiped out the old debt and powered the new Aston Villa towards a healthier future.

'One of the problems at the Villa in the sixties was the board,' explained Villa's legendary left-back Charlie Aitken, who made a club-record 660 appearances from 1959 to 1976. 'The board didn't want to spend any money and none of the directors put any money into the club, which wasn't being run properly. I could see that a mile away. We had a beautiful training ground that they sold to builders for something like £25,000. So we had to go to places like Delta Metals and Fort Dunlop and train at these factory grounds. Doug and Pat Matthews rejuvenated the club when it was on its knees. It was an absolute disgrace what was going on – there was no money anywhere. There was very little to get excited about at Villa other than representing the club and being part of its history.'

Goalscoring winger Harry Burrows further emphasised the point of how Villa's frugality was hurting its development and reputation among the players. He helped Villa win the inaugural League Cup in 1961 with a goal in the two-legged final and continued to find the net frequently thereafter. But in the 1964/65 season he asked for a rise on his £20-a-week salary. The new manager Dick Taylor continually refused him until Burrows finally had enough and slapped in a transfer request. Taylor then offered him the raise, but it was too late – the damage was done. Stoke City, supposedly inferior to Villa, bought him and soon doubled Burrows' wages. He became a hero with the Stoke fans for the next eight years. Villa's frugal culture has been a common theme through the years.

Ellis became a director and chairman-elect at Villa Park on 17 December 1968, joining the club as part of a rescue operation. The old club was widely respected but mostly for its pre-war feats. It had won English football's top league six times, but never since 1910. It had won the FA Cup seven times, but only once in almost fifty years. Villa's lack of success on the pitch was a clear indictment and reflective of its off-field leadership. The club was edging towards bankruptcy when Ellis arrived. 'You could write your name in the dust, window frames were rotting, the smell of failure and imminent financial ruin hung in the air,' recalled Ellis. Even catering operations were inadequate. A favourite story from one frustrated club insider of the time recalled how a catering assistant refused to sell the last pie on a match day to a supporter because she was saving it for 'a regular'. Things had to change.

The total assets of the club then, including the stadium and the land, were £203,770. Until the share issue, there were debts of over £200,000, while attendances had dropped alarmingly. Tougher times and relegation to the Third Division were almost inevitable, but Ellis was not to be deterred. He translated his business skills from the travel industry to football and was a pioneer in encouraging the football club to develop sophisticated hospitality boxes, starting in the Trinity Road Stand. He also resourced a public relations employee – Eric Woodward – because he felt Villa's image needed improving in the regional and national eye. He contributed himself in that regard, announcing in his first press conference – with the bravado that marked his reign throughout – that he wanted Villa Park to become a 365-day-a-year multi-purpose stadium, adding, 'I want Aston Villa to be another Real Madrid.'

While Ellis was notoriously egotistical, he was also commercially savvy in a way that benefitted Aston Villa hugely in those early days of financial recovery. His ravenous appetite for the club to generate income was never better displayed than when he struck a deal with local car sales outlet Bristol Street Motors. Ellis wrote in his autobiography *'Deadly Doug'* that BSM agreed to pay the club £3,000 if the company's advertising hoarding received at least three minutes of TV air time throughout the whole season. Prior to the final game, it looked as though the £3,000 would be lost due to a lack of brand exposure. Enter Ellis, who would rather have poked knitting needles in his eyes than lose £3,000 of advertising revenue. He addressed the players in an effort to ensure the camera's attention was on a particular area of the pitch, where the advert was placed. Some managers would not have appreciated such distractive thoughts, but this was Doug Ellis and it was his club. So what happened? Winger Willie Anderson collapsed in a heap injured – supposedly – just in front of the relevant advert. The physiotherapist's treatment was captured perfectly in front of the branding on television. Anderson earned a £100 bonus for his ingenuity and Villa banked the £3,000.

Once ensconced in his new project that was the rebirth of Aston Villa Football Club, Ellis invited Harry Kartz onto the board along with Harry Parkes, who had played for Villa between 1939 and 1955 before establishing an eponymous sports shop that became well-known in Birmingham. Kartz also had Villa in his heart, having been a supporter since his father took him along from an early age. 'My first game was in 1919,' a 101-year-old Kartz reflected at his Solihull home, shortly before his passing in 2016. 'I well remember goalscorers like Pongo Waring and Billy Walker and Arthur Dorrell on the wing, Frank Barson at centre-half, goalkeeper Sam Hardy and Tommy Weston at left-back. I saw all the old players of that generation. Villa was in my blood. I later joined the shareholders' association before Doug invited me onto the board, as we were friends from business. The club was having a bad time when I joined Doug. The finances weren't good but Doug sorted it all out.'

Jim Hartley, a self-made businessman from the motor industry, and Bob Mackay, a successful estate agent, were also added to the board. Dick Greenhalgh, with an engineering background, came on in August 1971, lasting just a year on a persistently squabbling board.

The old regime had already sacked manager Tommy Cummings as the team veered towards relegation to the Third Division. Arthur Cox was installed as caretaker manager, before charismatic Scotsman Tommy Docherty became Ellis's first manager after impressing Pat Matthews with his knowledge of the squad. The early interactions between Ellis and Docherty were amusing but laced with a hint of seriousness.

When Ellis inquired in his first meeting with Docherty why he wanted to manage Aston Villa, the manager-elect explained it was he who had been approached, by Pat Matthews, and not the other way around before ending his answer with '... Doug,' to which Ellis replied, 'Mr Chairman, if you don't mind.'

'You're not the chairman yet,' Docherty responded, swiftly. Ellis would soon take up the role.

As many a manager would later discover, there was only ever one winner when taking on Ellis. Immediately, attendances tripled and optimism grew with the dynamism of Ellis in the boardroom and the flamboyant, outspoken Docherty as manager. Docherty's initial task was trying to keep Villa in the Second Division while also attempting to strengthen the squad on a limited budget. It was a tough ask. The signing of Bruce Rioch, who arrived in July 1969 along with his brother Neil in a joint deal for £100,000 from Luton Town after Villa had avoided relegation, suggested the club was willing to invest again.

'Doug wanted to sign someone for £100,000,' remembers secretary Alan Bennett, who had arrived from Chelsea, where he was assistant secretary during Docherty's reign. 'Doug would have signed me if I'd cost £100,000. I'm not saying the Rioch brothers weren't worth it but Doug wanted to make a statement.' Docherty also signed Ian 'Chico' Hamilton from Southend for £40,000 despite having sold him when he was Chelsea boss.

The successful bid for the Rioch brothers was Docherty's eighth bid of £100,000 that summer, to emphasise his proactivity in the transfer market and the still-new board's willingness to back him. He tried to prise Jimmy Greenhoff from Birmingham City and also Tommy Craig from Sheffield Wednesday, but Villa were not an attractive proposition to everyone.

Results in the 1969/70 campaign demonstrated how the situation had to worsen before real progress could be made. The first game of that season saw the debuts of Bruce Rioch, Hamilton and Pat McMahon, but Ron Saunders' Norwich City team won 1–0. Results did not improve and Ellis showed early evidence of his ruthless streak when Docherty was fired after a 5–3 loss to Portsmouth on 17 January 1970, even though he was not even halfway through a three-year contract. He was the first of Ellis's eleven eventual managerial sackings; the two other managers who served under him – Graham Taylor and Brian Little – resigned.

'The Doc was a good manager but he wasn't as good a coach, while Arthur Cox at that stage wasn't a thinking coach either,' Bennett believes. 'I remember them being very optimistic in the summer I came in and after watching a pre-season friendly, Tom [Docherty] said, "What you think?" I told him I thought we would struggle. He didn't share my view.'

Former Villa player and ex-Wales international Vic Crowe was appointed as Docherty's successor in the month of his 38th birthday. Crowe had played at Villa for twelve years from 1952, and was on the staff as manager of the reserves. His initial four-month tenure resulted in relegation, but that time was long enough for the board to detect a general improvement in the team's play and earn him a longer contract. Villa's relegation in that 1969/70 season to the third tier of English football meant they had plummeted to the lowest point in their history. Never before had Villa played below the top two leagues, where they had to spend the next two seasons.

Out of darkness came light. During these desperate times there were encouraging signs that would help chart the club's journey back towards the top.

Crowe was not the board's preferred appointment but they realised with relegation looming and little money in the bank for new players, a higher-profile manager would not then have been attracted to Villa, so Crowe landed the job by default. Another former Villain, Ron Wylie, was hired as his assistant. Villa finished fourth in the 1970/71 season, missing out on the top two promotion places. The one major highlight was reaching the League Cup final at Wembley, having defeated Manchester United in the two-legged semi-final. The 2–0 loss to First Division side Tottenham Hotspur reflected little of Villa's attacking threat and ball possession in the match. Ultimately, two Martin Chivers goals settled the game, which still represented progress as Villa chased better times.

Shrewd transfer activity powered the squad's push for promotion back into the Second Division. Goalscoring winger Ray Graydon joined from Bristol Rovers in the summer of 1971, while Crowe also added the key signings of future captains and defenders Ian Ross from Liverpool and Chris Nicholl from Luton. These new recruits, made possible only because of the unexpectedly high gate receipts from Villa's League Cup run, helped secure Villa the Third Division championship.

Crowe and Wylie saw goals in Graydon – whether he was scoring or creating them with his pinpoint deliveries from the right flank – and he would become a club legend with 81 goals in 232 appearances, collecting two League Cups along the way. Graydon had struggled to make a successful football career initially; he trained with Bristol City as a teenager yet they rejected him before he had a single first-team opportunity. Local rivals Bristol Rovers instead gave him his chance and he flourished thereafter. 'I went up to Birmingham to meet Vic Crowe and Ron Wylie and signed for about thirty pounds a week but I would have signed for a penny,' Graydon recalled. 'I was just so overawed by the club. I'd never been there before and thought it was unbelievable to be wanted by a club that size. It was clear they were going places.'

Optimism had returned to Villa Park.

Third Division Villa Host Pelé

*'It needed someone with drive and enthusiasm to shake Aston Villa
out of its very serious malaise and Doug Ellis did that.
When I joined the board in '72, he was all about doing what was right
for the club. He spent so much of his life at Villa.
You can't fault his drive and enthusiasm through those years.'* – **Alan Smith**

WHILE PROGRESS WAS BEING MADE ON THE PITCH, THE BOARD
started to develop the club off it. They purchased their Bodymoor Heath training
ground, located half a mile from The Belfry golf course in rural Warwickshire,
from a local farmer for £65,000. The 20-acre site was opened in December 1971.
Director Harry Kartz immersed himself into improving youth development to
encourage a better feeder system, designed to filter talent into the first team. There
were clear examples that Villa during this era were willing to place faith in youth.
Jimmy Brown made his Villa debut at Bolton Wanderers on 17 September 1969
when aged just 15 years and 349 days to become the club's youngest first-team
player. He became Villa's youngest captain three seasons later, aged 19. But in 1975
new manager Ron Saunders chose to sell him to Preston North End and Brown
completed an unfulfilled career by retiring at 28.

The two-legged FA Youth Cup final victory over a Liverpool team that included
future England star Phil Thompson in 1972 was the first measurable reward for
Villa's new vision towards youth. And that title was won while Villa were still a
third-tier club. 'Doug and I ran the show at Villa and it was Doug who asked me to

improve the youth set-up,' revealed Kartz. Chief scout Peter Doherty, who managed Northern Ireland in the 1958 World Cup and later spotted Kevin Keegan at Scunthorpe United for Liverpool, led that process. 'We used to go all over the country,' Kartz added. 'I didn't get paid for this role and I was so passionate, it cost me my engineering business. While I was busy with Villa, my executives formed their own company and took most of my business with them. I don't blame them; I was always at Villa.'

The club's newfound dedication to youth was further vindicated when it produced first-teamers like Brian Little, John Gidman, Bobby McDonald and goalkeeper Jake Findlay, who all played in that FA Youth Cup final.

The progression of right-back Gidman and forward Little represented some of the club's most pleasing development work – ever. Both were capped by England – though only once, which many Villa supporters regard as a travesty of justice. Nonetheless, any disappointment at their lack of an international career was somewhat compensated by their hero status with the Villa faithful. Ellis's delight at the flourishing youth project meant he took on a role with some of its success stories in keeping with that of a supportive uncle long into the future.

Gidman derived from what he describes as a 'Liverpool daft' family, so naturally he was desperate to fulfil his father Jack Gidman's dream and play in the red of Liverpool – at a time when Bill Shankly had cultivated a winning mentality. He was on course to do just that when he became part of the schoolboy set-up at Anfield – until the legendary manager shattered his and his father's dream.

'Shankly was a brilliant manager, a legend,' Gidman recalled. 'I didn't have a lot to do with him, until he called me in the office and told me I was shit.

'[Former England goalkeeper] Tony Waiters was in charge of their youth team and he didn't fancy me because I'm not a yes-man. He advised Shankly to get rid of me. So Shankly called me in and read the reports that I had no skill and the wrong attitude to be a pro footballer – anything you needed to be a pro footballer I didn't have! I was almost sixteen and they wanted me to quit, but my father made me stick with Liverpool. He said, "Look, you're not the brainiest, you're not going to get a job, so stay with it and keep earning."'

Fortunately for Gidman, Waiters moved on and Liverpool club stalwart Ronnie Moran came in and converted him into a right-back from a winger. Liverpool eventually released him all the same; although Moran had requested a rethink on Gidman, Shankly refused because he had already sent the release letter to

Gidman's parents and didn't want to look foolish. He was rarely a man to go back on a decision.

Liverpool's loss was Villa's gain as they stepped in and offered Gidman a one-month trial. Frank Upton was Villa's youth coach and he comforted the youngster before his trial with the words, 'If Villa don't sign you, I know Chelsea will.'

Gidman was given five games to prove himself. At the end of his trial he was called into manager Vic Crowe's office.

'I expected the same Shankly, "Sorry, son, you're shit" speech but he said, "We're going to give you a year as a pro." I couldn't shake his hand quick enough. I got into the first team within a year after we won the Youth Cup. And I never looked back. That's a time in a kid's life when you sink or swim. I owe everything to Villa for coming in for me. They gave me a second bite of the cherry.'

Gidman's natural innocence on a football pitch that powered his rampaging right-wing attacks was mirrored by his personality in those rookie days. Goalkeeper Jim Cumbes soon exploited that trusting nature before Gidman wised up to dressing-room humour. 'I wound Giddy up on the coach when we were travelling to Cardiff, asking him if he had got his passport because we were playing in Wales. He ran to the front of the coach panicking to the manager that he'd not brought his passport.'

Brian Little, older brother of Alan who was also part of the Villa youth system without going on to achieve the same success, arrived in the West Midlands from the northeast in 1968 as a fifteen-year-old. Although Ellis and his new board would not then have been aware of Little in those gloomy late-60s days, his potential would not be concealed for long. His goalscoring exploits later contributed to Villa's League Cup wins of 1975 and 1977.

'Scouting in those days was totally different as it is today with academies,' remembers Little, who first trialled at Port Vale and then other clubs such as Leeds United, Sunderland, Newcastle United, Manchester City and West Bromwich Albion.

'I turned up at Villa in '68 when Tommy Cummings was manager and Malcolm Musgrove was his assistant. Malcolm is from the northeast and was related to my mum's family. He was classed as my Uncle Malcolm really, which probably wasn't technically true but that was how I always knew him. Malcolm was told by one of the family that young Brian has been to Leeds and various other clubs, so he sent someone to watch me and I was invited down. This sounds a bit corny but it's true, the minute I came to Villa Park it felt right and I thought to myself, "If they offer me an apprenticeship, I'm coming here." They were in Division Two at the time but it didn't matter. I just wanted to go to Villa.'

Jake Findlay joined as an apprentice in 1969 and stayed until his eventual sale in 1978, though his Villa career did not go on to be as successful as those of Gidman or Little, specifically due to a personality clash with future manager Ron Saunders. He was scouted aged fourteen while playing county schools football for Perthshire in Scotland against Fife. Peter Doherty was soon at his family home asking his parents if he could travel down to Birmingham for a trial, which he sailed through.

'There was a lot of emphasis on discovering young talent at Villa then,' Findlay recalls. 'Peter Doherty improved the standard and emphasis on scouting all over the country. They were struggling in the Second Division when I signed at a time I could have gone to Rangers, Celtic or a whole host of other clubs instead. But I liked the way Doug Ellis and Peter Doherty treated the youngsters and assured our families that we would be well looked after.' Villa didn't always make the right calls on whether a player had what it took to make it. They signed future two-time European Cup winner Garry Birtles on schoolboy forms but released him. He later turned up at Nottingham Forest to play a significant role in the club's golden era. Some years later, Brian McClair was an apprentice at Villa, before he too was released and went on to win a raft of honours with Manchester United in the 1990s.

Aside from better youth recruitment, Ellis was intent on ramping up the club's profile during Villa's 1971/72 promotion-winning season in the Second Division. An ambitious invitation was extended to Santos, the club of Brazil's triple World Cup winner Pelé. They accepted and played at Villa Park in an exhibition match on 21 February 1972, which witnessed a crowd of 54,437.

Santos were no strangers to these kinds of games and in fact they were so lucrative the club raked in approximately £100,000 for a European trip; this, while they struggled to break even in domestic games. Overseas trips kept them solvent, but seemingly the Santos bosses overcompensated: the Aston Villa brochure for the game claimed Santos averaged one hundred games a year. Villa paid around £10,000 for the privilege, which Sheffield Wednesday and Stoke City had enjoyed in previous years. The fixture was a significant statement by Villa and few clubs playing in the third tier of their national pyramid could have managed it.

The Villa fans were nearly deprived of the star attraction, however, for the legendary Pelé delivered a stunning ultimatum to Ellis on the day of the match.

'I took Pelé round Birmingham for a city tour in my Rolls-Royce and he turned to me and said, "I can't play tonight,"' Ellis remembers. 'I almost had a heart attack because we had sold over 40,000 tickets on the strength of Pelé playing. He then said he would play if we paid him another five thousand pounds. I had no choice but to pay him, otherwise we would have had a riot on our hands.' Clearly, when the middleman agreed the deal between Villa and Santos, the player whose appearance mattered most had not been adequately recompensed; not until Ellis settled the matter.

The match itself, which Villa won 2–1, came during the so-called 'three-day week' when Edward Heath's Conservative government introduced curfews on commercial enterprises for electricity use during the miners' strike, when coal was in short supply. Floodlight use was banned so the club had to hire generators to light up the spectacle, which was to have an evening kick-off in the back end of winter. Harry Kartz, with his engineering knowhow, sourced the generator company and it was subsequently rigged up for the local government's safety officials to inspect. They had ordered it to be run with all the lights on for three hours the night before the event to ensure it would be safe on the night. Those tests were subsequently passed.

All seemed to be going fine until 45 minutes before kick-off when the chief electrician contacted secretary Alan Bennett to say there was a problem. The water cooling system, rigged up courtesy of an extra-long hosepipe that was run from the changing rooms and through the car park, was not working and there was a serious overheating problem.

'We discovered that a certain H.D. Ellis had parked his car on top of the hosepipe, which wasn't allowing the water to cool the generator,' Bennett recalled with a smile. 'So we had to ask him to remove it. People were arriving in droves by then so if we had not found it we would have been in serious trouble.'

More problems were to arise. The next hurdle was linked to the four floodlights powered through the generator. Each tower had its own switch and they each warmed up one after the other. By this time, the players were limbering up on the pitch, with just two towers on. Before they could switch the next two on, the electrician identified another problem. He informed Bennett that if all four towers were used there was a strong likelihood the generator would be overloaded and blow all the fuses, leaving the whole ground in darkness. When the trial had gone ahead the night before, there were not so many other power sources in operation, like catering and merchandise booths. They had no choice but to play with three operating floodlights – two on the Trinity Road side of the ground and one on the Witton Lane side. Doug Ellis was unhappy. 'This is ridiculous,' he snapped at Bennett during the half-time interval. Ellis insisted something be done to rectify the situation. The pressure was on, as Ellis was not a man to disappoint.

'Doug's seat was in the Trinity Road directors box so at half-time I consulted the electrician and asked if we could power both towers on the opposite Witton Lane side and remove one of the Trinity Road towers,' said Bennett.

'"That's much better, Alan," Doug said from the directors box as he took his seat for the second-half.'

Ellis was oblivious to the fact one of the towers behind him was out but at least he was happy. The only man who was visibly unhappy was the Santos goalkeeper, who saw the darkened tower change ends with him, though Villa winger Ray Graydon also recalled Pelé complaining. The 2–1 victory over Santos gave the players a substantial shot of self-belief ahead of their promotion challenge. Graydon, who scored the second from the penalty spot after crossing for Pat McMahon's first goal, felt it was a significant step for Villa on their climb towards a brighter future. 'It was massive, just to be playing Pelé and Santos, I thought I was dreaming,' Graydon commented, still with a hint of disbelief in his voice more than forty years later. 'It was like the Harlem Globetrotters coming to town. I remember running by their left-back so many times through that game. When I reflect, I imagine the poor lad was knackered because they were always travelling the world for these kinds of matches.'

A spectator that night was soon to become Villa's defensive kingpin and captain. Ian Ross, a 24-year-old Scotsman, had played just 48 times for Liverpool since 1966 and was surplus to requirements at Anfield. Ross was initially reluctant to sign for Villa and was understandably miffed that Liverpool had agreed to sell him to a Third Division club. Bill Shankly gave his blessing for Ross to go down to Birmingham for transfer talks just when Villa happened to be hosting Santos. That fixture said much for the ambition of the club. By the time of the final whistle, Ross's mind was made up: he was going to sign for Villa. Next day he held contract talks with manager Vic Crowe. While these negotiations were ongoing, Ellis hovered outside, itching to become involved in what was then the manager's domain. Crowe left the room temporarily only to be met by a curious Ellis, who was informed that Ross was almost there but was stuttering a little.

'Mind if I have a crack at him?' Ellis asked.

Crowe could hardly deny his employer so he went in and came back out two minutes later, instructing Alan Bennett to find the forms as Ross was signing. Ross later revealed to Bennett that Ellis had offered him one thousand pounds a year more than the sum he had allowed Crowe to offer, seemingly just so he could demonstrate it was he who had edged the deal over the line, even with the player as good as convinced already.

As Crowe led Villa back into the Second Division, highly charged and sometimes poisonous political agendas in the boardroom threatened to disturb the club's progress.

Ellis, regarded by his fellow board members as an egomaniac who courted the limelight too often, was the subject of a 'no confidence' vote in August 1972. Although still in favour with the many minority shareholders who well remembered his emergency takeover four years earlier, his lack of popularity with the fewer majority shareholders resulted in his temporary ousting as chairman, with Jim Hartley replacing him. Ellis was unwilling to accept such a humbling defeat and his spat with Hartley was resolved at an EGM the following month, when a stage was erected on the pitch with the Witton Lane stand stuffed with vociferous shareholders. The fallout meant that Hartley, Bob MacKay and Dick Greenhalgh were removed from the board, while Harry Kartz, who had temporarily resigned his directorship, and legendary former Villa player and manager Eric Houghton were elected as new members, with Ellis reinstated as chairman. Former England cricketer and lifelong Villa supporter Alan A.C. Smith also replaced Harry Parkes as a director.

Smith, who played six Test matches, later served as secretary of Warwickshire County Cricket Club, and as a selector of the England cricket team and chief executive of the Test and County Cricket Board for ten years from 1986. He had been introduced to Villa by his father before the end of the Second World War, so the club was in his blood. Smith remained a Villa director until 1978 and in those six years he witnessed a great deal of political upheaval, with Ellis always at the centre of any wrangle.

'There were periods when it was not so argumentative,' he reflected drily. Smith was initially proposed by Ellis as a candidate to replace Parkes. Ellis also invited Villa Park regular and future club chairman Sir William Dugdale and

Bristol Street Motors executive Harry Cressman onto the board in April 1973.

Despite the infighting and vote of 'no confidence' against him, Ellis was still seen as the man to take Villa forward. 'I wasn't involved when Doug came in but I'd been a Villa supporter since a small boy and it was very sad to see the parlous position that Villa had got into by the end of the 60s,' Smith commented. 'It needed someone with drive and enthusiasm to shake the club out of its very serious malaise and Doug Ellis did that. When I joined the board in '72, he was all about doing what was right for the club. He spent so much of his life at Villa. You can't fault his drive and enthusiasm through those years.'

Goalkeeper Jim Cumbes, a member of the team which won both the League Cup and promotion in 1974/75, acknowledged it was Ellis's optimism and passion for Villa that persuaded him to drop not one but two divisions to sign for £35,000 on 25 November 1971. He and John Osborne were alternating the goalkeeper position at West Bromwich Albion and when Villa approached him, he was out of the side. It was a huge decision for Cumbes because he had already risen from Tranmere Rovers in the Third Division to West Brom in the First, so he justifiably wondered whether he wished to drop two divisions again. Villa's crowds, though, were bigger than Albion's and Cumbes detected that superiority.

'As soon as I walked into Villa Park I thought, "Crikey, this is a big club,"' Cumbes recalled. 'I spoke to Vic Crowe on the Wednesday and they wanted me to sign before Thursday afternoon to play on the Saturday. I told Vic I needed to go home and think about whether I would sign. He understood but wanted to know by the next day as he needed me to play at Oldham on the Saturday. I left his office and as I walked past the chairman's room, Doug said, "Well, have you signed, Jim?" I told him I was going home to think about it. He replied, "Jim, you should never have to think twice about joining a club like this." I always remembered that and as I was driving home I thought, "Wow, I like his confidence, this is a club going places." It is funny how things can go because if I had not signed on that Thursday and left it to the Monday, Tommy Hughes could have played, kept a clean sheet and Vic Crowe might have thought, "Why do I need a new goalkeeper?"' Cumbes's debut would be a 6–0 win at Oldham Athletic.

Villa narrowly missed out on successive promotions in 1972/73, finishing third when two teams were promoted. Crowe failed to build on that progress and, instead, results slipped. The 1973/74 season ended with an underwhelming 1–1 draw at promotion-chasing Leyton Orient, to secure a modest league finish in fourteenth position. A change in team management appeared to be needed and Ellis duly made it. Crowe was sacked.

With such a steely focus on Aston Villa, Ellis took his eye off the ball as far as his own business went and his travel agency at 44 Cannon Street in Birmingham faltered badly.

'We had this huge pegboard that showed how many bookings we had made and to which country and how many flights were sold etcetera,' Ellis recounted. 'Well, if the bookings were completed, the pegs would be green, but if they were not sold or if business was incomplete the pegs would be red or yellow. I can tell you with the amount of time I was spending at Aston Villa, my business was suffering and there were far too many red pegs on the wall. I lost a quarter of a million pounds in one year. 'I realised if I wanted to be hands-on at Villa my travel business would continue to suffer – so eventually I sold it.'

That moment would come in 1976. Ellis then had nothing to distract him from what would become his life's work.

Ron Saunders:
Genius? Ace Motivator?
Bully?

'Ron frightened the life out of me at first, I struggled to get on with him.
We had a clash of personalities from day one. He revelled in winding me up and
would test me all the time.' – **Brian Little**

IN THE YEAR THAT BILL SHANKLY EXITED THE MANAGER'S SEAT AT
Anfield, Aston Villa continued their evolving revolution by hiring a man whose
achivements later proved arguably as monumental to them as Shankly's were to
Liverpool. For Ron Saunders' reign at Villa saw him take the club out of Second
Division mediocrity to the top of the First Division, eventually leaving a deep
footprint in Europe.

Villa toyed with the prospect of appointing a more high-profile boss. World
Cup-winning manager Sir Alf Ramsey was sounded out after his sacking by the
Football Association for failing to lead England to the 1974 World Cup finals, but
he refused to move from his Ipswich home. Ramsey instead recommended his
East Anglian neighbour, Saunders. There was also some curious self-promotion by
Brian Clough and his management associate Peter Taylor, who had won the league
championship with Derby County in 1971/72 yet had fallen out with the Sam
Longson-led Rams board, resigning in October 1973. Clough met with Ellis at a
Lichfield restaurant to discuss the Villa manager's position but the meeting only
confirmed to Ellis that a partnership would not be a good idea.

The rendezvous ended with Ellis concluding, succinctly, 'Look, Brian, it would never work. There can only ever be one boss at Aston Villa – and that's me.'

Intriguingly, Saunders and Ellis each had significant egos and were rarely united when they led Villa in their respective roles, but somehow they managed to coexist and much of that was due to Saunders' preference to keep a low media profile. The media to Saunders was more a psychological tool to use for motivating his players or deceiving future opposition. Therefore, that left Ellis enough room to develop his own public profile.

It wasn't the first occasion Clough had touted himself for the Villa manager's post; eighteen months earlier Ellis, Vic Crowe and Alan Bennett travelled to Derby's Baseball Ground to sign left-back John Robson. While Crowe, Bennett and Robson were completing the formalities, Clough and Taylor openly declared their interest in managing Villa, which a stunned Ellis politely dismissed. Later in his career, Clough regretted never having the opportunity to manage Villa, which he regarded as the biggest club in the Midlands despite his own Nottingham Forest team's subsequent European success.

The Clough rumour, following Crowe's dismissal, was loud enough to have reached the dressing room and goalkeeper Jim Cumbes felt deflated when it never materialised. 'Our disappointment and surprise at Vic leaving was tempered by the fact we all thought Brian Clough was coming in,' said Cumbes. 'Most of us thought, "This could be fantastic – big club, big manager." It didn't happen of course so there was a feeling the eventual new manager Ron Saunders was a bit of a second choice.'

Ron Saunders was born in 1932 in Birkenhead, ironically just eight miles from where his eventual employer and sparring partner Doug Ellis was born, in Hooton. Saunders' management style was built on endeavour and discipline and employing a psychology that had players guessing whether they had played or trained well enough to win his favour; a mentality that later worked for Alex Ferguson. Midfielder Pat Heard, signed by Saunders in 1979, colourfully described what it was like to play under him.

'He was calm but he had that fear factor also; in a strange way he was like your dad,' said Heard. 'He would invest all this trust in you and you felt you wanted to please him. He was never a ranter or a raver in the dressing room. His work was done on the training ground in midweek. Before the game, he would casually sit next to each player and say, "Now you know what your job is don't you, son?"

So you'd say, "Yes, boss." And he'd say, "Because you know where you'll be if you don't do your job, don't you – back in the reserves …'" Saunders knew he wanted to be a football manager from his mid-twenties and was aided by the education he received from playing under respected coaches like Bill McGarry and Bob Stokoe at his two final clubs, Watford and Charlton Athletic. Stokoe was an infamous disciplinarian whose methods might not be tolerated by modern-day professionals, but when Saunders became a manager he took aspects of Stokoe's approach into his own style. Saunders' background as a prolific striker in the 1950s and 60s, notably with Portsmouth where he scored 145 league goals, helped him command a level of respect from players and staff. Yet his profile was not all that high initially as a manager. That came later. He commenced his management career with a two-year spell at Southern League outfit Yeovil Town, prior to a four-month stint at Oxford United, where he helped them stave off relegation from the Second Division by three points. One of his charges then was a veteran wing-half who didn't make the grade as a rookie at Villa in the late 50s but who would himself go on to a successful management career at West Bromwich Albion, Manchester United and Villa, Ron Atkinson. He remembers Saunders' managerial philosophy in those four months at Oxford.

'I was probably the only one at the club who thought we would stay up before he came as most of the boys had lost faith,' recalled Atkinson.

'When Saunders came in we were very impressed; he was the first tracksuit manager I saw, as Arthur Turner [Saunders' predecessor] was seldom around except on match days. Ron put a big emphasis on the work ethic. He didn't do much tactical stuff on the training ground; his focus was on fitness. We played a bit route one and he was very big on hitting the ball into the channels inside the full-back. He would tell our striker, "You run, you run and you run and when you stop running we'll take you off and put someone else on who will.'"

Even in those days, before Saunders had developed much of a CV, he was a tough man-manager who would leave his players with little doubt of what he expected of them. Oxford had progressed through the divisions and had a team devoid of 'names'. They were a hard-working unit and Saunders would not have had it any other way. 'We had a crucial game at Craven Cottage at the end of March,' remembered Atkinson. 'Ron said to us, "We haven't come here to win, we haven't come here to entertain, we have come here to not get beat." And he finished with the words, "If we score, they don't." Then after we scored with the first kick of the match, we had to hang on for 89 minutes – but we did it. I reckon I put more balls into the Thames that night than it had ever seen before. But I learned quickly that was how Ron wanted us to play.'

In the next stage of a blossoming management career, he was recruited by Norwich City on 1 July 1969 with the sole aim of achieving promotion to the top tier of English football. Saunders not only managed to earn them promotion for the first time in their 70-year history in 1972, he also steered the Canaries to the League Cup final against Tottenham a year later. The key difference between Saunders at Norwich and his subsequent ill-fated challenge at Manchester City was the lack of egos involved. Whereas Man City's team of internationals rejected his uncompromising 'my way or no way' regime, the Norwich players embraced his methods that again centred on fitness. Saunders' philosophy was about ensuring that even if the opposition were superior in quality, they would not be in fitness, drive and commitment.

'Ron came across as a dour disciplinarian but that was his style and was what we needed then,' believes Dave Stringer, who was Saunders' centre-back at Carrow Road. 'He dragged us out of the Second Division after we had been stuck there for ten years. We needed someone to pull us together in a no-nonsense way and that was what we got with Ron.

'He surrounded himself with honest, hard-working players to get the job done. He was strong on discipline and if you didn't want to do things his way, you were out. There was no fear of upsetting anyone. Some players couldn't handle it and the insecure ones fell by the wayside.'

If Saunders was appreciated in the dressing room at Norwich, he wasn't as popular in the boardroom – a common theme through his management career. He clashed with Canaries' chairman Sir Arthur South, who arrived in 1973. South had a strong personality and was not one to share key decisions on club affairs. Both wanted to run the club and after an almighty row, the manager resigned.

He was recruited by Manchester City just a week later as the permanent successor to Johnny Hart. More power battles awaited him – but this time with the players.

Saunders indicated from the outset he wasn't frightened to shake things up, despite coming in after a highly successful period in which City had won the league championship, the League Cup, the FA Cup and the European Cup Winners' Cup within three years under the management of Joe Mercer and

Malcolm Allison. Saunders' abrasive methods delivered a League Cup final appearance on 2 March 1974 when they lost to Wolverhampton Wanderers, but also created such disharmony among senior players that they embarked on a mutinous campaign to influence his dismissal that chairman Peter Swales was happy to support. This act sparked distrust within Saunders of so-called 'star' players who had relationships with club directors. That feeling of suspicion stayed with him for the rest of his management career – and was significant in the way he conducted himself at Villa.

'I only knew him as "Ron Saunders: Villa manager" and he talked to me a lot about things,' said his former goalkeeper Jimmy Rimmer, who became one of Saunders' few confidants after he signed for Villa from Arsenal in 1977. 'At City he tried to get rid of the lads who were doing their talking upstairs [to the directors]. I knew the likes of Franny Lee, Mike Summerbee and Denis Law and they were in Peter Swales' ear a lot – Ron didn't like that. His attitude was, "If you have a problem, come and see the manager, not the chairman," which I agree with. Once people go behind your back, respect is lost.'

Such decorated players as Law, Summerbee, Lee, Colin Bell and Rodney Marsh resisted Saunders and their collective opposition was ultimately rewarded with his sacking. But were City any better off for the removal of Saunders? Across the next 37 years, they would win only one trophy – the League Cup in 1976. Only the emergence of wealthy overseas ownership changed their fortunes through lavish spending on prestigious global talent. Ironically, the star players Saunders attempted to remove left anyway, as their futures at City were no more secure under the management of Saunders' successor, their former team-mate Tony Book, who also set about revolutionising the team but in a more respectful manner. Law retired the same year; Summerbee left the following year to finish his career at a lower level, with Burnley, Blackpool and Stockport; Lee departed for two seasons at Derby County before retirement; and Marsh was three years out from the end of a career that tailed off with a spell in America. Bell was the only one who remained for any length of time, retiring in 1979 with his final game ending in a 3–2 defeat – to Saunders' Aston Villa.

Book, who had been caretaker manager before Saunders' arrival, was one of his few allies as his assistant. He remembers the sorry ending to his reign after a run of one win in his last ten games.

'Ron was still living in Norwich at the time, so after we lost 3–0 at QPR – which turned out to be his final game as manager – he went home separately and the lads caught the train back. When we arrived at Piccadilly Station in Manchester, the chairman was waiting on the platform for us. He pulled our skipper Mike Doyle aside and it soon became clear Ron would be gone.

'I liked Ron and I didn't have a problem with him but he was a sergeant-major figure and he didn't treat the likes of Denis Law or Mike Summerbee any differently to anyone else despite what they had achieved. These players were used to a more relaxed regime under Malcolm Allison, who was a great coach and ahead of his time. Ron wasn't prepared to tiptoe around egos and sometimes you need to handle players differently.'

What then motivated the Doug Ellis-led Aston Villa board to recruit Saunders on 4 June 1974, after a fractured, thankless six-month reign at City? The answer is similar to Norwich: because Villa were drifting under Vic Crowe and desperately required strong leadership. In Saunders, they found their man.

Secretary Alan Bennett had been impressed with Crowe for most of his tenure, especially his leadership during promotion from the Third Division. But he also felt he lost his certainty of direction towards the end. 'He and Ron Wylie almost ended up as a partnership – when we needed a strong leader,' Bennett recalled. 'The Villa board were right in deciding the Crowe–Wylie partnership was not going to improve matters. Saunders was as good a manager Villa could have recruited then. He gave Villa the drive that was lacking.'

Saunders' unshakeable determination to implement a winning mentality shone through from the outset, bravely rebounding from his City travails. On signing his initial three-year contract, he told the directors he would lift Villa back into the top flight. Twelve months later he had achieved just that, while also winning the League Cup in the same season. He looked to freshen up the squad almost immediately, returning to Maine Road to make the terrier-like Frank Carrodus his first signing, without approval from Ellis or the Villa board.

'I received a call late one night from Ron, who was staying at the Penns Hall Hotel, just outside Birmingham,' Ellis recalled. 'He informed me he had signed Frank Carrodus for £100,000. I had never even heard of Carrodus. I was furious and drove to the hotel to speak with Ron.'

There, the two who would become the most significant protagonists at Villa over the next decade, sat on twin beds facing one another. It was their first dispute of many.

They wasted little time in getting to the point – small talk wasn't their style.

Ellis: Ron, you do not sign players, you can merely recommend players to the board. You have no business agreeing transfers without our knowledge.
Saunders: Your opinion on any footballer is 110 per cent irrelevant. This deal is done. I've agreed it with City.
Ellis: We will see about that.

The chairman researched Carrodus and discovered him to be 'a hard-working journeyman' kind of footballer, so he eventually approved the transfer – but for £90,000. A power struggle had begun – and it never stopped. It was, frankly, the tale of two huge egos. In fairness to Saunders, it was not uncommon for managers of that generation to sign players or even agree transfers without board approval.

'That was my first head-to-head with Doug,' Saunders reflected, 'and I came home feeling mad because Doug said he was not sure about the player. 'I said, as many managers told their chairman, "You do your job and I'll do mine."'

Throughout Saunders reign, player opinion of them both was divided. They would either be in the Saunders camp and suspicious of Ellis, or they were closer to Ellis and feeling unappreciated and disenfranchised in Saunders' rapidly developing revolution. Villa's star trio of the 1970s, John Gidman, Brian Little and Andy Gray, were all regarded like sons by Ellis, with the former two having been recruited into his ambitious new youth system pre-Saunders. Other players were wary of even being spotted talking to the chairman.

Rampaging right-back Gidman had a frosty introduction to life under Saunders. It was a precursor for the remainder of their relationship. Saunders knew Gidman strengthened his team but was loathe to offer the kind of encouragement and praise Gidman deserved. Therefore, the player sided with Ellis when any political agenda was raised among players which was rare, to be fair. The fact Ellis owned a travel agency that provided players with holidays at favourable prices endeared him to some. In fact, Gidman had just been on an Ellis-arranged holiday in Famagusta, northern Cyprus, when he returned to learn that Saunders had succeeded Crowe. He was told to meet his new manager at Villa Park at three o'clock. Gidman arrived at ten to three and was kept waiting half an hour before a blunt exchange ensued. On Gidman's entrance into the manager's office, sparks soon flew.

Saunders: Who are you?

Gidman: Well, who the fuck are you?

The mood between them never improved.

Gidman added: 'I'd heard what had gone on at City and how he didn't like names; he apparently treated the likes of Bell, Summerbee and Lee like shit. Guys at the end of their careers deserved more respect than that but that was his style.'

Brian Little, a creative and skilful forward, was not Saunders' typical kind of player, with graft and endurance favoured above all. Tireless midfielders like Carrodus and his successor Des Bremner typified the 'Saunders Way'. 'Little would have been regarded as a luxury player by the manager, but Saunders was savvy enough to know a successful team needed the balance Little brought, in the same way mercurial winger Tony Morley was an irreplaceable cog in his First Division title-winning team years later.

'Ron frightened the life out of me at first, I struggled to get on with him,' Little acknowledged. 'We had a clash of personalities from day one. He revelled in winding me up. He would test me all the time, like calling me into his office and playing mind games so I would walk out thinking, "I've had enough of this, I will show him at the weekend," and then have a stormer. I thought I'd won then because I had played well and got one over on him but he knew what he was doing all along. He was a master psychologist.'

Saunders' Manchester City background was a significant precursor to his Villa tenure, as he realised he needed to align himself with the senior players. He knew he could not afford to charge into another club, upset the seniors and expect to succeed. Therefore at Villa the seniors were invariably afforded a certain amount of leeway and could be excused for playing a game of golf on a Thursday even though Saunders forbade it so close to a match day. They could also survive his wrath if they went out for drinks when he would probably have preferred them not to. Saunders looked on both breaches of protocol as a kind of team bonding and so saw merit in certain misdemeanours. Brian Clough was the same – if players wanted to have a drink, they could as long as it was with teammates, not privately. Youngsters rarely enjoyed the same freedom. Saunders generally spoke differently to the more experienced players like Ian Ross, Chris Nicholl, Dennis Mortimer and, later, Jimmy Rimmer, Ken McNaught and Peter Withe. 'There was a dual respect with those guys,' Little said, 'and there was respect also for the youngsters, but the difference was if you stepped out of line only fractionally you quickly got a clip round the ear. It was like having a strict teacher at school.'

The youngsters lived in fear of Saunders and that atmosphere remained throughout his reign. Players came and went but the attitude of treating youngsters harshly remained constant. The rookies soon came to understand the rules: If you did well and earned his favour, he didn't say a lot; if you did OK, he said less; but if you did not perform very well in a match or training, he would have plenty to say. Any youngster at Villa who clashed with Saunders' hard-line methods or who needed praise to excel rarely prospered, with Jake Findlay, Steve Hunt and Bobby McDonald obvious examples. A lack of ability was rarely the problem. Hunt even went on to play for England on two occasions.

'That was how it was in the 1970s,' Hunt reasoned. 'I am not sure if it was bullying but he was certainly intimidating. We didn't see eye to eye, which is why he got rid of me, I suppose, but he never bullied me. He could be hard on players and it was almost like he was pressing for a reaction, the right reaction, where you went out and played the game of your life. But not all players react like that, do they?'

Those such as Little and latterly Gordon Cowans and Gary Shaw survived because, allied with great ability, they also developed a thick skin to Saunders' tough-love approach.

'We spent our lives trying to win his approval and that was the style that worked for him,' Little admitted. 'If you passed him in the corridor you were like a rabbit in the headlights, but he had only got to wink at you and that was enough, it was like, "Thank God for that, I must be in his good books." He probably wasn't as bad as all that and he was more than likely playing a game. But as a youngster you don't see that. His style wouldn't be allowed nowadays, but I would not have had it any other way.'

Few players would contest Saunders' management of young players at Villa was extreme. Many claim he was a bully. Allan Evans, who arrived at Villa from Dunfermline in 1977, was nicknamed 'Psycho' by the Villa fans due to his unwavering bravery as a whole-hearted defender. He was less intimidated by the manager than most, though still felt that if the manager's style was to be judged by modern-day standards, a dim view would be taken by the politically correct.

The wealthier players of post-millennium times might choose to oppose Saunders and possibly take to social media to air grievances. Nothing stays in-house for long now and questionable treatment of players or staff would be dealt with more harshly, as was the case when Paul Lambert's assistants were fired in 2014. But as Ken McNaught pointed out: 'There were no HR departments in the 70s.' Managers were allowed to go about their business as they deemed fit, even if their methods did border on bullying; 1970s management was a different time – what was motivational coaching back then is today's bullying. Certainly Saunders' son Ronnie said that his father considered himself a manager who tried to motivate players, but not all players appreciated his approach.

'If you judge Saunders' methods on how things are now, absolutely; what we regard as bullying now, yes it was, one hundred per cent,' said Evans. 'But that is how it was then. If you were not in the first team, he didn't want to know you. So what? Get in the first team!'

That chance would have been a fine thing for goalkeeper Jake Findlay who, after winning the FA Youth Cup in 1972, was expected to go on to become a first-team regular. However, he played just fourteen league games before departing for Luton Town in 1978. Not all those years of exclusion can be levelled at Saunders. But Villa's goalkeeper during the success of the early 1980s, Jimmy Rimmer, arrived a year before Findlay's exit and he observed why he felt Saunders froze Findlay out. Rimmer, curiously, was the third established keeper signed ahead of Findlay after Jim Cumbes pre-Saunders and John Burridge, while even rookie Nigel Spink was signed from non-league Chelmsford Town before Findlay exited.

'Jake had so much ability but Ron thought he was just messing about all the time,' said Rimmer. 'That was just Jake. He couldn't help it; that was who he was. Some people have that kind of character. What would Ron have been like with Paul Gascoigne? Ron couldn't handle characters sometimes.' Indeed, the manager who signed him for Luton, David Pleat, described Findlay as 'a loveable Jack-the-Lad'. So too was Burridge. And those kinds of characters rarely won Saunders' favour.

Charlie Aitken was more critical of Saunders' treatment of Findlay and felt he picked on him because he was overweight and unfit. 'Ron nearly killed him,' said Aitken. 'Ron used to force him to train until he was almost vomiting blood. It was terrible.' Saunders was obsessed with his players being in peak physical condition and so the combination of Findlay's playful behaviour and a seemingly casual attitude towards training would have been Saunders' motivation for his rough treatment.

Nigel Spink recalled how Saunders used to order his players to run up and down steep country hills for pre-season training. 'Not long after I joined as a £55-a-week rookie, I was last to finish that fitness drill and was at the back with Jake when all the others had completed it,' said Spink. 'Us keepers never enjoyed those types of runs. Anyway, I was on all fours and was ready to give up and Saunders said, "OK, son, if you want to give it up, go and get a shower." But Jake said, "No way, Spinky, we're finishing this, otherwise he'll never let you forget the fact you quit." It seemed to me Jake was speaking from experience. But fortunately, I always got along with Ron.'

Findlay himself is in no doubt he was victimised.

'I was bullied by him – one hundred per cent,' said Findlay. 'Other players were too. Bobby Mac McDonald, Stevie Hunt, Keith Masefield – it was mainly the youngsters. He had a way of talking to you that made you feel little.'

Left-back McDonald, who opted against giving an interview for this book, was worthy of more opportunities than he was given by Saunders, according to Findlay and other teammates. Instead, Gordon Smith was eventually brought in from Scottish side St Johnstone to take his place. 'He was a really nice lad but wasn't in the same class as Bobby,' Findlay commented. The ex-England player-turned-manager Gordon Milne was happy to sign him for Coventry City after a recommendation by his assistant Ron Wylie, who had known McDonald at Villa.

Milne, widely regarded as one of football's nice guys, was not surprised with the uncompromising reputation Saunders developed because of the way he played. Milne earned fourteen caps for England in the 1960s and in doing so crossed paths with his future managerial rival in the West Midlands. 'Every manager has his own way,' reasoned Milne. 'When Ron played he was a competitor and was tough, was a hard man and no-nonsense, you knew you were in a game. That was his personality and he was never going to change. Senior players can handle a bloke like that a bit better, though the youngsters might think, "Bloody hell, this bloke's a bit tough."' Saunders' motives were based on improving players, but Findlay considered his methods flawed as he himself needed reassurance and an arm around the shoulder, which was not Saunders' way.

Findlay wasn't the only goalkeeper to receive rough treatment from Saunders. The man who was intended to be his and Jim Cumbes' replacement – John

Burridge – suffered in a similar manner. In fairness to Saunders, Burridge could be something of a clown figure and usually sought humour in any situation no matter how serious, which was never going to endear him to a manager who was often regarded as being humourless. Other managers, like Ron Atkinson perhaps, might have appreciated this light-heartedness around the group to add balance to the dressing room. Given some of Burridge's pranks, though – like exploding an inflated sick bag above Saunders' head while approaching a runway in the knowledge the manager was a hoPeléss flier – he was always likely to incur his wrath. Burridge eventually submitted a transfer request to escape life at Villa.

'Saunders was a real bully-boy,' said Burridge. 'You can bully a midfield player or bully a defender or a forward, but you can't bully a goalkeeper. A goalkeeper needs to be full of confidence at all times. If a manager is slagging you off, then your confidence nosedives. You always get remembered for your mistakes and Saunders made damn sure I remembered all of mine. I was on the verge of a nervous breakdown. I had it out with him in his office one day and he called me a "pussy" – maybe I was, but to play in goal for a club like Aston Villa at such a tender age, you had to be a certain type of person, mentally unbreakable.'

Burridge's replacement, Jimmy Rimmer, was almost four years his senior at 29 and had the experience of playing at Manchester United and Arsenal. Rimmer was the role-model type that Saunders appreciated.

'Ron was hard on people and he was probably harder on those who weren't stars of the team,' said Andy Gray, who was *the* star for Villa in the 1970s, though the manager despised the term 'star'. 'He didn't give me a hard time very often to the point where I felt he was bullying me. If I was injured he might goad me at times into coming back quicker but that was only because he wanted me back in the side. He didn't bully me and I wouldn't have allowed him to. There are definitely players, though, who would say that they have been bullied by Ron Saunders – definitely. I wouldn't argue with that.'

The manager's harsh approach was not reserved solely for the youngsters. Leighton Phillips, Saunders' second signing from Cardiff City, felt his manager had something against Welshmen such was the regularity of the criticism towards him. 'It was only as I got older,' Phillips recalled, 'I realised he did a good job – whatever his methods. He was a master psychologist who always wanted more. You'd never done enough for him.'

Another senior player, Jim Cumbes, shared a cordial relationship with

Saunders. He detected, though, a quirkiness of character that was difficult for him to fathom. At a Professional Footballers' Association dinner in London in 1974, comedian and Birmingham City supporter Jasper Carrot was the speaker. His allegiance to Birmingham had never been a secret and neither did Carrot wish for it to be, so he flaunted it and made a comical remark about how Ron Saunders was sacked by Norwich, sacked by Manchester City, so it was wonderful that City's bitter rivals Aston Villa had recruited him. Seemingly, all in the room fell about laughing and at this moment the television cameras panned in on Cumbes' laughter, which he came to rue. On Monday morning at the training ground, Saunders grilled Cumbes.

'Did you give Carrot that line?' inquired Saunders.

'It was ridiculous,' Cumbes recalled. 'Ron could be very paranoid. He didn't trust many people. Maybe that was a result of what happened to him at Man City.'

On Saunders' management, Cumbes added: 'I don't like over-criticising people but Ron was a bit of a bully. He wouldn't punch you in the face but if he didn't like something you were saying or something you were doing he would punch you. We were staying at a London hotel on a Friday night for a game on Saturday and were having an evening meal as a team. Suddenly I felt this hefty thump on the back of my shoulder. I turned round and it was Ron. He said, "What you doing eating a prawn cocktail? You can't have that the night before a match. It could upset your stomach for tomorrow," and he had it taken away. There were times when he could be really nasty but that was his way of trying to get the best out of you. Whereas Vic Crowe would be understanding and would cajole you along, Ron would beat you down hoping you would fight back through your performance.'

Shocking revelations maybe, but this was the 1970s and memories should be interpreted in a way that was consistent with the generation. Managers in those days generally ran not just the team but the whole club, which was a regular irritation to Doug Ellis, of course, who himself craved control. There was no one higher in command than the manager in the players' eyes.

Allan Evans, who was to become Ken McNaught's central defensive partner for five years from 1978, felt players who were tough in character generally survived the Saunders regime. Evans regarded a Saunders rollicking as motivation and would thrive on such occasions. 'I liked Ron a lot,' Evans said. 'If you did what he asked he would back you one hundred per cent and would never criticise you in public. Even if you had a bad game he would back you. But if you were a moaner, he never liked that.' Evans learned the hard way. After cementing his place in the first team in the 1977/78 season, he left training at one o'clock, just like the rest of the first-teamers. As soon as he reached home there was a phone call – from Saunders.

'Where are you?' the furious manager asked.

'I came home like the other first-teamers, gaffer,' Evans replied.

'You haven't earned that right yet, son!' Saunders fumed. 'Get your arse back to the training ground now!'

Evans could not jump back into his car quickly enough.

That was how Saunders extracted the best out of his team – by denying them a comfort zone. Gordon Cowans commented, with a wry smile: 'The only time Ron put his arm around you was if he craftily wanted to smell your breath to see if you'd had a drink the night before. The senior players had a lot of freedom with him, but not us youngsters. But it was all about driving us on.'

Ironically, Saunders was strongly in favour of promoting youth from within – Gary Shaw, Gary Shelton and Lee Jenkins all made their Villa first-team debuts in the 1978/79 season, with Shaw and Jenkins still seventeen-year-old apprentices. Cowans, Brendan Ormsby, Ivor Linton, Gary Williams, Colin Gibson, Charlie Young, Noel Blake and more were all given first-team opportunities by Saunders while still teenagers so he most certainly wasn't anti-youngster, quite the opposite. He was just a punishing taskmaster.

While the manager had no shortage of detractors for his stern methods, many more appreciated how he created a winning culture. Tony Morley was older than McNaught yet was regarded in the same way as the younger Shaw and Cowans because he was a joker in the dressing room and preferred the company of the younger players. Therefore, he was given zero encouragement by the manager. Years later, though, Morley is thankful Saunders brought his best football out of him, which led to his winning six England caps.

'In all my time at Villa I don't remember him ever praising myself, Gary or Gordon, though he would praise other players,' Morley remembered. 'He never wanted us to get too big for our boots. It was all part of his psychology to get us working harder in games. I could score a great goal but rather than praise me he would ask, "But how many tackles did you make?" If the answer was "two or three" he'd simply reply, "Not enough!"'

Saunders ultimately turned his players into winners. He was well aware of his reputation but did not lose sleep over the naysayers who poured scorn on his tough regime.

'I cannot honestly say I know whether or not my players like me,' Saunders said during his latter Villa days. 'I'm not one little bit concerned, either, about being the winner in a popularity contest. I hope and believe that my players respect me not only as a person but as a professional manager who knows his trade inside-out. That, to my way of thinking, is what really matters.'

How Can a Manager Get Rid of a Chairman?

*'Doug wanted to run the show, absolutely everything and
Ron wouldn't let him have anything to do with the playing side of things.
They weren't too good together.'* – **Harry Kartz**

MANCHESTER UNITED HAD BEEN CHAMPIONS OF EUROPE SIX YEARS earlier in 1968. By the 1974/75 season, they were a Second Division club. It should not have come as any surprise that Tommy Docherty's side rebounded back into the top flight at the first attempt. Less predictable was Aston Villa's promotion as runners-up under new manager Ron Saunders, especially after their mediocre finish in fourteenth place the season prior. Saunders arrived with a reputation for agitating senior players in the hope of sparking a revolution at Manchester City. He was equally uncompromising as Villa's manager, but he learned to choose his battles. His chief adversary soon became the chairman, Doug Ellis.

Despite the commonly held belief that manager and chairman must be in sync to achieve best results on and off the pitch, Ellis and Saunders managed to confound the norm by succeeding against a backdrop of acrimony. Saunders was always ready to lay down a marker to Ellis as if to suggest, 'You might be the chairman, but I am running things around here.' This was never more apparent than when Saunders instructed the coach driver to leave Ellis behind when he was late, in the days when directors used to travel on the team bus to away games. Steve Stride, then assistant secretary, had to drive ahead so they could catch up with the team.

'We were certainly not close as chairman-manager relationships go and were not on one another's Christmas card list,' Ellis admitted. 'But he was a good coach and football manager so I was happy for him to be at Aston Villa.

The summer of '74 at Villa was largely about Saunders consolidating his message to his players of how he wanted to play. In his typically dogmatic way, the players were advised if they did not believe in his tactics, they would not make the team. He demanded total commitment towards training and those who did not share that view were banished. While he led with an iron fist, he was not against players thinking creatively towards tactics. Ray Graydon, who worked towards his coaching badges from the age of 25, commented: 'Although the way we played was always going to be *his* way – and he would tell everybody that and would be very strong on that – Ron also used to give us licence to come up with ideas. I worked a lot on throw-ins and free-kick routines. Ron would then say, "Yes, I like it, I'll use that," or "No, I don't like that."'

Saunders' playing style was different to Crowe's, with a preference for moving the ball forward more quickly'. That suited many of the players who were instantly won over by him. Charlie Aitken considered Saunders 'a revelation' at first.

'I heard about his time at City and how he upset the senior players,' Aitken said. 'He knew he couldn't carry on like that when he came to Villa and his attitude was very good. His training was good and he corresponded well with everybody. He was very meticulous and each player knew his job. He would have the youth team play us in training, in the same way that the opposition we were preparing to face would play. Tactically, he was spot-on.'

Holte End favourite Brian Little and his fellow attackers Graydon and Keith Leonard, and later John Deehan and Andy Gray, were rarely used in team training sessions. Quite often they would only be deployed for the final ten minutes in practice matches, as they were instructed to hone their finishing ability separately. Saunders was more interested in fine-tuning his back four and midfield into a tight, organised unit and would have them playing as an eight- or nine-man group against the youth team that was at full strength with eleven. The emphasis was focused towards defence and suffocating the opposition from passing the ball for too long, through pressing energetically. 'I used that same training drill when I went into coaching and many people would pay me compliments like "Your team is hard to beat",' Little said. 'Much of that should be credited to what I had learned from Ron. He had the players totally drilled in winning the ball, keeping their shape and scrapping for the ball.'

Even the formation was inventive. Villa regularly played a 4–3–1–2 system with Little tucked in behind a front two. 'No team played like that in those days,' Little continued. 'The next team to employ it was Ipswich with Eric Gates in the hole. Ironically, Ipswich tried to buy me, so there is little doubt that Bobby Robson was looking at Saunders' methods and trying to put me in that role behind the front two. Ron was ahead of his time. If you look at the way the game is being played now, it is almost as though we have gone back to the tactics Saunders was using in the 70s. None of us realised it then but the man was a genius.'

In terms of preparation, fitness was afforded great attention. Saunders never wanted so-called 'names'; he wanted a 'team' that worked hard for one another. Therefore, one of the methods he employed to outfox oppositions that might include more of a celebrity line-up – whether Kevin Keegan, Johan Cruyff or Kenny Dalglish – was to ensure his players were fitter than those they were facing so they could outrun and outpower them. A club does not need to be affluent for its players to be able to harass their opponents for ninety minutes.

When Villa's quest for promotion to the First Division began, sceptics soon questioned whether Saunders was the right man after they won just two of their first eight matches in that 1974/75 campaign. A comprehensive 3–0 win at First Division Everton in the League Cup, though, suggested his message was seeping through. Villa were seventh in the league table at Christmas, but kicked on with an inspired second half of the season that saw them lose just one league match, ensuring a second-place finish.

They took nineteen points from their last available twenty when it was two points for a win, completing the season with eight consecutive victories. The season-ending match was a 4–1 win at third-placed Norwich, who they also defeated 1–0 to win the League Cup at Wembley.

'It took until after Christmas before Ron's methods started to click,' Frank Carrodus admitted.

'Once we got into our groove, I have never known a spirit like it. Every game we just knew we were going to go out and win. We thrashed Norwich 4–1 even with me and Giddy up front. Their manager John Bond said to us afterwards, "I don't know what you fucking lot are on ..."'

Villa's only league defeat after New Year was a 1–0 loss in a bruising encounter at Leyton Orient thanks to a goal by the India-born Ricky Heppolette. 'It was a really rough game,' Little recalled. 'Gee, there were some tackles flying in. They had a player called Tom Walley and he was the only one who ever battered big Keith Leonard. He sorted Keith out a treat and it was probably the only time that happened.'

Promotion was secured with two games remaining after a convincing 4–0 win at Sheffield Wednesday, teeing up some marathon celebrations. Secretary Alan Bennett had arranged for a crate of champagne to be on the team bus in case promotion was achieved that evening to accompany them on the journey home on the M1. Their hosts and bottom club Wednesday also handed over a crate despite their own travails. 'There were twenty-four bottles to keep the players and staff going,' remembered Bennett. 'But we had to stop at an off-licence for another crate before we even got out of the Sheffield traffic on the way back to Birmingham.

'The manager joined in to a certain extent, but he was more of a brandy man.'

If anyone deserved a plastic cup of champagne that night it was Graydon and Little, whose 27 and 24 goals respectively had shot Villa back into the First Division, while the thirteen goals from midfield by 'Chico' Hamilton should not be undervalued. Graydon had actually netted eighteen times before the turn of the year. Leighton Phillips, though, considered the unheralded contributions of right-back John Gidman and left-back John Robson as equally significant. 'Robbo was the best defender in the club,' Phillips remarked, 'while Giddy was so good going forwards that their left winger used to mark *him*, not the other way around.'

Promotion complemented the League Cup that was won on the first day of March against Saunders' former club Norwich. Saunders had become the first manager to lead three different clubs to the League Cup final in successive years, after the Canaries lost to Tottenham in 1973 and Man City fell to Wolves a year later.

In the week leading up to the Wembley showpiece, it became clear to the Villa players that Saunders would not accept anything other than a victory because of his bitter fall-out with Norwich chairman Arthur South. 'He positively hated their chairman and he wasn't a great fan of John Bond either, so he was desperate to win,' Jim Cumbes revealed.

Saunders revelled in the use of kidology and mind games. He pulled Little and Cumbes aside on the Friday before the final to tell them he was leaking a false story to the media that both of them were struggling with flu and were doubtful for the game, but reassured them they would definitely be playing.

'He was doing what might now be described as "a Mourinho" to give Norwich something to think about,' added Cumbes.

Along the way to the final, Cumbes identified a softer, compassionate edge to Saunders, who would probably have been described by some of the players as dictatorial. The goalkeeper recalled the aftermath of the League Cup semi-final second leg against Chester City. Villa were 2–0 up before Chester came back to level the scores.

'I was partly responsible for their second, even though it was an awful, wet and muddy night,' Cumbes acknowledged. 'I caught a ball but as I landed it fell from my grasp and they scored. I thought it might cost us a place at Wembley but fortunately Brian Little scored a third and we went through. Afterwards in the dressing room it was a lively atmosphere with plenty of Wembley talk but I spent some time on my own in the showers just reflecting. Then I felt this punch in between my shoulder blades – it was Ron Saunders. He handed me a glass of champagne and said, "Get that down you!" It was his way of saying "forget it" – so he did have a sympathetic side.'

The final, contested by two teams who would both be promoted at the end of the season and attended by a crowd of 95,946, was hardly befitting of the occasion. Norwich veteran Dave Stringer suggested the game was so devoid of excitement it had the Saunders hallmark all over it, given his influence on both teams. Bond was still trying to add the flamboyance instilled in him from his West Ham United upbringing. 'It was a dour game and I had one save to make, which wasn't that difficult,' Cumbes said. 'I could have had my lunch in the goalmouth. We expected a much tougher game ... but they didn't turn up; we outplayed them.

'It was a dangerous game, though, as we didn't convert our pressure into goals. Their goalkeeper Kevin Keelan kept them in it. For us Frank Carrodus was unbelievable that day and must have covered every blade of grass. Frank was typical of the side's hard-working attitude.'

Graydon's winner originated from a Hamilton corner that Chris Nicholl headed towards an empty net and was destined for a goal before Mel Machin dived to hand-ball on the line, conceding a penalty. Graydon's spot-kick was tipped onto a post by Keelan, before he controlled the rebound and scored. Graydon netted six times in seven games either side of that final and was seemingly unstoppable – at least before the victory lap. He celebrated with the jubilant Villa fans, and was shaking a few hands when one overexuberant supporter pushed him forward and brought on severe leg cramp that deprived him of a lap of honour.

'I made up for it in the changing rooms,' said Graydon. 'I wanted to savour every moment so I got into the big bath last and stayed there to reflect on what we had done. I noticed that the lads had left about half a dozen plastic cups on the side still half-full of champagne and I swam across and downed every last one of them.' Graydon not only left London with his winners' tankard but also a slice of Wembley turf that he had removed the day before the final and kept moist in his hotel-room sink. He later placed it proudly in his garden in Sutton Coldfield.

There were chaotic scenes at Wembley. An Italian restaurateur by the name of Lorenzo, known to the Villa players, somehow talked his way into Villa's dressing room while bringing along his friend and a crate of champagne, which always helps when gate-crashing a party. Within minutes, Lorenzo, draped in a long fur coat, dived into the bath.

'It was a crazy situation as the champagne flowed quite freely,' Cumbes recalled.

There was a celebration on the night at Villa's team hotel with family and friends. Match-winner Graydon remembers fondly that his dad was able to see him play the final and then join him for a few beers afterwards. 'I walked Mum and Dad back to their taxi and for the first time in my life I heard Dad swear in front of Mum. I pointed out to him I'd never heard him swear before in front of a lady. He said, "Son, if you ever have a boy, and if he ever plays for Aston Villa, and if he ever scores the winning goal in a cup final at Wembley, make sure you fucking swear!"'

Ellis and the Villa board sanctioned a tour of the Caribbean at the end of the season to reward the players for their League Cup triumph and promotion. The players viewed the trip as a holiday and were delighted when the engine of the *Cunard Adventurer* malfunctioned on the eve of a match against a Barbados XI. While passengers scrambled up on deck to find a lifejacket, Ray Graydon was oblivious to the drama while watching Steve McQueen flick *The Towering Inferno* in the cinema, until a power cut denied him the ending. The prospect of drifting on a broken boat in the Caribbean Sea with a rum punch was seemingly more attractive than lacing up boots for an ultimately meaningless friendly after a tiring season. Not that a restless Barbados crowd shared that view. Fortunately for them, Ellis chartered a plane to fly the team to the game from their unscheduled stop in Caracus, Venezuela, as he felt he had to honour the fixture, which they did.

According to Ellis, Saunders insisted on leaving the tour early with his wife so he could collect his Bell's Manager of the Year award from Eric Morecambe at the Café Royal in London – and then be flown back to the Caribbean. Two years later, Saunders refused permission for Andy Gray to travel to London from Birmingham to receive his then-unprecedented double award of the Professional Footballers' Association's Player of the Year and Young Player of the Year prizes. Ron Saunders Jr, though, wished to put the record straight as far as what Ellis insinuated. 'Yes, he and my mother were flown back for the award, but they did not want to go. Dad has always been a terrible traveller and never even took long-haul family holidays. Doug and the club insisted he went and pushed him to go. Mom had to go too as she and Dad were on the same passport that the whole party was travelling on.'

The manager was also presented with that award in front of the Villa fans before the Leeds United match on 16 August. Intriguingly, 1974/75 was a good season for the lower tiers of English football as all four League Cup semi-finalists – Villa, Man United, Norwich, and Fourth Division Chester – together with FA Cup runners-up Fulham, Football Writers' Association Footballer of the Year Alan Mullery, then a Fulham player, and Manager of the Year Saunders all came from outside Division One.

Having achieved such rapid success in his first season, Saunders quickly became untouchable and all-powerful among the players and even in the boardroom, which was an irritation to Ellis despite his pride in the club's success. Saunders' influence grew and grew on the players and *his* way was always the *right* way. There were no grey areas. And as far as the directors were concerned, who could argue with a manager who had just won promotion and the League Cup in his first season? As much as Ellis respected Saunders' achievements, he was never comfortable with the manager's penchant to be involved in all club matters, whether agreeing transfers without directors' approval or cosying up to sympathetic ears in the boardroom. Ellis accepts he may have interfered too much in team matters but was more damning of Saunders and his fellow board members.

'Ron certainly made a habit of sticking his nose in business that did not concern him, like going around talking behind my back to other members of the board,' said Ellis, who was unhappy with the politics and atmosphere around the boardroom then. 'They made the mistake of listening to the manager more than me on too many occasions.'

Other directors could live with Saunders' desire to have more involvement in club matters than Ellis was comfortable with. The irritation worked both ways, for Saunders took umbrage at Ellis's keen interest in what was happening on the training ground, sometimes on a daily basis. Saunders viewed Bodymoor Heath as his kingdom and any visit from Ellis was unwelcome.

'Doug wanted to run the show, absolutely everything, and Ron wouldn't let him have anything to do with the playing side of things,' Harry Kartz recalled. 'They weren't too good together.'

Rather than live with the status quo, Saunders used his power earned through the winning of silverware to share his thoughts with board members, canvassing discreetly against Ellis. And when Saunders realised he had persuaded them, Ellis didn't stand a chance in their power battle. That discomfort resulted in Ellis making way, rather than the manager, as directors turned against the chairman.

'As Ron became more and more powerful he ousted Doug Ellis from the chair by undermining him verbally and any way possible,' said Charlie Aitken, a long-time ally of Ellis and soon to become a victim of Saunders' ruthlessness. 'How can a manager get rid of a chairman?'

It is an unusual question but a fair one in this case as the stand-off ultimately culminated in Ellis being asked to make way for new chairman Sir William Dugdale in 1975, with Ellis stripped of his power, his public profile and, to some extent, his dignity such was the humiliation of the move. Ellis reluctantly slipped back to the rank of mere director, after he had steered the club's course for the previous seven years.

How tirelessly did Saunders really lobby support among Ellis's fellow directors? Was Ellis paranoid?

'I don't remember Ron ever coming to my house and I am unaware of him going to any other director's house,' said Alan Smith.

'I know he would talk football with Eric Houghton, but that should be no surprise given what Eric achieved in football as a player and a manager. Other directors knew Ron was uncomfortable with Doug going to the training ground as often as he did and we as a board felt Doug had not got it right and was spending too much time on the training ground and interfering too much with the technicalities of the playing side.'

Saunders' stance was, 'I've been appointed manager so let me get on and manage or sack me if you don't like the way I work.' He did not want anyone constantly looking over his shoulder, which was how he viewed Ellis's presence.

'Ultimately, Ron was an ambitious manager,' Smith added. 'He got most things right and was arguably the best manager Villa have ever had, certainly since the war.'

Ellis's undoing stemmed more from a clash at boardroom level.

'They were all successful in their own right but they found it difficult to blend in, because of their egos,' then-secretary Alan Bennett said. 'Doug wanted to do things his way when he was chairman and that didn't always please the rest of the board. Doug upset people [on the committee] and didn't listen to them.'

Steve Stride detected a permanent atmosphere at boardroom level and viewed proceedings within the club as looking rather like a case of 'the manager and the rest of the board versus Doug Ellis'.

Alan Smith and Harry Kartz were both brought to Villa by Ellis yet they eventually turned against him on countless occasions, especially Kartz, who sided with the anti-Ellis camp in 1975 and again in 1979 when Ronald Bendall took control of Villa, leading to Ellis's departure, albeit temporarily. The movement to eject Ellis from the chair was not a sudden one according to Smith, who revealed it had been discussed throughout the summer of 1975. The directors often spoke among themselves behind Ellis's back and the hot topic was, 'Doug is spending too much time on the training ground and getting involved in things he shouldn't be getting involved in.' They felt it was not a chairman's job to be on the training pitch two or three times a week.

'Our collective concern was that we [couldn't] keep Doug in check,' Smith recalled. 'The manager should not have the chairman constantly watching training and interfering and wanting to be in all the photographs. The rest of the board felt the chairman was very important but should essentially be taking a back seat.'

Ellis reflected on those days with a clear annoyance still present in his voice. He was especially miffed by the way directors he had introduced to the club eventually sided against him. He and Kartz had been close allies at one stage and, in fact, it was Kartz who persuaded Ellis to buy a racehorse which they called El-Kar Ellis-Kartz. The purchase was simply fun for Ellis but would have meant more for Kartz, who was quite partial to a punt on the horses. Ellis's superior wealth allowed Kartz to live his dream of being a racehorse owner. 'We would go over to France and race it and had some good days together,' Ellis reflected.

'But Harry Kartz wasn't always the most loyal of friends and would side with Ron more often than he should have.'

The political fallout in the boardroom was unpleasant for all, but to Kartz it paled in comparison with other battles he had fought in his life. He had been an RAF gunner from 1940-46, flying in a Wellington bomber out of Honington airbase in Suffolk. He looked back with pride on the 'many missions' he flew over Germany.

'I had one or two scares in the war,' said Kartz. 'While we were dropping German ration books over Hamburg, we were caught in a searchlight but the pilot managed to get us out of that one. It put the arguments inside the Villa boardroom into perspective.'

New chairman Sir William Dugdale did not have Ellis's history of rebuilding Villa and staving off impending bankruptcy, but he did possess the diplomacy to handle the egos of Saunders and Ellis. Dugdale was an impressive individual despite not having a significant football background, other than being a lifelong Villa supporter. He had seen Billy Walker and Eric Houghton, a fellow Villa director in the 1970s, score in the first match he ever saw – a 4–2 win over Leicester City in 1932. Dugdale achieved more than most in a colourful life that came to an end in 2014. He was awarded the Military Cross for his bravery during the Second World War after fighting campaigns in North Africa and Italy; he rode in the Grand National; piloted aeroplanes in round-the-world races; was a qualified solicitor; and was chairman of the Severn Trent Water Authority, among other roles. Ellis dismissed Dugdale in his autobiography *Deadly Doug* as someone who was born with a silver spoon and lacked football know-how.

Alan Smith robustly rebuffed such an observation. 'Bill was born with a silver spoon in his mouth as much as his family was very wealthy and were very large landowners,' Smith conceded. 'But he was an extremely talented man. For Doug to say that is complete nonsense. Bill had got his heart in the club and had the club in his heart all his life. I saw him two years before he died and we talked about Villa. He had got a season ticket. He was every bit a football man as Doug. The difference was Bill was always very good with people.'

Director Harry Cressman was also loyal to Saunders, so allied to the support the manager enjoyed from Dugdale, Houghton, Smith and Kartz, Ellis cut an isolated figure on the Villa board. 'The next three years with Bill in the chair were outstandingly successful for Villa and that period led to the subsequent winning of the league championship and European Cup,' Smith added.

The ousting of Ellis and promotion of Dugdale was not the only development of significance in the boardroom that year, for a gentleman by the name of Ronald Bendall also emerged. Bendall, a Birmingham-born accountant who was tall with striking bushy eyebrows, was a tax exile living on the Isle of Man, who had made his millions by specialising in liquidations. At that time he was merely aspirational and seeking closer relations with the club to appease his Villa-mad son, Donald, even if he had been first introduced to Villa by his father, Frederick. Bendall played football and rugby at school, though claimed to have been a better cricketer and golfer at youth level.

'My father was not an avid supporter,' Bendall said in an interview with the official club's match programme in 1978, 'but Villa became increasingly important in the family after I was married. We were season-ticket holders, though I did not feel really close to the club until Donald became a fanatic. I probably wouldn't be on the board today but for the interest which I developed from Donald's enthusiasm for Aston Villa.'

Bendall was welcomed on to the board in March 1975 and was vice-chairman within a year, succeeding Kartz.

Bendall's ambitions would gradually increase, to the point where Aston Villa would eventually become his and Doug Ellis would have little choice but to surrender his position and his shares, and to leave for pastures new. It was a power battle that simmered and gradually evolved; not like Ellis's conflict with Saunders, which was immediate and boiled continuously. Bendall slowly integrated himself into Villa, building alliances from his original standpoint of knowing no one but his friend and club president Trevor Gill.

In fact, one such alliance was created almost immediately with Saunders. The manager was still in the process of selling his house in Norwich in 1975 and required a bridging loan to buy a property he had identified in Solihull, on the outskirts of Birmingham. The Villa board refused to help when Saunders asked for it, though Gill and Bendall were only too happy to assist. On hearing of this generosity, Ellis and the board reversed their initial decision and were all of a sudden happy to help their manager. It was yet more evidence of the atmosphere between Saunders and Ellis, and also of the distrust between Ellis and Bendall.

Bendall spent £25,000 on shares to buy into Villa. The mild-mannered

Dugdale did not take kindly to Bendall, according to director Alan Smith. As undemonstrative and respectful as Dugdale was, he was no fool and soon looked on Bendall suspiciously. Dugdale had Villa's interests at heart – rather like Ellis – yet Bendall's motives were always puzzling such was the disconnect he seemed to have with the game.

'Bendall knew nothing about football,' said Kartz, who resigned his vice-chairmanship before Bendall took the role. 'I remember one game at Villa Park when he didn't even leave the boardroom after half-time. He wasn't a football man. He was only ever interested in being chairman. But I will say this for him; once he got there he wanted the club to be successful.'

The Arrival
Of Andy Gray

'After Andy Gray started banging all those goals in at Dundee United,
Jock Stein said if he could have swapped Andy for Kenny Dalglish he would have.
And I know he would have paid cash on top.' – **Maurice Freill**

ASTON VILLA SUPPORTERS WOULD SHAKE AT THE THOUGHT OF A history without Andy Gray. Yet only fate enabled his arrival to materialise, during Villa's first season back in the top flight in 1975/76. While a severe, ultimately career-ending knee injury to striker Keith Leonard sustained against Arsenal in September was a cruel blow for him and the team, it was the reason Ron Saunders moved so quickly for a replacement, who would later become a club legend. Gray was scoring prolifically in Scottish football and subsequently earned a £120,000 move to Villa two months shy of his twentieth birthday. He soon wooed the Villa fans with his all-action, committed displays.

'It is strange how things can decide people's futures because if Keith had stayed fit and scored goals in the First Division I might never have joined Aston Villa,' Gray admitted. 'But he got a bad one, which would have been a big disappointment to Ron as he was a massive fan of Keith's, who was a tall, strong, bustling, aggressive centre-forward.'

Leonard had scored four goals in eight games at the start of that season and clearly had more to offer. But Gray's introduction added a more potent dynamic to Villa. Put simply, he was vital to the shaping of a new exciting era at Villa Park. Gray was a fearless, powerful frontman and the ideal goalscoring outlet in Saunders' hard-working, well-drilled team.

Midfield powerhouse Dennis Mortimer arrived from Coventry City two months after Gray and added further power and quality to a developing side. History should reflect that these were Saunders' two most important signings. Mortimer's eventual captaining of the European Cup-winning team remains his ultimate legacy. And without Gray's goals, who is to say how well Villa would have fared in the mid-to-late 70s? Saunders would certainly not have been able to bankroll his final team reshaping without the British record transfer fee received from Wolverhampton Wanderers for Gray in 1979.

Gray had been born in the Scottish football hotbed of Glasgow and raised on a council estate by his mother, Margaret. He was the youngest of four brothers and the lack of a father figure after his parents separated when he was two meant he looked to his siblings for guidance. 'My relationship with my father was fleeting and sporadic,' Gray revealed. 'My brothers, though, were football-mad and all played at various levels.' Willie was the oldest brother and possibly the most talented but he had to go off to work when their father left and he became man of the house. James played for Clydebank and was an early inspiration to Andy, who would sneak into the dressing room and collect the kit to be washed. The next brother, Duncan, was not driven to play professional football so it was left to young Andy to live the family's dream.

Gray believed his chance of a football career had passed him by at seventeen until his goalscoring exploits for amateur team Clydebank Strollers attracted the attention of local scout Maurice Freill. The scout's badgering of Dundee United manager Jim McLean to give the kid an opportunity eventually resulted in a contract. Gray's impact at Tannadice would embarrass Rangers and Celtic, who traditionally outmuscled all-comers to the signatures of the best talent in the country, especially as Rangers fan Gray was plucked from their own back yard.

'After Andy started banging all those goals in at Dundee United, Jock Stein [the Celtic manager] said if he could have swapped Andy for Kenny Dalglish he would have,' Freill recalled. 'And I know he would have paid Dundee United cash on top. It's highly unlikely Dalglish would have made that move but it does emphasise Andy's impact.'

Jim McLean was the perfect mentor for rough diamond Gray in those rookie days. The manager would spend many an afternoon on the Tannadice pitch, hitting balls for the youngster to control, working on his movement, his heading and his finishing. 'I felt like I had Jim to myself for three years – it was just amazing,' Gray reflected. 'Extra training wasn't punishment for me, while my mates were down the snooker hall, having a game of golf and whatever else. I wasn't the most talented footballer in the world but I had an insatiable appetite to make myself better.'

With his meteoric rise came the inevitability of a move south. Brian Clough offered £75,000 to take Gray to Nottingham Forest, despite widespread scepticism of whether he could replicate his form of 46 goals in just 62 games south of the border. McLean rejected Forest's approach but was prepared to sell him to German club Schalke after a six-figure sum was offered on the advice of scout and ex-Rangers goalkeeper Gerry Neef. Gray spurned that offer for a move to England. He observed how the likes of Joe Jordan, Billy Bremner, Gordon McQueen, Graeme Souness, Eddie Gray, Archie Gemmill and many more had advanced their careers by moving to England and he craved the same.

Ron Saunders targeted Gray after a tip-off from his former Portsmouth team-mate Tony Barton, who was then scouting for Pompey before his eventual switch to Villa Park. The Gray transfer was significant in Barton's moving to Villa after his advice proved so valuable. Barton had scouted Gray when the south coast club were languishing near the bottom of the Second Division in 1974/75.

'They were trying to buy the crowd by bringing in experienced names rather than young talent, which is why the likes of George Graham and Ken Foggo came in,' explained Chris Barton, the eldest of the late Tony Barton's three sons.

'Dad told them Andy Gray was scoring goals for fun at Dundee United and they only wanted peanuts for him, but Pompey weren't interested because he was an unknown. So Dad called Ron Saunders and said, "My chairman isn't interested in this Scottish kid but if I were you I would get someone to have a look at him."'

Saunders subsequently instructed his head scout Neville Briggs to watch Gray and he was impressed by the kid's talent. Villa chairman William Dugdale subsequently completed the deal, negotiating with his opposite number into the early hours while at a water industry conference in Bournemouth, during his work for Severn Trent.

With no video footage of Gray to analyse, as would now be a minimum course of action to research a potential signing, Saunders' first proper view of his new centre-forward was on his debut – a 0-0 draw at Middlesbrough. Ray Graydon felt Gray's clumsy touch let him down at first but acknowledged his enthusiasm to train and improve was such he quickly became an asset. Frank Carrodus also identified that rawness in Gray but was impressed by his courage and will to win. 'His signing was crucial to our rise,' Carrodus said. 'What a tough, brave player he was. Andy was as brave as a lion.'

Villa played a vibrant brand of football that suited Gray. A headed goal on his home debut against Manchester United in a midweek League Cup match did much to settle his nerves and ease Villa fans' reservations about the relatively unknown striker. He managed his first league goal in front of the Holte End against Tottenham.

'The fans would no doubt have been thinking, "Has Saunders gone mad, signing this skinny kid from Scotland?"' Gray reflected with a chuckle. 'So it was nice to start with a few goals.

'I was lucky because kids at that age can reach a club and realise you've made the wrong move. But Villa was a great fit for me. I loved the club, the players suited my game – they were a great set of lads – and I loved Birmingham, it was a good place to be at that time. The Villa fans took to me because of my style. I always played as if it was my last game.'

There has long been a misconception about the relationship between Gray and Saunders. The manner of Gray's acrimonious exit to Wolves suggested he and the manager did not enjoy working with one another, which was correct for the last year of his first spell at the club. But from 1975 to 1978, Gray was appreciative of the mentoring he received from Saunders. Devout family man Saunders, though, never liked Gray's attraction to the city nightclubs. In fact, Gray eventually bought shares in one. But the player is adamant his disciplinarian boss never had any reason to be concerned about his off-field conduct. 'I was a good pro and never did anything I shouldn't have done,' Gray insisted. 'I never got drunk on a Friday night and turned up unprepared for a game on Saturday. I was a young man who enjoyed my life, but I was always aware of my responsibilities.'

Villa had their first taste of European football before Gray arrived, when they faced Antwerp in the UEFA Cup, courtesy of their 1975 League Cup triumph. The 4–1 defeat in Belgium and then a 1–0 reverse at home were reminders that, while something exciting was under construction at Villa, the team was still way short of stepping up to that next level.

The away leg came first on 17 September and Austrian striker Karl Kodat netted a stunning twelve-minute hat-trick in the first half. It was 4–0 at the break. Graydon scored Villa's first competitive European goal thirteen minutes from time but it was a mere consolation. Leighton Phillips at Cardiff, Ian Ross at Liverpool and Frank Carrodus at Manchester City had previously sampled elite European competition, but otherwise Villa's lack of continental experience was ruthlessly exposed by an Antwerp side that included future Netherlands and Manchester United manager Louis van Gaal.

'That game in Antwerp came too early for us,' Charlie Aitken insisted. 'It was a nightmare from start to finish. Even before the game the team bus dropped us off about 400 yards away from the ground and we had to walk in this blizzard. When we reached the changing rooms it was freezing and I remember Saunders trying to light this big boiler and it nearly blew up in his face when he put a match to it.'

Goalkeeper Jim Cumbes acknowledged the goals they conceded were poor and that he was partly culpable. He also felt, though, he was made a scapegoat for the loss – Saunders never picked him again. He was moved on to Vic Crowe's Portland Timbers in the North American Soccer League. Cumbes was one of several ex-Villains to play for the Timbers in that period, along with Brian Tiler, Tony Betts, Pat McMahon, Willie Anderson, Barry Lynch and Mick Hoban, while a young Peter Withe joined from Wolves.

'Once you weren't in Ron's plans he completely ostracised you and you were sent away to the farthest part of the training ground to practise with the reserves or youth team,' Cumbes said. 'He just didn't want to know you – that was his style.'

With Villa out of Europe and out of the League Cup, their main focus was establishing themselves in the top flight. Saunders then turned to Mortimer to bolster his squad. He was a commanding midfielder who would soon replace 'Chico' Hamilton. Saunders had twice attempted to sign Tommy Craig around this time, but the Scotsman spurned his advances. Ironically, the manager finally did capture Craig from Newcastle in 1977 on a four-year contract with wages of £250 a week and an annual £4,000 loyalty bonus. That was for a club record fee of £277,000, but he only stayed half that time and Saunders later admitted it was a mistake as Craig never delivered.

Mortimer, a 23-year-old Liverpudlian, had been nurtured at nearby Coventry City from youth level to first-team regular. His team-mate David Cross had played under Saunders at Norwich and therefore the Villa manager used that network to tap Mortimer up in an unofficial dressing-room environment; Cross duly conveyed the message that Villa wanted him. This was a typical way for clubs to reach a potential new signing, long before the general custom of agents being used. Mortimer's future was seemingly decided in fast-forward, before he had much time to consider the option of joining Villa.

He then met his manager Gordon Milne, which was less a discussion and more an unsubtle hint that he *had* to join Villa, as the chairman did not wish to lose the £175,000 transfer fee that had been agreed. Milne drove the player down the A45 to the Malt Shovel pub on the Stonebridge roundabout – a local landmark halfway between Birmingham and Coventry. As they said their goodbyes, Milne advised: 'There's no going back now, son.'

In the event, the formalities were completed at Highfield Road but soon it was Villa Park which would become his home for the next ten years, though it wasn't exactly a dream move for Mortimer at the time.

'Villa didn't seem that much bigger than Coventry then, in football terms,' Mortimer reflected. 'Villa had only just been promoted but it was clear they were building under Ron. I didn't know anything about Aston Villa then but I didn't know anything about Coventry either when I joined as a kid. I suppose just like the saying goes, I was sent to Coventry ... when I came down to the West Midlands, the only club I knew about or was interested in was Liverpool, having been a fan from childhood.'

Mortimer saw which way the wind was blowing and did not oppose the move; after all, the fee had been agreed: £100,000 up front followed by three interim payments of £25,000. Now it was just up to the player to negotiate his terms.

'Ron and I knew what wage we would go to,' secretary Alan Bennett recalled. 'Ron was given an annual wage budget once a season and it was up to him how he spent it. So after he spoke football and sold his vision of Villa to Dennis, we got around to money. It was a normal tactic of ours to offer just ninety per cent at first of what we were prepared to go to, as most players would always ask for more. So Ron said, "Dennis, this is what we can offer you." Dennis looked at the papers and said, "Fine, where do I sign?"

'Ron paused, looked at me and said, "Alan, I think we can do a little better than that, can't we?" So we went up another ten per cent, plus win bonuses and a signing-on fee. Dennis was happy and we got our man. It was all over in twenty minutes. It surprised me and Ron how quickly Dennis was prepared to sign, but he clearly felt unwanted at Coventry. Later, Ron and I were congratulating ourselves on how well it had all gone and I asked him what the attraction was and he said, without delay, "We need a captain."'

Ian Ross was still Villa skipper and Chris Nicholl was his successor. But Saunders had already identified leadership qualities in Mortimer, who did take over the role in 1977 after Nicholl was sold.

Mortimer made his debut in a 4–1 win against West Ham on Boxing Day in front of 51,000 supporters. His final game for Coventry at Highfield Road a week earlier was a 2–1 loss to Everton, attended by just 14,419. Milne was genuinely sorry to lose Mortimer, having admired his 'engine' and tough, determined personality.

'I knew early on we were not going to be able to hang on to Dennis,' Milne acknowledged. 'There was some hype created around his performances that encouraged clubs to think about signing him. Jimmy Hill [the Coventry chairman] thought we should take the money and use it to find someone else, probably for half of the money. Dennis wasn't knocking on my door for a move – he would have been more hurt that we were prepared to let him go. But I knew we were never going to go where Villa were going.'

Mortimer was one of three midfielders sold by Coventry that year; another of the three, Willie Carr, was mystified by the club's transfer policy, having considered Mortimer, Mick McGuire and himself as the youngest and most exciting midfield trio in the top flight of English football. They were all sold in quick succession, with Carr and McGuire heading for Wolves and Norwich respectively. 'I couldn't understand why they did that, but it was obvious Dennis was destined for better things,' Carr acknowledged.

That season, seventeen-year-old apprentice Gordon Cowans made his Villa first-team debut at Maine Road, his only appearance in that 1975/76 campaign. He would soon become a permanent member of Saunders' midfield trio along with Mortimer and both were later two-thirds of Villa's most celebrated midfield ever. When Des Bremner replaced Frank Carrodus in 1979, that midfield three was complete.

Cowans was discovered by Neville Briggs, who had admired his footballing talents since Gordon was nine years old. He finally recruited the youngster by visiting the family home in Mansfield after his father, Walter, had relocated from County Durham to work in the Nottinghamshire coal mines. Cowans' mother,

Norma, shrewdly used Aston Villa's interest in her son to the betterment of her husband. 'Please give my husband a job as well,' Mrs Cowans appealed to Doug Ellis, trying her damnedest to extricate her husband from the bleakness of mining. Ellis valued Briggs' opinion so much he was happy to oblige, and Mr and Mrs Cowans were appointed as the first managers of the hostel the club opened in the summer of 1972, which accommodated the Villa apprentices.

When Gordon signed his first professional contract in 1974, Walter changed jobs and became the kit manager, while Norma was able to move into a house of their own. By 1977, Cowans was playing in the League Cup final; though he missed the Wembley showpiece, he featured in the two replays. His opportunities increased after a broken leg sustained by Alex Cropley.

Despite the captures of Gray and Mortimer and the rapid development of Cowans, Saunders made a further signing of huge importance that season when bringing in new head scout Tony Barton. This was not a double act that came together by fluke. They had played together at Portsmouth from the time Barton joined from Nottingham Forest in 1961 until Saunders' departure for Watford in 1964; they even lived three doors from one another on Fortunes Way in Bedhampton. They became a solid professional partnership when Saunders invited Barton and his family up to the West Midlands for a get-together that masqueraded as an official interview. Their children played together while they chatted at Saunders' family home. The job was, of course, offered and accepted.

The official title of Barton's employment was 'assistant to the manager' but it was more of a scouting brief, to identify new players and compile match reports on upcoming opponents. Barton, a gentleman in every sense, was also charged with the less desirable task of informing youth players they were not being retained, not a role that came easy to him.

Barton knew he had joined an honest, down-to-earth regime as soon as he moved into his new home, when he had first-team players pitching up to help. 'I couldn't believe it when Frank Carrodus came in carrying a chair, telling my mum to put the kettle on,' recalled Chris Barton. 'They weren't superstars in those days, just friends of the family, and much of that attitude was attributable to Ron.' Even John Gidman, then on the fringes of the England team, would pick Chris up in his yellow Triumph Dolomite Sprint and drive him to Bodymoor Heath for a kick-about with the apprentices.

Tony Barton so nearly sidestepped a football career; he could have played cricket professionally after making it into Surrey representative sides as a left-handed, middle-order batsman and medium-pace bowler. Instead, he became a conscientious scout. He was out watching games at all hours. His wife Rosina, known as Rose, was accustomed to his return home around midnight, usually greeted by a slew of messages from managers seeking his opinion on players. 'David Pleat, Bobby Robson and Brian Clough were just three who would call him often,' recalled Chris Barton. 'It wasn't unusual to have Cloughie sitting in our front room. Dad was good friends with Bobby Robson because they started their careers at Fulham together.' The Barton–Saunders dynamic worked because they were opposites. Saunders was the strong personality in the public eye, while Barton was low-profile and went about his work with a quiet efficiency. The players would see Barton fleetingly at the training ground when he met with the manager.

That 1975/76 season saw further changes to the team, as Saunders attempted to phase out Vic Crowe's squad and introduce his own. Alex Cropley was brought in from Arsenal having recovered from two broken legs; his pedigree had earlier been apparent when he played twice for Scotland in 1971. Secretary Alan Bennett recalled an interesting aspect to that Cropley transfer. 'When we signed Cropley, the two managers, Saunders and Terry Neill, had agreed the deal on the phone and when we got down to London the fee had gone up by ten grand. Ron was absolutely furious and after that he put a recording device on his phone. We paid the extra ten grand – because we wanted the player.'

Then Luton Town manager David Pleat tells his own story of how Saunders later played this very trick on him when selling him Mick Harford from Birmingham City, raising the price by £50,000 to £250,000. 'I wasn't particularly happy about that,' Pleat reflected.

Saunders avenged Neill's negotiation antics and any bad feeling from that transfer a month later when Villa hammered Arsenal 5–1, with Cropley ensconced in the Villa midfield. Not that Arsenal manager Terry Neill was sad to lose him. He felt that with Liam Brady at left midfield and with Graham Rix coming through, he didn't need Cropley, so the move suited all parties.

Another player introduced that season who flourished under Saunders, having been signed by Crowe as a youth player, was striker John Deehan. Deehan initially impressed Crowe with a first-half hat-trick in a trial for Villa under-18s against an

England under-18s team at the club's Bodymoor Heath training ground. He was only playing after his father called the club to advise them his son was about to trial for Arsenal, adding that because he was a local boy from Sheldon and a Villa fan, would they give him a trial too? They gave him a chance and he lined up against fellow triallist Charlie Young, who played in the England team. In the canteen after the match, Deehan Sr met Crowe, Frank Upton and Neville Briggs and, once they ascertained he had definitely not signed any forms with Arsenal, they presented him with an offer of a two-year apprenticeship. He was in. As a result of his joining Villa, Birmingham City conducted a review of how they managed to miss a youngster whose family home was directly next to their training ground at Elmdon Park, where he played every Sunday.

Deehan made his debut as an eighteen-year-old in a 3–0 defeat at Ipswich on 1 November 1975. 'That was a tough debut, with Mick Mills, Roger Osborne and George Burley all really good players. The whole experience was something new. I wasn't used to big-match crowds and I actually felt unnerved when John Peddelty scored their first. The noise was so loud I thought one of the stands was collapsing,' he recalled.

'My career took off when Andy Gray arrived,' Deehan added. 'I was pretty much the next man in for a couple of years; as soon as there was an injury to Andy, Brian Little or Ray Graydon I tended to get the call.'

Saunders was never reluctant to throw a rookie into the team and favoured mouldable youngsters rather than experienced players who he felt were less receptive to his philosophy. In that regard, Saunders' ruthlessness was never demonstrated more than when he opted to move on Charlie Aitken, who held the club appearance record. Villa failed to win a single game away from home in that first season back in the top flight. It underlined Saunders' prediction that his side needed three years to adjust to the higher standard. Team rebuilding was a continual project. Cumbes had already been ousted and Aitken was next. He was banished from the first team after a streak of six games without a win that culminated with a 2–0 defeat at home to QPR, who narrowly fell short of being champions of England that season. It was not a temporary omission for the veteran left-back either; it was to be the end of his career in England.

Aitken knew his days at Villa were numbered when Saunders called him into his office and, while puffing on a cigar, verbally abused him. 'I'm not willing to share what he said but it was so embarrassing the coach Roy McLaren walked out of the room,' Aitken recalled.

There was no problem with Aitken's professionalism for he was arguably the fittest at the club, even at the age of 33. The fall-out between player and manager was as much a clash of personalities and cultures. Saunders was a working-class man from Birkenhead and came to be Villa manager the hard way, through earning the right with spells at non-league Yeovil, as well as Oxford, Norwich and Manchester City. Aitken was significantly different in character; he could project aloofness through his superior education and self-proclaimed insistence that football was financially a waste of his time – that attitude irritated Saunders.

'I played football not because I wanted to as I wanted to go to university and go into politics or something that I was interested in,' Aitken said. 'My initial plan was to go and try life at Villa but probably with the intention to return to school in Scotland, but I made the first team pretty quickly and stayed on.'

Aitken went to night school to learn French in his early days at Villa at a time when he found it difficult adjusting to a footballer's life. 'I was educated to a tremendously high level having gone to one of the best schools in Great Britain,' he revealed. 'I had to completely change my personality and had great difficulty adapting.' Aitken utilised that education to good use and became something of an entrepreneur while at Villa. He sold insurance, let property, was knowledgeable on jewellery and also had an interest in antiques. He would even set Doug Ellis's grandfather clocks at his house, a relationship that would certainly have made Saunders suspicious of Aitken.

'Tony Barton told me years later at a function that Ron didn't like me because I was financially independent of football and had other interests,' Aitken revealed.

The manner of Aitken's exit was harsh. He was forced to train away from Bodymoor Heath. Poignantly, after sixteen years' loyal service to Villa, the only person at the club who spoke to Aitken directly after his ousting – before he left for a swansong in the USA with Pelé's New York Cosmos – was Ellis. Even Ellis was something of a peripheral figure himself by then with Sir William Dugdale in the chairman's seat. It was a complete changing of the guard throughout the club – and the manager was behind the plot.

Paisley's Liverpool 'Blown Away'

*'This wasn't just a good Liverpool team, you are talking here about
the best team in the world at that time ... Villa put on what was probably the best
performance you will ever have seen against us at that time ... As the goals
kept going in I remember myself and Emlyn looking at each other, speechless.
We were all shell-shocked.'* – **Phil Thompson**

IF 1975/76 WAS A SEASON OF TRANSITION, THE NEXT CAMPAIGN witnessed a meteoric improvement that culminated with another League Cup triumph and a courageous attempt at an unlikely league title win, Villa finishing just six points behind eventual champions Liverpool. There was one result, though, in a ground-breaking campaign that exemplified their upward curve.

Not often do even the best of teams manage near-perfection, but on a wintry Wednesday night in Birmingham on 15 December 1976, Aston Villa achieved just that with a slick, thumping 5-1 victory. And not against just any side, but a Liverpool team that retained the league championship and became champions of Europe for the first time at the end of that campaign, while also losing in the FA Cup final. Villa's win was a monumental event. Never again in that era were Liverpool taken apart in such a brutal manner. It had been a decade since any side had inflicted such pain on the Reds, when Ajax beat them by the same scoreline in a European Cup tie. Liverpool would win the league eleven times across eighteen seasons. Teams just didn't boss them around like on that night. Villa had weaknesses – but they played to their strengths. Ron Saunders, who played for

Everton and supported Tranmere Rovers in his youth, always regarded Liverpool as the benchmark for what his Villa team were trying to achieve: prolonged success.

'This wasn't just a good Liverpool team, you are talking here about the best team in the world at that time,' commented Liverpool defender Phil Thompson, who still recalls the match with a lingering hurt and disbelief having endured a torrid ninety minutes. 'Villa were a fantastic team then and on this particular evening they put on what was probably the best performance you will ever have seen against us.

'And it was the most incredible noise I have ever heard at a football match in my life, which is quite something given the amount of big-night atmospheres Liverpool experienced in those days. It was deafening. As the goals kept going in I remember myself and Emlyn [Hughes] looking at each other, speechless. We were all shell-shocked. It was 5–1 at half-time and there were some harsh words said but it wasn't a time for bollockings; we were so good then that we all knew our jobs. We had just been totally blown away.'

Liverpool had legends throughout their ranks, either established or at least in the making. Two-time European Player of the Year Kevin Keegan and England stars like Ray Clemence, Hughes and younger talents Phil Neal, Thompson and Terry McDermott. There were 438 international appearances in that side after they had all retired, compared to Villa's 82 and 58 of those were courtesy of Wales' defender Leighton Phillips.

Andy Gray opened the scoring in the tenth minute, while his fellow striker John Deehan made it 2–0 in the twelfth. Deehan added a third ten minutes later before Brian Little put Villa four goals up without reply by the 31st minute. By the time Gray struck a fifth on the stroke of half-time, four minutes after a goal by Ray Kennedy, it was game over. The victory could have been even more emphatic. It wasn't a night to single out individuals but one player not on the score-sheet but who was unstoppable was Dennis Mortimer, a boyhood Liverpool supporter who slipped the Reds' scouting net. He made both Deehan goals, Gray's second and fouls on him saw Thompson and Kennedy yellow-carded. His forcefulness in midfield powered a Villa display that shocked the footballing world. Supporters from as far away as Australia called into newspapers and television stations to check if the score was correct.

'We were just outstanding,' recalled Little. 'You have games where you can play well but out of twelve attempts only one or two might go in. But on this night, it was one of those games where every attempt went in. We wiped the floor with them. We absolutely slaughtered them and there were shock waves everywhere.' Phillips suggested the result might easily have been 8–1 had Villa been more fortunate, having hit the woodwork three times.

There was not one television camera present, pitifully for Villa, to capture possibly the club's most crushing, most polished display of all time. Cameras were instead at the Baseball Ground for the league clash between Derby County and Arsenal, while an Under-21 international between England and Wales at Wolverhampton's Molineux stadium further sponged up the media coverage in the region. Ironically, both of those other matches were goalless. Liverpool had beaten Villa 3–0 at Anfield three months prior, so few would have predicted this kind of freakish result. But it was no fluke, as Villa made significant strides that season – they were third in the table after thrashing Liverpool, and the league title was something to aim for.

'It was a great year,' Andy Gray reflected. 'After we beat Liverpool, we were flying and all of us thought we would have a chance of winning the league. We certainly felt we could win something – that was an absolute certainty. In the league we were competing against a great Liverpool side, but with a bit more luck we could have run them even closer for the title. The team we had was good enough to win the league.'

Few would disagree with Gray's statements, though Saunders was expert in reminding his players they needed to do more. There are managers who would use such a rousing performance to boost team confidence and instil in them supreme belief … 'You beat the champions 5–1 so you are a great team, you can win the league.' That wasn't Saunders' way and possibly was the greatest difference between him and Bill Shankly. Kevin Keegan spoke of his first meeting with the fabled manager when he was told, 'You're going to play for England, son,' even though he was a twenty-year-old rookie at the time. Phil Thompson's confidence was boosted in a similar way by Shankly at a tender age.

Saunders, though, preferred understated congratulations and a reminder that a good display meant nothing unless the next game and the game after that saw a similar level of commitment. Saunders' buzz phrase was to expect '110 per cent effort' from his players. While the manager did not wish to harp on about this genuine destruction of Liverpool, the players knew as a group and individually what they were now capable of. Mid-table mediocrity was no longer good enough.

Villa approached the Liverpool game following a morale-boosting 3–1 win at Elland Road against Leeds and their many celebrated names like Eddie and Frank Gray, Peter Lorimer, Joe Jordan, Paul Reaney, David Harvey and Trevor Cherry. While sceptics might say a fresh-faced, hungry Villa exploited an ageing Leeds team the wrong side of their glory years, there was nothing further from the truth with Liverpool. 'We ripped into Liverpool with pace, got the ball down, moved it forward and put them under severe pressure,' Gray recounted. 'They couldn't cope with the tempo we played at or the balls flying into their box. We pummelled them and Ray Clemence was shell-shocked at half-time. It was an amazing evening.'

So bamboozled were Liverpool they were beaten 2–0 at West Ham three days later, before they gave themselves a metaphoric slap across the chops and woke from their slumbers. What made Villa's margin of victory all the more incredible was the fact they were not at full strength. They were without their reliable centre-half and captain Chris Nicholl, owing to a broken nose, and he watched and he watched from the stands – in awe. Regular goalkeeper John Burridge was also missing, though his absence was felt less as his replacement Jake Findlay was an under-rated keeper and unlucky not to have appeared in more first-team games. Nicholl's loss, though, meant eighteen-year-old rookie Charlie Young came in for just his second match after debuting in the previous game at Leeds. Furthermore, new signing Alex Cropley was forced out of the game with an injury in the 56th minute and another eighteen-year-old, Mike Buttress, came on to make his career debut. Both Young and Buttress failed to make the grade at Villa and ended up at Gillingham. But on this night, they did just fine.

Young, born in Cyprus and the son of an English-born serviceman and Welsh mother, had been converted from a centre-forward and was spotted while representing Chester Schoolboys by an unlikely scout – John Gidman's father. Leighton Phillips, who guided his central defensive partner Young through the breathless encounter, reasoned that Saunders' penchant for organisation and work ethic meant a local Sunday League player could have been fitted into the team without him looking out of place.

'You wouldn't have dreamed of putting Charlie into a game like that at that stage of his career,' Frank Carrodus commented. 'But Saunders had little choice, which was a measure of the injury problems we were having that season.

'We absolutely battered Liverpool and had so much pace going forward – it was a delight to play in. We had also beaten Arsenal 5–1 a couple of months before so we were catching fire and taking teams apart. It was only the injuries that stopped us from winning the league. I tore knee ligaments on that bloody awful pitch at Derby in the same game that Andy injured his ankle, which caused us to both miss the second League Cup final replay. If we could have kept everyone fit I believe we would have won the league.

'Our casualty list was so bad Good Hope Hospital called the club to ask if they would return their crutches as we had something like eleven pairs.'

Phil Thompson concurred that Villa were genuine title contenders that season. He knew a few of their players as more than just opponents, having gone to school with Dennis Mortimer, played in the same Liverpool youth set-up as John Gidman and played for England's junior teams with Brian Little.

'They had the power of Andy Gray, the menace of young John Deehan and Brian Little was the catalyst for them that night – he was a great player and turned us inside and out. Ray Clemence was beaten by outstanding goals – there were no horrendous mistakes. The ball was literally flying into the back of the net.'

Little credits Saunders for the freedom he played with that caused Liverpool so many problems. The manager issued him with defensive instructions for when Villa didn't have the ball, but then gave him carte blanche to express himself when they were in possession. Little could pretty much do as he wanted and that suited player and team.

'That's another example of how Ron Saunders was a genius as a manager,' said Little. 'We hear about the modern-day "Number 10" position but that was basically what I played. Ron wanted me to try and stop their full-backs from attacking when we didn't have the ball but when we did he gave me licence to roam.

'We had the most organised team, run by the most disciplinarian manager in the whole country.'

For Scouser John Gidman the match represented one of the most satisfying moments of his career. To destroy the title-holders in such a way, the European champions-to-be whose previous regime had decided he was not good enough to wear the famous Liver Bird crest, meant this result tasted sweet.

He especially enjoyed seeing the manager with whom he clashed so often silenced when he would normally have meted out measured criticism in an effort to get further improvement. 'We totally outplayed Liverpool with all their stars and the Villa fans were stunned,' Gidman recalled. 'We were in the dressing room at half-time and Saunders barely said a word. What could he say? He just said,

"Have a cup of tea." He wasn't the type to praise any fucker anyway but how could he criticise that night?'

Another player who was enjoying the sweet smell of success was nineteen-year-old striker Deehan, who had only broken into the first team in the previous season. He would have been an unlikely starter against Liverpool had it not been for a long-term injury to Ray Graydon, who sat out four months of the campaign following a robust tackle from West Bromwich Albion's Len Cantello. Graydon's misfortune was Deehan's opening.

Deehan has vivid memories of that shocking evening: 'For the first goal, I can still picture John Robson motoring down the left wing and just before he reached the by-line he put his foot through the ball and I was waiting towards the far post, but before I could get to it, I saw Andy come from nowhere and deflect it into the top corner to put us 1–0 up. I scored two minutes later when I had an opportunity to skip inside, beat Emlyn Hughes and shoot to the far post. We never let up from there. My second, which made it 3–0, went through the legs of Ray Clemence.'

The Villa players were euphoric after the match and bottles of beer were passed around the dressing room freely; it wasn't your average victory for a midweek league match. 'We all went out that night,' recalled Jake Findlay. 'We started at the Bagot Arms because Leighton Phillips was pally with the manager there, then we went into town to Sloopy's nightclub. That was our nightclub and the Blues players tended to go to Rebecca's. We still weren't done there and finished up at the Elbow Room where George Best and Black Sabbath would occasionally visit. We wrapped it up in the early hours. Saunders didn't mind because that was the done thing in those days; he saw a night on the town as being good for team unity.'

The late-night drinking exploits and the physical exertion of the Liverpool game might have taken their toll on the players and affected their performance in the game three days later at home to Newcastle. Villa scraped a 2–1 win, though, which demonstrated that such a display against the Reds was never likely to be seen again. It was a once-in-a-generation performance and result. But a vital trait of Ron Saunders' teams was the ability to win matches when not playing to their optimum.

One familiar pattern that was soon resumed centred on the selection of Findlay. He played in the Liverpool and Newcastle games but as soon as Villa lost 3–2 at their bogey team Middlesbrough, he was dropped for the returning John Burridge.

Findlay did not play again for three months, even though the goalkeeper felt that he had played well at Ayresome Park.

'I don't know why I was dropped,' he revealed. 'It was difficult playing a game when you knew you would be out again even if you played well. It was only later in my career at Luton when I toughened up mentally and could handle it. I should have made a stand to leave Villa much earlier than I did because I was never given a run of ten or fifteen games, which would have given me more of a chance to establish myself.'

Villa might have finished closer to Liverpool or even surpassed them if their form on the road had been better. While they lost just once at Villa Park that season, to Birmingham City, they went down twelve times away from home. John Deehan, reflecting back on that successful campaign, blames Saunders and the senior players for not recognising how close they were to achieving something special.

'I'm convinced if we were more professional and could have closed out more away games, we would have won the league,' Deehan claimed. 'Those six points we lost the league by were only three away victories instead of silly defeats. Saunders could have given us a bit more information and said, "It's great we're winning at home but can we transfer that form on the road?" He was a manager who liked routine: jumping hurdles on a Wednesday, naming the team on a Thursday, an intense training session on a Friday, everyone knew their jobs. But to me he failed to point out there was a great prize ahead if we stopped getting beat away from home. It was a shame nobody, not just the manager but a senior player like Chris Nicholl or Dennis Mortimer, looked at that away form and challenged us to be better.'

Cup Hero Skipper Discarded by Ruthless Boss

'I saw Villa as my club after six years there and I didn't want to go. My family was happy, we'd finished fourth, won the League Cup. It was a complete shock to be sold, though I admire Ron Saunders for his ruthlessness.' – **Chris Nicholl**

VILLA'S TRIUMPH IN THE 1977 LEAGUE CUP FINAL WAS A LONG-awaited event that went on, and on, and on, until finally a result was settled – to the relief of the players as much as the fans and anyone else who had an interest in this drawn-out finale. 'It was a farce,' commented defender Leighton Phillips. 'The only good thing is that Villa paid us three bonuses, one for each match. We had a few beers after the second replay but we were keen to get back to Birmingham and move on with our league form.'

Could you imagine Manchester United or Arsenal in modern times playing in three finals just to claim one trophy? In total, Ron Saunders' men spent 960 minutes on the pitch to win their third League Cup, from the second round when they ousted holders Manchester City through to the conclusion of the final's second replay against Everton – a three-match saga attended by 210,000 spectators in all. Villa were fortunate in being drawn at home for the ties against Man City (3–0), Norwich (2–1), Wrexham (5–1) and Millwall (2–0), but their endurance was tested to the maximum by such a long campaign in which Brian Little amassed ten goals, including a hat-trick in a semi-final replay against Queens Park Rangers – this after the customary two-legged contest could not separate the sides.

The first game with QPR was a goalless draw at Loftus Road followed by a two-apiece stalemate at Villa Park, leading to the semi-final play-off. The replay was staged at Arsenal's Highbury stadium because Rangers won a coin toss for choice of venue. Secretary Alan Bennett said Villa would likely have chosen Molineux if they had won the toss. Brian Little ensured the third clash with QPR was settled in ninety minutes with a clinical hat-trick, though midfielder Dennis Mortimer set up two of those goals with typical surging advances from deep.

The original showpiece final at Wembley Stadium on 12 March was as much of an anticlimax as could be; a drab goalless affair. Everton manager and former Villa player Gordon Lee summed it up succinctly: 'The first game wasn't very good and it was more memorable for me for being my wife Irene's birthday.'

Leighton Phillips was equally uninspired by the football that both teams served up in front of the 100,000 crowd. 'On the day, the occasion got to a few of the lads – it was a terrible game to play in and must have been terrible to watch.'

The draw at Wembley set up the first replay at Sheffield Wednesday's Hillsborough ground four days later, the first time it had staged a major game as a neutral cup venue. The 1–1 draw came after Bob Latchford's last-minute equaliser cancelled out Roger Kenyon's own goal. If the second replay had less of a sense of anticipation, with a whole month going by before the teams reconvened at Old Trafford on 13 April, the match itself offered the kind of entertainment that had been greatly missing from the first two clashes as Villa prevailed 3–2 after extra time.

Villa's casualty list was expanding by the time the second replay arrived, with star striker Andy Gray ruled out due to an ankle ligament injury and Frank Carrodus with a knee problem – both sustained at Derby County's Baseball Ground, regarded then as something of a mud-heap. Another key man, marauding right-back John Gidman, only made the Old Trafford game after having a pain-killing injection before kick-off to repel a groin injury. Captain Chris Nicholl, too, played with a heavily bandaged left foot that he had turned in a pothole, again at the Baseball Ground. It is Nicholl's goal that this final is best remembered for, as his forty-yard strike surprised everyone and rocketed into the Everton goal to level the score at 1–1 with ten minutes of normal time remaining, after Latchford had given the Toffees a 38th-minute lead. Nicholl's goal made it into a poll for the 25 best League Cup moments in 2010 to mark the competition's fiftieth anniversary.

'Most of my goals were headers and usually mistimed headers that came off my nose,' the former Northern Ireland defender joked. 'The ball came out to the halfway line and one of their lads came at me so I dropped one shoulder and he went that way, someone else came at me so I dropped the other shoulder and left him standing. And I had no other shoulders to drop and just panicked as it was on my left peg – my wrong foot – so I put my foot through it and watched it fly into the top corner.' The ever-dependable Brian Little scored Villa's next two goals as they won after extra time.

Gordon Lee, who won the very first League Cup as a player with Joe Mercer's Villa in 1961, had been a runner-up in the competition in 1976 when his Newcastle United team went down to Manchester City. It would remain the closest he came to winning anything with the Toffees before his eventual departure in 1981. The former right-back thought the cup was set to be wrapped in Everton's blue and white at 1–0 late in the game at Old Trafford, until Nicholl shattered Everton hearts with his stunner. 'I'm pretty sure he never scored a goal like that in his life before or after.'

Villa's League Cup success came at a cost. The resulting fixture pile-up of eight games in twenty-four days in April weighed heavily on the relatively small squad. Villa's bold attempt at an unlikely league title win was affected by the amount of games that led to multiple injuries and fatigue. Nonetheless, another trophy win was a fine achievement, which gave Ron Saunders his second League Cup triumph in the four finals his teams had reached in five years. Villa also qualified for the UEFA Cup and that, subsequently, set up more mouth-watering adventures, culminating with a quarter-final against Barcelona.

Villa banked a record £500,000 from the three finals, which helped fund the £1 million development of the Witton Stand. The club's debt had been mounting so the League Cup success and associated income from the sale of corporate boxes, turnstile revenue and a donation from the club's internal Development Association to the tune of £250,000 soon wiped out the debt, though Saunders was always ready to test the board's willingness to release more funds for new signings. The manager was constantly plotting ways to improve what he had.

The three-match final and those added funds led the manager towards another key signing. Saunders was continually, and ruthlessly, assessing his squad in his drive to achieve more. Few would then have known he had identified Nicholl, his captain and defensive rock, as being one such player he was prepared to move on. His fellow defender Leighton Phillips believed Nicholl had at least another three seasons to serve Villa – as was the general view. Yet Saunders had already lined up the man he wanted to replace Nicholl with.

Everton's Ken McNaught had impressed him by marking Andy Gray so well in the first two finals at Wembley and Hillsborough. McNaught would prove a shrewd acquisition by Villa, even though Saunders almost bought Luton Town defender Steve Buckley, having already agreed a fee of £145,000 for his services, until Hatters boss Harry Haslam tried to hike up the price. In the short-term, Nicholl's departure upset various sections of the club. Secretary Alan Bennett revealed Nicholl's sale was the one exit that the William Dugdale-led board disagreed with Saunders on, but nonetheless they allowed him to run the team his way. Nicholl was approaching his 31st birthday at this time so was hardly past his prime.

'Ron was very suspicious of senior players so once you got to thirty, he was keen to move you on,' Nicholl reasoned. 'That stemmed from his experiences at Man City, which changed him. I felt we had an excellent relationship, but as I was his captain maybe he felt I had too much influence. I saw Villa as my club after six years there and I didn't want to go. My family was happy, we'd finished fourth, won the League Cup. It was a complete shock to be sold, though I admire Ron for his ruthlessness.'

The first Nicholl and the players knew of his departure was the day Southampton manager Lawrie McMenemy arrived at Villa's team hotel in Marbella, where they spent their end-of-season break. With that, Nicholl became a Southampton player.

Shortly after Nicholl's exit another senior player, Ray Graydon, who was nearing thirty, learned that Saunders was ready to offload him too after receiving an offer from Leicester City manager Frank McLintock. A late switch, though, took Graydon to Coventry City instead. Graydon felt the writing was on the wall when he witnessed the sale of his good friend Nicholl, who he had taken his coaching badges with. He did not wish to leave but also did not want to be left on the fringes at Villa when Coventry were offering him first-team football. 'Ray had a reputation for running up and down the right wing, putting in as many balls into the box as anybody else could,' Sky Blues manager Gordon Milne said. 'And we had two people [Mick Ferguson and Ian Wallace] who would always be in there trying to get on the end of those crosses. Ray was a good pro around the young lads and that was what we needed.'

As for McNaught, he was 22 but was looked upon as a senior player as soon as he arrived at Villa Park such was his confidence, maturity and physical stature – all qualities that Saunders admired for a man so young. The loyal Scot was reluctant to move because of the way his first manager, Harry Catterick, had personally tapped his parents' front door in Kirkcaldy while he was a teenager to arrange his move south of the border. But this was now a different time and McNaught felt unappreciated by Gordon Lee. 'I didn't want Ken to leave, but centre-half was one position where we had a few options with Roger Kenyon, David Jones and Mick Lyons,' Lee said. Like with Graydon, once McNaught detected he was not wanted he was very receptive to a £200,000 transfer to Villa.

'I was about to leave for the States when Ron Saunders first came in for me,' McNaught recalled. 'Just before I went I said, "No disrespect, Mr Saunders, but I have this holiday booked and I'd like to go." I was visiting my wife Maureen's aunt and uncle in Detroit and we then drove down to Florida. We were out there for a month. When I came back I wondered if Villa had bought anybody in the time I'd been away. They'd had their most successful campaign in many years the season just gone, but Saunders was still dismantling that team to build another. I carried on at Everton for the time being and went on a pre-season tour to Germany. On our return, Gordon Lee called myself and Mick Lyons into his office and said, "Which one of you two wants to go to Villa?" I found out that was a bluff and Saunders only wanted me.' McNaught challenged Lee on his decision to sell him after he had not missed a game for a season and a half, but Lee's mind was made up and so McNaught slotted into a new-look Villa defence alongside Leighton Phillips.

Exciting things were happening at Villa following the fourth-place league finish in the 1976/77 season – their best top-flight finish in 44 years. With 76 goals, they had scored more than any other club – Liverpool managed 62 – but, crucially, Bob Paisley's champions had conceded seventeen fewer, 33 to Villa's 50.

Andy Gray's contribution was recognised when his peers voted him as PFA Player of the Year and Young Player of the Year. Unfortunately for Gray he was blocked by his disciplinarian manager from attending the function in London on a Sunday evening to collect his prestigious awards, supposedly because there was a match three days later. Never before had a player won both Player of the Year awards. Cristiano Ronaldo and Gareth Bale are the only players to have matched Gray's achievement in subsequent years, which emphasises the scale of the feat. ITV were concerned that the winner of the two biggest prizes would not be present at the ceremony so Derek Dougan, chairman of the PFA, offered a chauffeur service from Gray's house with a commitment to return him home by midnight to appease his manager. Still Saunders blocked it. Dougan then tested Gray's resolve.

'When it was clear I wasn't going to be there Derek asked me to give one of my awards up and said that if we do it we can't tell anyone that I had actually won both,' Gray revealed. 'But I thought, thankfully, "No, if I have won both awards I'm going to keep both." Nine times out of ten at that young age I would have said to Derek, "OK, take one away," but I held firm, thank God.'

At the time, Gray did not appreciate the magnitude of his achievement as the award was only four years old. He was a rookie, new to English football, and suddenly he was being told that he was the best footballer in England. Therefore, he was a little overawed by the attention and adulation and didn't fight Saunders because he saw him as his boss who he needed to obey. It is only in the intervening years, seeing all the great players collecting their awards, he has come to appreciate his sacrifice. Gray is clear that if he had his time again he would defy his manager.

'I would have jumped in the car and gone to London to pick up my awards,' Gray insisted. 'He was wrong to block me, but it was a measure of his dislike for star players. Ron felt the hard-working, unsung heroes like Frank Carrodus and Ken McNaught – both fine players but who never grabbed the same headlines as I might have – should receive those kinds of awards. I never forgave Ron for not letting me go and as the years passed I felt stronger that he was absolutely wrong to do that. It was thirty years before anyone emulated what I did, so there are only three of us to have achieved that double. That's special, and it was special for the club, but Ron didn't think that. He didn't like one of his stars being feted. He didn't like players getting headlines and making themselves into heroes. He was all about the team, but what he failed to realise is that if you have a successful team it will mean you will have successful individuals. People who score goals will collect the most headlines, which wasn't something I chased, it was just my job.'

Saunders admitted years later that he should have handled Gray differently, which was a rare admittance of wrongdoing by a man who was always so sure of his own methods. 'At the time, he felt it was the right thing to do even though family members and close friends questioned him on why he stopped Andy from going,' Ronnie Saunders Jr revealed. 'Dad thought after a big night in London, he'd only get half a game from him the following Saturday – and that was if he didn't come back with a groin strain.'

Saunders knew he had to strengthen his squad further with a UEFA Cup campaign approaching the following season. McNaught replaced Nicholl, Graydon's sale offered regular first-team football to John Deehan, and Saunders wasn't done there. He never trusted Jake Findlay enough to promote him into the first team when John Burridge's transfer request was accepted and subsequently acted upon. Therefore, he recruited a young goalkeeper from Chelmsford Town in January 1977, Nigel Spink, who he saw as one for the future. Spink impressed Saunders with his potential and when he came to sign his first proper contract with Villa, the rookie keeper knocked on the manager's door to complete the formalities. He was soon in for a rude awakening that would prepare him for life under the strict, unpredictable manager.

'I'm not signing you here in my office, son,' Saunders said. 'You're not that good yet. We will go into the car park and do it there.' It saved Spink from the plastering career he was planning to undertake along with a life of non-league football.

So, as far as goalkeepers were concerned, Saunders was left with Findlay, who he was keen to offload, the outgoing Burridge and an inexperienced Spink. Saunders made a new goalkeeper a priority. He consulted his head scout Tony Barton and other contacts around the country in an effort to find his new number one, before settling upon a player who had just made his England debut but was not wanted at Arsenal. Terry Neill, the Gunners manager, was keen to recruit his countryman Pat Jennings from his old club Tottenham and so there was no future at Highbury for Jimmy Rimmer.

Barton was a friend of the chief scout at Arsenal, Gordon Clark, who had helped facilitate a move to Villa for Alex Cropley when he was unhappy at the Gunners. Clark explained to Barton there were a number of clubs interested in signing Rimmer, including Ipswich Town. According to Rimmer, Neill offered him a new five-year contract in March 1977 but also advised him that Jennings would be coming in over the summer. Rimmer was suspicious of Jennings' pending arrival and refused to sign the contract in the hope of better financial terms or another club moving in. In the event he was right to delay. Once he heard of Villa's interest in him he was keen to move, as he never settled in London and was not a popular figure at Arsenal, according to Neill.

'Jimmy Rimmer was a terrific goalkeeper and an excellent trainer but was a strange sort of lad,' Neill said. 'He could get tense, a bit nervy and superstitious.

He did a great job for Villa, but for me Pat Jennings was the greatest ever so it would have been tough for Jimmy to have stayed on and played.'

Neill did not delay once he knew of Villa's interest in Rimmer. He signed Jennings for £40,000 at 9.30 a.m. on a Wednesday and sold Rimmer for £95,000 at 12.30 p.m. the same day. While it seemed like a dream transaction for the Arsenal boss, Rimmer was equally delighted to be leaving a club where the manager saw him as an oddball 'with no personality'. At Villa, though, he would soon become Saunders' closest confidant among the players, so he was appreciated at last. The memory of Villa's 5–1 win the previous year against a Gunners team including Liam Brady, Alan Ball and Malcolm Macdonald was still in his memory, too, so he was well aware of his new team's potential.

'Villa struck me as a big club and I only wanted to join the biggest clubs,' Rimmer explained, having started his career at Manchester United. 'I never really settled in London and I never felt all that welcome at Arsenal. But that wasn't the case at Villa. Ron bought me because I had plenty of experience, especially after Chris Nicholl had just left. Ron and I met up every Thursday, privately, to talk about the game and he was always keen to know how the other clubs I had been at did things. I would tell him what the likes of Matt Busby did at United and how Bertie [Mee] operated at Arsenal. Ron believed in me and I was always adamant in our conversations that we would win things with the way he was building the team.'

Another player recruited in 1977 was Scottish rookie Allan Evans, considered then a rough diamond. He became a club legend over many years, but initially he had to earn his stripes. He was just a part-time footballer at Dunfermline, driving a fork-lift truck every day and playing matches twice a week, hardly having time to train properly. He did enough, though, to attract the attention of Villa scout Tony Barton and Leeds United were also on his trail after watching him score for Dunfermline, as a striker. His plan was to go to both clubs for a trial. But after three days at Villa, Ron Saunders pulled him aside and sounded him out about a move to the West Midlands.

'Despite my lack of fitness compared to the other lads who trained full-time, Ron saw enough in me,' Evans recalled. 'I told him I had a trial at Leeds planned and I would see how that goes. Leeds were my team as a boy because of Billy Bremner and Peter Lorimer so I was excited by that opportunity. But I thought after that Leeds might not want me and I could ruin my chance with Villa, so I joined Villa there and then and never looked back.'

Evans moved south to the West Midlands with wife Gillian, their two children and St Bernard dog, and their lives were soon to be transformed. Villa did not know it then but, in buying Evans after the signing of McNaught, they had secured the second member of what later became one of the club's best-ever central defensive partnerships.

Cruyff and the Screwed-Up Team Sheet

*'I told Saunders, "I'm disgusted by what you said, the things I've done for you, the games I've played for you when I've been strapped up, when I have been injected – there's not a part of my body that hasn't been injected to help the cause of playing for Villa and you over the last three years, and you tell people I'm a cheat? We're finished!"' – **Andy Gray***

THE MIGHTY BARCELONA WERE NOT EXACTLY THE DOMINANT force in the 1970s that they have been in the more recent Messi years but they were still a force. Especially for an Aston Villa side still only in their third year back in the top flight of English football. This UEFA Cup quarter-final was a mouth-watering event for Villa, whose rebuilding under Ron Saunders was ahead of schedule and exceeding realistic expectation. There was one overpowering factor that made the Catalans a substantial obstacle, for within their ranks was the Dutch playmaker Johan Cruyff, the iconic player of the 1970s. Villa's capable, industrious professionals had to find a way to compete with and even try to defeat this threat. 'They had superstars, we didn't,' was goalkeeper Jimmy Rimmer's assessment. 'We never classed ourselves in that way. That's how we won games – we believed in ourselves and helped each other out.'

Cruyff had announced he was departing the Camp Nou at the end of the 1977/78 season and so, with his farewell beckoning, there was a determination within the club to mark his exit with a major trophy. In the event, they did win the domestic Copa del Rey but they felt a UEFA Cup triumph would leave a greater legacy and was within their grasp. The fabled Dutch manager Rinus Michels was in his second stint as Barça manager; FIFA named him Coach of the Century in 1999 for leading Ajax, Barça and the Netherlands to some wonderful successes. The romantics of European football were keen to see the Michels–Cruyff double act combine triumphantly. In March 1978 Aston Villa were blocking their path to the last four of the UEFA Cup and Saunders was not in any way interested in Cruyff's reputation or aspirations of a happy swansong.

'My abiding memory of that game is actually before the kick-off,' Brian Little recalled. 'Ron Saunders was reading out their team sheet and when he got to Cruyff he paused, squinted a little and said, "Joey Gruff". With that he crumpled up the team sheet and threw it on the floor! But as good as Ron was with his psychology, it didn't help us this time. Cruyff absolutely tortured us. He was brilliant. I had never seen anything so quick over three yards. He was incredible, immense. Ron decided not to make any special plans for him, but we should have. Ron, as was his way, didn't want to give them too much respect.'

Cruyff, the man who inspired Holland's path to the 1974 World Cup final, could not be contained. Aged nearly 31, he was still a magician with a football at his feet and he orchestrated the first leg at Villa Park, when the club received £7,500 for the rights to televise the game. The Dutchman scored in the twentieth minute after dispossessing Gordon Cowans in midfield before embarking on a run which ended with a strike from 25 yards. Leighton Phillips accepted the blame for allowing Cruyff too much space and not tackling him, while Rimmer also conceded he should have made the save.

Rafael Zuviria's glancing header made it 2–0 with ten minutes remaining and Barça were seemingly set up for a comfortable second leg at home. It was then that Cruyff gestured towards the bench to be substituted after sustaining a knock to his Achilles from Frank Carrodus. He would likely have stayed on and seen the game out had the score been different but he felt he had done enough, the game was won and it was time to claim an early shower. Phillips' defensive partner, Ken McNaught, applauded the maestro on his way off, as much out of relief at not having to mark him any more as admiration of his performance. 'It was just a master-show,' McNaught reflected. 'You couldn't mark him, though you'd try. If he wanted to play in a space, he would find that space like all great players do. Just when I thought I had him under control, he was gone.'

After Cruyff hobbled off in the 82nd minute to a standing ovation from the visiting and home support, the match turned in Villa's favour, almost as if they had gained a three-man advantage. Just the very sight of Cruyff's exit to the tunnel buoyed Villa and, somehow, goals from McNaught with a diving header in the 87th and a tap-in by striker John Deehan in the 89th minute earned them an unlikely draw to level the tie.

Cruyff's departure was the obvious cause for the turnaround but another change that made a difference was the introduction of Allan Evans for his Villa debut. He came on for right-back and namesake David Evans, but played in what was then his regular position of striker with utility man John Gregory filling in at right-back. Evans' physicality was much-needed in what was a brutally competitive cup tie. The Scot was later nicknamed 'Psycho' by the Villa supporters and he gave an early indication why that would be so. His shoulder-barge on Barcelona goalkeeper Pedro María Artola caused him to miss his catch and the ball dropped loose for Deehan to tap home. It was a euphoric moment for players and supporters but, as Carrodus conceded, the team was lucky to escape defeat that night and the players generally believed they played better in the second leg in the Camp Nou.

'The home tie was one of the roughest games I ever played in,' Brian Little recalled. 'They were no angels in that Barcelona team. One of the lessons we took from those games was just how tough these top teams were; they kicked lumps out of us. There was a lad called Migueli – he followed me everywhere and kicked the hell out of me. It was hard to play against them; they were so physical and ruthless.'

The second leg was always going to be tough and became even more arduous when John Gidman was sent off after just 22 minutes by the Turkish referee, Doğan Babacan, for kicking out at their Argentinian winger Zuviria. Still, Villa took the lead through Little in the 57th minute and were 3-2 ahead on aggregate and appeared to be on course for a monumental upset that would have spoiled Cruyff's farewell party. However, the Catalans scored twice in the last 23 minutes to take the tie 4-3 on aggregate, despite a last-minute chip from McNaught that hit the top of the crossbar.

'With Giddy getting sent off early we didn't have the legs later on,' Phillips said. 'They put the Argentinian on Giddy and must have known that he could be erratic. He wound Giddy up by diving all over the place.' There was a general sense of what might have been had Villa kept eleven men on the park, but none of Gidman's teammates blamed him for his dismissal. His manager, though, who never needed an excuse to berate the outspoken right-back, was far less impressed.

Gidman wasn't the only culprit on the night for Deehan also acknowledged his inexperience cost his team when Migueli scored Barcelona's equaliser.

'Saunders kept shouting at me to fight my corner so this one time the ball came to me, I chested it and threw an elbow at the man behind me who I thought was [Carles] Rexach but was actually Migueli and I knew straight away I'd made a mistake,' Deehan recalled. 'This bloke lost it and chased after me until he calmed himself. He got me back though by scoring their first goal when I was his designated marker. They took a corner and I thought, "I can go and head that out," so as I went to clear the danger this Barcelona player came from nowhere with a flick-on, straight to the unmarked Migueli to score. Saunders didn't bollock me but he certainly pointed out that I lost my man. He was more disappointed at Giddy's sending-off.'

Villa's European sojourn came to a halt there in Barcelona but they had won much respect from home and abroad for taking Cruyff and his team to the wire for a place in the last four. Barça crashed out to PSV Eindhoven in the subsequent semi-finals. Saunders' team was incredibly fit from their pre-season hill-running routines and that allowed them to defend from front to back. Villa's UEFA Cup campaign began with 4-0 and 2-0 victories against Turkey's Fenerbache, a 3-1 aggregate win over Polish outfit Górnik Zabrze and then another 3-1 aggregate triumph over Spaniards Athletic Bilbao.

The campaign was ground-breaking for Villa as their best-ever Euro achievement but it meant so much more for some of the players and none more so than Ken McNaught, who arrived from Everton one week before the season started. He never had a pre-season after a drawn-out transfer saga and found it difficult to play alongside Leighton Phillips, who preferred a sweeper role, which was not what McNaught was accustomed to. He was more about one central defender taking care of the left side and the other the right side while covering for each other, too. Even training sessions could be uncomfortable, for McNaught was accustomed to controlling high balls and laying it off to cultured midfielders like Martin Dobson. But Saunders would stop training and lambast McNaught every time he tried to 'play' his way from defence. 'If I wanted you to do that I'd have signed Roy McFarland,' Saunders would say. Eventually McNaught understood his role, as a reliable, no-nonsense central defender.

It all made for a nightmarish beginning at Villa for the Scot as the supporters barracked his every nervous error. Scout Tony Barton had spent many hours working on bringing McNaught to Villa and his son Chris said his father thought at one stage he would prove to be a 'monumental cock-up', but the European campaign and his eventual partnership with Allan Evans remedied the situation and prevented an early move away from Villa Park.

'It seemed the harder I tried the worse it got,' McNaught reflected. 'The fans were giving me stick and it was only when Saunders came out and said, "The lad's had enough stick, get off his back," that things improved. He stood up for me and never once dropped me. He had a point to prove and he knew I'd get over it. The game where things changed was Górnik Zabrze when I scored two. After that I never looked back.' McNaught's form also improved once he moved his wife Maureen and their two Old English Sheepdogs to the West Midlands from their house in Formby on Merseyside. He had risked Saunders' ire on too many occasions through unsolicited dashes up and down the M6 against the manager's orders. Saunders was not short on snitches and players were more often than not rumbled when they opposed their manager's rulebook. Fortunately for him, though, McNaught was one of Saunders' favoured ones along with Jimmy Rimmer, Dennis Mortimer and latterly Peter Withe.

Saunders made Leighton Phillips his next high-profile casualty in his squad shake-up, a decision influenced somewhat by the traits he had detected in the more youthful Allan Evans, who he felt would be better served in a defensive role. Saunders revealed years later to his son Ron Jr that he would have liked to have kept Phillips and Chris Nicholl but his limited wage budget meant he had to be ruthless. After just three games as a striker, Saunders asked Rimmer and McNaught their opinions on playing Evans at the back and both agreed it was a tactic worth trying. Especially with Andy Gray returning from injury and with Brian Little and the free-scoring youngster Deehan up front. Evans had to be deployed elsewhere if he wanted to play. It also meant the short-lived experiment of playing the versatile John Gregory with McNaught was shelved. Gregory, too, was soon to be shown the Villa exit.

Evans recalled: 'Saunders came to me and said, "I'm thinking of playing you centre-back." I said, "Brilliant, I'd love it." I never looked back.' The first five games with the new-look McNaught–Evans pairing coincided with five victories, including a 6–1 demolition of Bobby Robson's vastly improving Ipswich Town, who won the FA Cup against Arsenal a week later. The 1977/78 season had proved another positive campaign with the UEFA Cup run and a top-eight league finish, even though it was four places lower than the season prior. John Deehan even received an England call-up for the prestigious international against Brazil. The proliferation of quality strikers then, with captain Kevin Keegan, Trevor Francis and Bob Latchford all in the starting XI, meant Deehan did not appear.

One major negative of this campaign was the broken leg sustained by Alex Cropley on 10 December against West Bromwich Albion at Villa Park. It kept him out of the game for exactly one year. Villa won a bruising encounter 3–0 but nobody was celebrating after this leg-break that was even heard by sections of the crowd such was the forcefulness of the tackle. It was Cropley's third such fracture and by far the worst, which effectively ended his career despite a few comeback attempts.

It was a cruel blow to someone who had been playing the best football of his career, six years beyond his only two appearances for Scotland while at Hibernian. Cropley blended fluently in a midfield trio that also comprised Dennis Mortimer and Frank Carrodus, and though the young prodigy Gordon Cowans was fast emerging, he would likely have had to wait for his opportunity longer had it not been for Cropley's misfortune. The midfielder who later became a taxi driver in Edinburgh acknowledged in an interview with *The Scotsman* newspaper that he was never the same after this injury, sustained following a late, high tackle from West Brom striker and fellow Scotsman Ally Brown, which snapped Cropley's leg at the shin when his studs caught in the turf.

'There are things about my football career that are vague in my memory, but that particular day I can well remember,' Cropley recalled. 'I remember how it happened, how I was lying and I can still smell the grass. I looked at my leg and saw a big hollow where the break was. The next thing I see is Andy Gray running from centre-forward to get the boy [Brown] by the neck. He had him up against the dugout wall.'

Unfortunately for Brown, though he enjoyed a successful and long career at the Hawthorns with 85 goals in over 300 matches, his name will forever be synonymous with the Cropley injury. Brown has never denied it was 'a bad tackle' but felt it was late rather than malicious, absolving himself from too much blame as the referee did not even book him for a challenge that he felt was no worse than many on that day. Brown's team-mate and fellow Scot Ally Robertson was a central defender who earned himself a reputation as an aggressive, no-nonsense player courtesy of his uncompromising approach. He was, therefore, often mistaken as the villain in the Cropley incident.

'I got the blame for it,' said Robertson. 'So many Villa fans associated me with that injury. I was a hard man as a player so it was an easy association to make. The fact I was called Ally too probably never helped.

'I trained with Cropley when I was an amateur as a teenager at Hibs, he was three years older than me and was a wonderful lad, the best. Later on we used to play against one another. Quite simply, Ally Brown would never have meant to hurt anybody. For him to do what he did, it was just a silly centre-forward's tackle. Ally is the nicest lad you could meet. It's sad because it was a nothing tackle and there were so many other things going on that were nasty tackles. It was a dirty, hard game and even without the Cropley injury there could have been three or four of us sent off.'

Another more controversial blot that season, which did not come to the fore for another year, was the manager's fall-out with star striker Andy Gray that occurred before the second leg against Barcelona. It was a serious enough disagreement to give Gray the motivation to leave the club he loved. He lost all respect for Ron Saunders through an episode that began with a training ground conversation when he was recovering from injury, three days prior to Villa's return leg at the Camp Nou on 15 March.

'I was getting treatment and Saunders came in – and he never came to the training ground at the weekend,' remembered Gray.

'At that stage I was really positive that I would be playing in Barcelona and was feeling ninety per cent fit. I thought that's what he would want to hear. But he asked me, "Are you fit today?" I said, "Well, no." Then he said, "If you're not fit today, I'm not taking you." I couldn't believe it. I told him, "I'm your best player, so if there's a good chance of me being fit, why wouldn't you take me?" But he just repeated himself that as I thought there was a chance I wasn't going to be fit, he would take someone else instead. He didn't even take me and as things turned out we took them very close. I might just have made the difference. Saunders denied Villa the opportunity to beat a great team like Barcelona on their own ground. I was a different kind of player and scored plenty of goals and with me in the team, we might just have surprised everybody.'

If that exchange was not hurtful enough to Gray, much worse was to come. On the Aer Lingus flight back to Birmingham after the game, Saunders spoke with a group of newspaper reporters and it was then that he accused Gray of cheating his manager, the fans, the players and himself by not playing.

One of those reporters was Peter White, who worked for the *Birmingham Post*

& Mail. He remembers Saunders making that comment in an off-the-record way, but nonetheless he said it. Nobody quoted the Villa manager, as that was the way relationships between players and managers and journalists worked. A trust existed. But, still, the damage was done.

'Nowadays I guess some reporters would plaster it all over the back page but we did things differently in those days,' White recalled. 'I was not much older than most of the players and I became good mates with players like Andy Gray, Brian Little and Dennis Mortimer so there was a trust between us that went further than player–journalist relationships. Although I never quoted Ron in my newspaper I still felt an obligation to Andy – who was a good mate of mine – to tell him what the manager had said. I didn't feel I was stirring or anything like that; I just made the point in a casual way that it's very obvious the manager doesn't like him very much. I have no regrets about telling him and certainly never thought at the time I was setting up a future British record transfer.'

Gray did not take the news of this character assassination well from his journalist friend. At the next opportunity, Gray stormed into the manager's office and vented his feelings.

'I told Saunders, "I'm disgusted by what you said, the things I've done for you, the games I've played for you when I've been strapped up, when I have been injected – there's not a part of my body that hasn't been injected to help the cause of playing for Villa and you over the last three years, and you tell people I'm a cheat? We're finished." I went on to say, "I don't want to play for you any more, I'm going to ask for a transfer and I'm going to get on with my job until I move. I want to go!"'

He played throughout the 1978/79 season under protest and still in dispute with his manager, who deliberated over the transfer. Saunders knew it would be for the best for him and the player if a move was sanctioned but he faced opposition from the board, especially director Doug Ellis.

'People thought I was staying when I got on with my job but that was me just being professional and doing my best for the football club. I told Saunders I had no respect for him any more and would definitely be leaving.'

And he did, to Wolverhampton Wanderers for a British-record fee, but that was not until September 1979, coinciding with the latter days of Ellis on the board. Following the Barcelona tie, Saunders was also close to having an opportunity to leave Villa Park when Leeds United chairman Manny Cussins asked the Villa board for permission to speak to him about the vacant manager's post at Elland

Road. But Villa denied them permission and it is highly likely Saunders would not have entertained the option either.

The 1977/78 season ended with a trip to Spain after Saunders approached the board and requested £10,000 to send the players away for a week. Despite the European adventure, the board felt the team had not won anything and did not deserve such a reward. They concluded with Saunders, though, that if he could source the funds his request would be accepted. The manager then raked through his contacts book and brokered a pre-World Cup friendly match between Villa and Sweden, which was subsequently played in Gothenburg.

'The board was then happy for the team to go to Spain,' club secretary Alan Bennett said, though Saunders did not make it to Spain and underwent eye surgery instead and met up with the team in Sweden. Coach Roy McLaren was ordered to ensure the players trained while they were in Spain so they did not arrive in Sweden 'looking like a bunch of drunkards'. It was easier said than done because the players did not fear McLaren like they did Saunders. The coach and secretary, though, had a lucky break at a time when they knew they would have a hard time instructing the players to train after a long, hard season.

'On the first day in Spain, the players were lounging around the pool when this beautiful, blonde German girl walks over to me and Roy and inquires, "I hear you are in charge of the Aston Villa football team? I am Heidi and I look after the hotel entertainment. I was hoping your players could help me with some fitness demonstrations for the guests?" We called Dennis Mortimer over and he took one look at Heidi and promised to assemble the boys right away! We ended up going to Sweden in good shape, as the fitness work didn't seem so boring all of a sudden.'

'My Biggest Hate was the Villa'

'I would have killed to beat the Villa,
but as hard as we tried they always used to beat us.'
– Alastair Robertson

WITH CHELSEA, TOTTENHAM, LEEDS, MANCHESTER UNITED AND Manchester City all in transition, the power base of English football was changing in the mid-to-late 1970s. Liverpool were still winning but the sudden emergence of Brian Clough's Nottingham Forest created a football power from the East Midlands. Villa's League Cup win and fourth-place league finish in 1976/77 and West Bromwich Albion's growth under Ron Atkinson's management also showcased a spike of improvement from the West Midlands as well. Meanwhile Wolverhampton Wanderers, Birmingham City and Coventry City were competitive and mostly established in the top flight.

Though Villa and West Brom were battling for supremacy in the West, Derby County were well past their Championship-winning highs of 1972 and 1975, and it was Forest who now claimed overall superiority in the region. The country would follow and, soon, the continent. Clough and his managerial sidekick Peter Taylor masterminded miraculous results having steered Forest to promotion from the second tier in 1977. A year later they would win the First Division against all the odds. And if that wasn't enough, Forest then claimed successive European Cup victories in 1979 and 1980. Their rapid success somewhat dwarfed the steady yet encouraging growth that was going on at Villa Park, as well as the Hawthorns for that matter.

Ironically, Clough employed a similarly basic philosophy to Ron Saunders inasmuch as he wanted his defenders to defend and keep the ball out of his own team's net and any positive forward play from them was a bonus. Once his attacking players were in possession he wanted them to express themselves, with pace and flair.

Gordon Milne and John Barnwell, the respective managers of Coventry and Wolves at that time, both feared West Brom more than any other force in the Midlands because of their danger in attack with players like Laurie Cunningham, Willie Johnston, Cyrille Regis and Tony 'Bomber' Brown, with the grit and determination of Bryan Robson, John Wile and Len Cantello supporting them. It was an exciting combination.

Villa's star striker Andy Gray remembers the challenge of taking on Forest to be so much more testing than West Brom or any other side in the region.

'West Brom had a decent side under Big Ron and Jim Smith was doing a good job at Blues, so it was a vibrant region to be a part of then,' Gray said. 'And around that time there was also Derby, Leicester, Coventry, Wolves and Forest, so the Midlands was an unbelievable place to be. It's such a shame many of the teams aren't there now and that rivalry has gone.

'But when we speak of the best of them then, Cloughie won the league so they had to be the best team in the Midlands, but we were very close behind them. We were better than West Brom. I felt we could beat West Brom any time and most times we did that. They had a terrific side as they showed when they went to Old Trafford and hammered United 5–3 [in December 1978]. But I always felt we had the beating of them.'

In support of Gray's comments, Villa played Forest six times over that late-70s period – four times in the league and once each in the FA and League Cups. Forest won on all six occasions. However, in six meetings with West Brom between 1976/77 and 1978/79, Villa won three, drew two and lost just once.

'My biggest hate was the Villa,' West Brom defender Ally Robertson openly admitted. 'I would have killed to beat the Villa, but as hard as we tried they always used to beat us. We used to beat Blues and then Blues would beat the Villa and we as a team would think, "How on earth have they lost to them?" We could beat Forest at home though they usually beat us at their place. But Villa … we could batter them but they'd always win. I don't know how or why. Maybe we wanted it too much and we tried to do things we weren't used to.' There is a perception that the really vicious derbies tended to be Villa against Birmingham, West Brom against Wolves and Forest against Derby. However, John Deehan explains that while he was most excited by any Villa–Blues clash, there was always something in any of the Midlands derbies. He was part of the Villa side that struggled to gain favour from Clough's well-disciplined unit and he knew all about their threat, having represented England Under-21s with Tony Woodcock and Viv Anderson, while there were other chief protagonists such as Peter Shilton, John Robertson and Kenny Burns. In fact, Burns, like Trevor Francis two years later, made the switch to Forest from Birmingham City and so was never in need of any motivation against Villa. Deehan was still a rookie in those days but he had to learn fast about the blood and thunder of derby-day football.

'Kenny Burns threw his arm out at me in one match and caught me in the throat and I could barely speak,' Deehan recalled, with a chuckle. 'I was gunning for him after that. Maybe out of innocence of youth I got him back with an elbow and split his lip open. His defensive partner Larry Lloyd said to me just after, "You stay over this side of the pitch with me now, son, and we'll see it through together." I think he was genuinely worried for me on one hand but also putting me off my game on the other. They were a tough duo at the back.'

Deehan was raised in Sheldon, a Birmingham City stronghold. His father, though, who worked at the nearby Jaguar factory, raised him as a Villa supporter. Naturally, that fixture always meant more to him but his first experience of 'second-city' derbies coincided with a two-season period from 1976 to 1978 when City won all four clashes. To further emphasise the wood that City had on Villa then, in the 1976/77 campaign when Villa finished fourth in the First Division, they lost just once at home in the league – to Birmingham City. No matter how successful Forest were under Clough and Taylor, Aston Villa were always the club all the others wanted to beat in the Midland derbies. Maybe it was their rich history and stature, which had been restored through the 1970s. But there was no doubting Villa were the 'Manchester United of the Midlands', the club all its rivals raised their game by an extra ten per cent against.

'Villa was the big game for me,' acknowledged West Brom's legendary midfielder Tony 'Bomber' Brown. 'The coaching staff at West Brom would always instil in us that Villa were the enemy and that has stuck with me. It was great, I love local derbies, there's nothing like them. I know traditionally Wolves are supposed to be our old enemy but I have to say Villa–Albion was the big one for me because we played against one another more times.'

Despite the needle that existed on match days, the managers of the various Midland clubs enjoyed a convivial friendship and afternoon rendezvous after training between the likes of John Barnwell, Brian Clough, Jim Smith, Ron Atkinson and Gordon Milne were not uncommon. Most of them had rubbed shoulders with one another in the lower leagues at some point as they sharpened their teeth in management – with Atkinson playing for Ron Saunders at Oxford. The one man who was less close to the rest was the devout family man, Saunders. The other managers liked and respected him but they did not socialise.

'There was nothing wrong with Ron and I never had a problem with him, but you couldn't get close to him like you could with other managers,' Gordon Milne revealed. 'I would say to my assistant Ron Wylie that Ron seems a bit guarded. And Ron would reply, "You've got to be guarded working for Doug!" And Ron Wylie had been at Villa as Vic Crowe's assistant so he knew all about Doug.'

Ron Atkinson became all too aware of Saunders' antisocial nature. He remembers calling Saunders to console him after he was sacked by Manchester City. Yet when he took the West Brom job, he said the Villa boss was the last of the local managers to phone him and that was only because they had business to discuss.

'Ron was very single-minded,' said Atkinson. 'He wasn't bothered about winning popularity contests. Whereas with me, if I was going to watch a game I would call Jim Smith and say, "I'm going up to Liverpool to watch a game, do you want to come along and travel together?" I would never have made that call to Ron.'

It was not only the managers who learned to put to one side their local differences in the interests of socialising with their neighbours. Ally Robertson, as competitive and aggressive as players came, acknowledged that however ugly things could become on the pitch, any bitterness and hatred was left right there on the field. After the final whistle, he would always look to shake the hand of his adversary, whether it be Andy Gray, John Richards or whoever else. 'We would always have a drink after the game, maybe even see each other up Liberty's [the nightclub] later on the night. I used to kick ten bells out of Gary Shaw and we'd then see each other on the town and just laugh about it. It was a lovely time to play football.'

Andy Gray's penchant for the Birmingham nightlife was clear when he invested financially in the Holy City Zoo venue. It became a hangout for teammates and local adversaries. Strangely, contrary to popular opinion, it was never a problem with Saunders and Gray acknowledges one of the nicest gestures the manager ever made towards him centred around his nightclub, which Gray only visited on the odd occasion, as opposed to every night as might be assumed. There was a First Division game on Wednesday, 7 March 1979, against Bolton Wanderers at Villa Park, which just happened to be the day of the launch of the nightclub under Gray's ownership and he was expected to be present early in the evening, which was highly improbable. However, Saunders then shocked Gray with his unusual offer. 'Ron came to me and said, "I hear your club is opening tonight?" I said, "Yes." He said, "I tell you what I'll do, if we are winning well at half-time, and you've played well, I'll take you off and you can go down and support the boys." I couldn't catch my breath – and he was true to his word. I walked off at half-time when we were leading 3–0, I'd scored one, and Ron let me be on my way. All the lads were like, "Where are you going?" I said, "I'm off now, boys, I've given you a 3–0 lead, don't mess it up!" [The final score was 3–0.] I don't believe anyone who knows Ron would believe he did that.'

Gray preferred wine bars to the sort of typical pubs the majority of Villa's fans would frequent. He soon became known as a regular celeb who might be spotted enjoying the Birmingham nightlife and even became an acquaintance of the members of burgeoning pop group Duran Duran, as his club was located not too far away from the Rum Runner, where Duran Duran formed and played live. Gray was more familiar with the management of the band and frequently played tennis with Mike Berrow, one of the two brothers who put Duran Duran together.

'We all used to go out,' Gray revealed. 'It was a great scene, it was a fabulous city, always buzzing. And in terms of the football, there was ourselves, West Brom and Birmingham City all in the top league so the banter was great. There were lots of other Midlands clubs around there too.'

Ron Saunders' ongoing revolution, meantime, continued to evolve and a further injection of youth in that 1978/79 season was a significant step towards Villa's subsequent success. Midfielder Gordon Cowans was now established as a regular first-teamer as was Allan Evans. Striker Gary Shaw was introduced and so too were full-backs Colin Gibson and Gary Williams. Ironically, Shaw made his first-team debut at Bristol City's Ashton Gate ground while still an apprentice, coming on for the final thirteen minutes, and it was there, sixteen months later, that he firmly announced himself with a hat-trick in a league match. Fittingly, Shaw's rapid development came at a time when Villa officially bade farewell to retired striker Keith Leonard, who had his testimonial on 25 September 1978 when the current Villa team played the 1975 League Cup-winning side. Leonard's team-mate from that '75 final, John Robson, was also granted a benefit game after he was forced to retire having been tragically diagnosed with multiple sclerosis. It was a time of change all round, some of it forced on the manager, some not. Youth was Saunders' focus as he sought to complement the seniors like Dennis Mortimer and Jimmy Rimmer with young legs.

Colin Gibson and Gary Williams quickly impressed the manager and would eventually vie for the left-back role during Villa's glory years. But at this stage, they were still hungry young rookies. Gibson was so desperate to become a footballer he moved 170 miles north from Bridport on the south coast up to the West Midlands. He knew very little about Aston Villa but that was not important to him. Playing the game professionally and being involved with a club in the upper echelons of the game was.

Gibson was a Chelsea supporter as a boy. His scant knowledge of Villa was such that he did not even know they were based in Birmingham. He knew Birmingham City were there, for obvious reasons, but not Villa, until he was scouted and subsequently educated on the club's history and geographical positioning. 'It then started to dawn on me that I was coming to a huge football club,' Gibson recalled. 'I really appreciated the fact I was joining a big club, which was maybe not seen to be as big as Liverpool but still was threatening to go places.'

Gary Williams had no such difficulties given that he was born and bred in nearby Wolverhampton. Williams journeyed to all of the major Midlands clubs for schoolboy trials and actually rejected offers from West Bromwich Albion, Wolves, Birmingham, Derby and, further afield, Plymouth Argyle, as his gut feeling told him Villa were offering more opportunities to the youngsters and playing their apprentices in the reserves, not only their surplus senior players. 'That was the key for me and it turned out to be a good decision as I mostly played in the reserves in my first year as an apprentice,' Williams said. 'I was a central midfielder for my school and the county team and I had not played anywhere in defence until I went to Villa. Once I got to Villa I started out at centre-half, then at full-back. I made my first-team full debut at left-back against Nottingham Forest but I hadn't played there before in my life. I was most comfortable on my right foot.' Williams' first task as an apprentice was to clean the boots of first-teamer Bobby McDonald. Ironically, Williams eventually succeeded McDonald and his replacement in the left-back role Gordon Smith.

Saunders always had his eye on the youth players who he felt good enough to challenge for first-team places. Goalkeeping rookie Nigel Spink impressed the manager with his attitude from the get-go, though had to be patient for his chance as understudy to the ever-present Jimmy Rimmer. But it was still an upward curve for Spink considering he had arrived from non-league Chelmsford Town after West Ham manager John Lyall told him he'd never make a footballer. He had been ready to give up on football, before Tony Barton spotted him and he signed on at Villa for £55 a week.

Youth certainly had its chance under Saunders, but not all the rookies around the squad, tried or untried, were able to make the cut. Striker Joe Ward was signed from Clyde for £35,000 but was never able to make an impact, making just three appearances after his debut at Manchester United on 24 February 1979. Others who failed to establish themselves included Willie Young, Mike Buttress, Charlie Young, David Evans, Ian Hendry, David Hughes, Keith Masefield, Lee Jenkins, Terry Bullivant, Gary Stirland, Robert Hopkins and Noel Blake, though the latter two would both later sign for Saunders at Birmingham City and become first-team regulars. Ivor Linton stayed at Villa Park for six years and eventually won a retrospective European Cup winners' medal, specially commissioned by the club, for his appearance as a substitute at Dynamo Berlin, but he only started sixteen games before he was moved on to Peterborough in 1982. Gary Shelton was an £80,000 signing from nearby Walsall and actually enjoyed his best season in 1978/79, chipping in with seven goals in nineteen league games from midfield, but he too was unable to cement his position.

Allan Evans, at least, was one rookie Saunders gambled on who paid the club back with such loyal service it is difficult to quantify. But he did have to earn his breakthrough in those early days, once he replaced Leighton Phillips as Ken McNaught's central defensive partner. Evans was on a pittance of a wage when he first joined Villa, so once he made the first team he plucked up the courage to ask his intimidating manager for a contract renegotiation, in the summer of 1978. He was without a club car, unlike his teammates in the first team, and he craved the day he would earn one as part of his financial package.

'I wasn't worried about the wages – the car meant more,' Evans recalled. 'Saunders offered me a meagre rise of about an extra forty quid a week but he laughed when I asked for a car. I told him I was disappointed and left. He called me back about half an hour later and told me I could have the club car. That was Ron's way of looking after me but just making me feel like he had done me a favour. Halfway through the next season, I was doing really well but my wages were still well below everyone else so I knocked on his door again. I told him I felt I deserved a wage that put me in line with the higher earners at the club. Ron paid very little attention to what I was saying, almost like he was distracted by more important matters. Then he said, "I need you to do a bit more," and I said I couldn't do any more, we got into a mini-argument and I left with a bit of an atmosphere.'

Evans acted like he played – with brutal honesty and transparency, leaving little to the imagination. Although they are usually admirable qualities, with Saunders one might argue it was pure naivety. Certainly, Evans was taken to task over his manner with the manager, even if he did have his way ultimately with his wages. The Scotsman was hauled into Saunders' office the following day and warned about his conduct. Evans added: 'Ron told me, "I don't like you coming into my office demanding things. Don't do it again!" I said, "But gaffer, I think I've earned that rise." Then he went, "I know, that's why we're going down the club this afternoon to sort you out a new contract. Now get out there and train." Sometimes you had to stand up to him, though I can remember on more than one occasion practising what I was going to say the night before as he was a fearsome customer to take on.'

While Evans' future at Aston Villa was settled for the foreseeable future, that could not be said about several other players, as Saunders was about to embark on his third and final team-rebuilding programme that would reap great rewards in time, but not before much upset among ousted players and anarchy in the boardroom.

All Change
off the Field

*'The Bendalls hated Ellis and that feeling fuelled their
appetite for buying more shares in the club. Every time they did that,
it was like a punch on the nose to Doug.'*
– Steve Stride

BRIAN LITTLE RARELY HAD MUCH INTERRACTION WITH THE
boardroom or the directors, but he did happen to witness the comical early
introduction of Ronald Bendall and his son Donald to life at Villa Park. Bendall Sr
was reversing his Rolls-Royce when Donald, who was supposed to be waving him
back into a safe parking position, failed his father as the luxurious 'Roller' shunted
against a wall. Bendall Jr just said casually, 'That's far enough, Daddy!'

Little's amusement was interrupted by thoughts of 'Who are these guys? They
must have a few bob.' Little never took much notice of boardroom figures or, as he
succinctly put it, 'those sorts of people'. The manager was the manager and they
would be all-encompassing in those days of autonomy. Indeed, to the Villa players
Ron Saunders was the manager, the chairman and pretty much everything else.
Why is this anecdote relevant? Because these two gentlemen may have emerged
initially as joke figures, but in time their influence and wealth meant Aston Villa
Football Club would become theirs.

This would not happen, though, before years of boardroom upheaval that usually saw the manager at the centre of any disagreement.

Ron Saunders never stopped plotting and planning for a more auspicious future on the pitch and his buying and selling from the latter half of 1978 to the end of 1979 gathered pace. He set about creating what would become the third and final team of his tenure. Life in the boardroom, meanwhile, was equally eventful and, ultimately, divisive.

The whole of the 1970s rarely saw harmony among Villa's directors, as infighting, one-upmanship and power battles reigned supreme.

'That was the main reason why I left,' secretary Alan Bennett remembered, of the time he resigned after ten years at the club to take up the same position at Leicester City in 1979. 'I recall commercial manager Eric Woodward saying to me sometime in the mid-70s, "I'm getting fed up of standing with my back against the wall," meaning he didn't want to be stabbed in the back by anyone. Myself and Eric didn't take sides but the problem with that was if a director didn't see you as being with them, they automatically concluded you must be with their rival.'

The infighting was one reason why Bennett left Villa. The other reason typified a habitual weakness of the club – refusing to pay a sufficient salary to retain top players or, in this case, staff. Bennett was highly regarded within Villa and across the English game. Leicester offered him 33 per cent more than he was earning at Villa, who waved him on his way with a 'Good luck' as opposed to trying to improve his terms after ten years' service.

The fractious atmosphere upstairs at Villa was not unrelated to team matters. Ron Saunders had the backing of the board to the extent that he manipulated and cajoled his way to near-overall control of the whole club. He wasn't just a football manager; he was more a general manager. But the one man who often opposed him and who was suspicious of him was Doug Ellis. Saunders and Ellis had a lingering distrust of one another right from the time the manager made Frank Carrodus his first Villa signing in 1974, prior to receiving approval from then chairman, Ellis. Their relationship never improved thereafter, though Ellis generally accepted that Saunders was good for the club because of his abilities to manage the team.

Once Ellis lost the chairmanship in 1975 to William Dugdale, though, his grip on the club slipped, until his complete exit was sealed in 1979. That humiliating departure was accelerated in no small part by the presence of the Bendalls, notably Ronald.

Bendall Sr had little regard for football and only a passing interest in Aston Villa. His involvement was almost a favour to his Villa-fanatic son, Donald. But once ensconced in club matters and once horns clashed between him and Ellis, his natural ego and competitiveness of not wishing to lose in business took over.

'Ron Bendall started buying up shares in Villa to oust Doug as soon as he was voted onto the board,' fellow board member Harry Kartz said. 'He and Doug used to fight one another for the shares.'

Bendall said in an interview in 1978 that owning Villa was never his primary intention during his early years as a major shareholder, though Ellis would care to differ. As the years passed, the situation changed, though Bendall always maintained publicly he merely acquired shares when they were offered him. Quite simply, Ronald Bendall did not understand football, which was why he never interfered in team affairs when he was director or, eventually, owner. Of course, Saunders enjoyed that added autonomy. Bendall's indifference to football matters meant he rarely clashed with fellow board members in their meetings, unlike Ellis, who would often bemoan Saunders' overspending in the transfer market or on player wages. That landscape widened the gulf between Ellis and the rest of the board.

Steve Stride was promoted to secretary from assistant to replace Alan Bennett in 1979, after working his way up the inner ranks of Villa. The club could not have employed a more passionate employee, for Stride was a Villa supporter from boyhood who would go on to serve in the position until 2006. It was a job he adored, having pretended to be Gerry Hitchens back in the early 60s. Around that time, he was bought a season ticket for the Trinity Road prior to the 1962/63 season as a reward for making it through to grammar school. Stride began at Villa in 1972 on £23 a week as an administrative assistant after sending a letter for a job to Ellis. By 1981, he was earning £11,000 per annum, which was £3,750 more than future manager Tony Barton.

Stride had a front-row view of the boardroom fallout. 'The Bendalls hated Ellis and that feeling fuelled their appetite for buying more shares in the club,' said Stride.

'Every time they did that, it was like a punch on the nose to Doug and a signal to keep out of club business. Of course, Ron [Saunders] loved that.'

The Bendalls were not all that popular themselves within the club, but were just more popular than Ellis with the people whose opinions mattered – Saunders and fellow board members. Stride describes Bendall Sr as a big, towering lump of a man who would sit in his office telling crude jokes to which office staff felt obliged to chuckle along politely, if uncomfortably at the same time. 'Donald was the same,' said Stride. 'Just like a rich man's son, whose dad had bought him a toy; he was a pillock. He would hang around and people just wanted him to go away – he became a nuisance around the club.'

A volatile wind of change initially swept through the boardroom at the club's Annual General Meeting on 17 August 1978. Harry Kartz, who had been vice-chairman from 1972 to 1975, was installed as chairman by default after Dugdale, Harry Cressman and Alan Smith resigned as directors eight days earlier.

Their resignations were in protest at Bendall's and Ellis's refusal to give Saunders the three-year rolling contract he requested. It would have meant that if he was ever dismissed he would earn three years' pay. Ellis, especially, robustly opposed this desire of the manager. An angrily worded joint statement from the three outgoing directors read:

> We have as you know advocated strongly for many months that a new contract, with immediate effect, for Ron Saunders was essential to the continued success of the club. Ron Saunders has brought the club from a position of mediocrity in the Second Division of the Football League to a place among the world elite. To our way of thinking the club should have acted towards Ron Saunders in a way which not only he but his coaches, the players and the supporters would have regarded as giving him security and continuity of control, to which he is justly entitled. Our failure to persuade the board about this has placed us in the invidious position that we and in particular Bill are forced to defend in public and, in the immediate future, at the Annual General Meeting a decision to delay the offer of a contract, a decision which we believe and have always believed to be profoundly wrong.

And off they went, out of the boardroom and the club.

Ronald Bendall remained on the board as vice-chairman, along with Ellis and Eric Houghton, with Donald Bendall joining them. It was an ever-changing landscape in the boardroom as the Bendalls snatched a firm grip of any shares going spare.

Directors' interests in Aston Villa as at 30 June 1979 shares £5 each:

	Special shares As at June 1978 / and June 1979		Ordinary shares As at June 1978 / and June 1979	
J.H. Kartz Chairman	3	3	31	31
R.F. Bendall V.Chair	360	374	19,233	19,530
H.D. Ellis	278	288	5,172	10,018
W.E. Houghton	1	1	12	12
D.J. Bendall	21	24	1,178	1,311

Source: AVFC library records

Kartz, on taking up his new role, indicated all was not well in the boardroom. He reserved his sharpest barbs for Ellis, whose ongoing opposition to Saunders was rarely appreciated or welcomed.

'I regret what has happened because I personally believe we had a board of tremendous potential,' Kartz said. 'However, when so many differing personalities are together in one boardroom I suppose it is always possible that something may happen.' He added, 'All I want is for us to have a harmonious board, so we can back the manager, players and staff. They must feel as though they have the entire board backing them if we are to continue our progress towards the top of English football.'

Events that preceded the boardroom tussle centred on heated discussions surrounding Saunders' new contract but also Ron Bendall's plan to have his son Donald join him on the board. It was Alan Smith's turn to seek re-election, in which case he was prepared to sacrifice himself in favour of speaking out on behalf of Saunders and the need to keep Villa's successful manager happily in his post. Smith had the support of Dugdale and Cressman, but once all three resigned it only served to empower Ronald Bendall all the more. But Saunders was at least handed a one-year extension to his rolling contract, so something positive did come out of the public furore. His salary rose from £25,000 per annum to £29,044. 'The act of resigning was all orchestrated with the intention of getting Ron Saunders a new contract because he had manifested himself to being a good manager by that point,' Smith recalled. 'So our action accelerated that process.'

As personnel on the board shifted, one thing remained constant: Ron Saunders' power and influence on club matters, especially transfer and wage issues. Harry

Kartz felt Saunders 'was no-nonsense yet was awkward to get along with' but he always appreciated his football management skills over any political agenda. Saunders was the manager who stopped directors from travelling on the team coach, but Kartz accepted the policy if it helped team unity.

'I knew how to handle Ron Saunders – you had to let him run the show, certainly as far as the playing side was concerned anyway,' said Kartz. 'I'm a Villa man and what was best for the Villa was right by me.'

Bendall and Kartz, and William Dugdale before them, were no messiahs in being able to co-exist harmoniously with Saunders. They just did what was needed. It was normal during that era for managers to be strong and crave a certain degree of control, while benefitting from the support of a right-hand man. Saunders had the control, and the support of Roy McLaren and Tony Barton. The autonomy Saunders enjoyed was only how Alex Ferguson managed later at Manchester United. Various managers of Saunders' generation ruled with an iron rod, like Brian Clough, Bill Shankly, Jock Stein and more. So if there was anything abnormal about the status quo between manager and boardroom it had more to do with Ellis's backbiting against the manager.

This background eventually paved the way for the greatest boardroom change of that time when Ellis departed Aston Villa altogether; a humiliating exit for a man with such a large ego and a painful one too, for his heart was firmly attached to the club. The move had been brewing with his gradual distancing from the other board members, while his relationship with Saunders was always tempestuous. Ellis believed he was ultimately the victim of back-stabbing and that his position on the board was untenable when Ronald Bendall pushed Kartz forward as the new chairman in 1979. That, in spite of Ellis being a more natural frontman for the club, as he had been between 1968 and 1975.

Kartz rejected Ellis's claims: 'I don't think he was stabbed in the back – he was simply voted off the board.' Ellis initially attempted to instigate the removal of the Bendalls and Kartz, writing a letter of his intention to the club secretary on 17 September 1979 that he sought their removal at the next AGM. But his aggressive tactic backfired on him.

Ellis finally agreed to sell his shares to Bendall on the understanding that if he ever sold them, they would be offered back to Ellis at the same rate. The spat ultimately meant Ellis was forced to sit powerless on the sidelines, like a scolded child watching his friends play the most enjoyable of games while he watched on from a distance. He was left deeply upset that the club he had helped to build from the brink of financial ruin, with a youth system he had funded and nurtured, had slipped from his grasp.

Ellis had no official role at Aston Villa from his resignation on 14 December 1979 to the date of the Bendall's eventual withdrawal on 30 November 1982, which coincided with the club's most successful period in their history. Villa stalwart Eric Houghton followed Ellis out of the boardroom by resigning his directorship on 31 December 1979.

Irrespective of the personal differences within the boardroom, Ellis's issues with Saunders was at the root of all his problems. It was his failure to win the backing of other board members against Saunders that alienated him as an isolated figure among the club's hierarchy. Indeed, Frank Carrodus saw it that way. 'Doug made the mistake of trying to take on Saunders when he was too powerful. You can't oust a manager who has won promotion, two League Cups and generally improved the team's league performances and got the club back into Europe.'

With Ellis gone, the club's spending registered less of a concern for the boardroom as the wage bill for the playing side of the club rose by 158 per cent from June 1978 to June 1981. Bendall and Kartz gave Saunders a freer rein on transfers and wage hikes – and the balance sheet showed as much, even before Ellis had actually sold his shares and exited the Villa stage. The long-term consequences of the spending were overlooked, however. Saunders would bring success to Villa Park.

Annual Wage Bill for Manager, Coaches and Players
including levies and bonuses

June 1978	£397,622
June 1979	£574,767
June 1980	£847,855
June 1981	£1,026,329

Source: AVFC library records

105

All Change
on the Field

'[Trevor] *Francis had asked for a transfer and a full discussion took place*
on the club's possible action should the transfer request be granted.
The manager agreed to inquire from Birmingham City's manager [Jim Smith]
the situation the following day.' – **AVFC board room minutes**

THE YEAR 1979 WAS A YEAR FOR REVOLUTION. CONSERVATIVE PARTY leader Margaret Thatcher defeated Labour's James Callaghan to become the United Kingdom's first female Prime Minister on 4 May, commencing an eleven-year reign that would split the country between lovers and haters of her hard-line policies.

Two days earlier, world-famous rock band The Who performed their first concert since the death of their iconic drummer Keith Moon, kicking off their *Who Are You* tour at the Rainbow Theatre in London.

Music trends were also changing; electro-pop reached number one in both the single and album charts as Gary Numan led the way with his hit song 'Cars'. Synthesiser bands and New Romantics such as Duran Duran and Spandau Ballet would soon exploit that movement into the early 1980s.

In cinemas, sci-fi made arguably its most significant footprint as a genre with the release of Ridley Scott picture *Alien*, starring Sigourney Weaver. The movie grossed more than $100 million and spawned a lucrative franchise in subsequent years. *Star Trek: The Motion Picture* was released the same year and began another film franchise that led to eleven films over the next three decades.

Radical changes were also afoot at Aston Villa. If ever proof was needed of Ron Saunders' ruthlessness in his quest to achieve more success, then it was delivered from the summer of 1978 to the latter half of 1979, especially.

Even though Villa came within six points of a shock league championship title in 1977 along with a League Cup triumph, followed by a UEFA Cup quarter-final appearance in 1978, it was not enough for the manager to remain loyal to a large contingent of his first-team squad. The European adventure masked shortcomings that Saunders was all too aware of that an eighth-place league finish and two premature cup exits did expose, despite a horrendous injury list. Further, there was growing division in the dressing room with some players wholly supportive of their manager come what may, while others chose to fight him and his methods. Saunders could tolerate players he did not necessarily like personally but who still performed for him on a Saturday afternoon and Wednesday evening. But as soon as those differences caused dressing-room unrest, then the manager knew he had to act.

He had already offloaded his former captain and defensive rock Chris Nicholl a year earlier to show how sentiment would never be an obstacle for him. When he took stock of his squad in summer 1978, he felt he needed yet another shake-up to achieve the success the club expected of him and which he demanded of himself. This desire was only strengthened in the following season by a horror run of injuries to players like Alex Cropley, Andy Gray limited to fifteen games in the 1978/79 season due to knee troubles and Frank Carrodus knee problems restricting him to just six appearances all season. John Robson's cruel diagnosis of multiple sclerosis led to his early retirement.

The framework, though, was in place. In Jimmy Rimmer, Saunders had the experienced, reliable goalkeeper he did not identify in Jim Cumbes, Jake Findlay or John Burridge; centre-back Ken McNaught had overcome a difficult baptism to eventually prove himself as Chris Nicholl's replacement; Allan Evans' development from Scottish rookie to English top-flight defender was good enough to bring about Leighton Phillips' subsequent exit that year; while Dennis Mortimer and Gordon Cowans were firmly ensconced in the centre of midfield. The attacking tip of his armoury was potent and robust, with Andy Gray, John Deehan and Brian Little, but nonetheless was still an area in line for change.

Gray, Findlay, John Gidman and John Gregory were never Saunders' favourites and were all sold over the next eighteen months, along with left-back Gordon Smith and midfielder Tommy Craig. Even players who had served him well, and loyally, were not spared. The sale of Deehan was, though, a surprise given his goalscoring exploits at such a young age.

Incoming transfers within this period who would become key players included Tony Morley, Des Bremner, Kenny Swain, David Geddis and, briefly, Gary Shelton.

The signing of Geddis sparked boardroom debate as Saunders agreed a deal with Ipswich Town without his board's approval, reasoning he had to move fast as West Bromwich Albion were chasing him as well. Saunders' son Ron Jr explained the real reason why his dad occasionally 'went solo'. 'He would find that the press got hold of the information, so he would sometimes give the board the odd red herring [to expose the leak]. Dad wanted no contact with the press until the deal was done as this would mess things up or create an auction and the price would go up. He was very shrewd with his business.'

The new arrivals coincided with the rapid growth of young players Colin Gibson, Gary Williams, Brendan Ormsby and Gary Shaw, who notched 22 goals in 21 Central League appearances and five goals in Villa's triumphant Southern Junior Floodlit Cup campaign of 1978/79.

'Ron was an expert in changing things around and regenerating his team,' Brian Little said. 'When you are one of the lads you get a bit upset if one of your mates is sold off, but good managers know when to shake things up.

'There was no middle ground with Ron. You were either in as a player, or you were out. And when you were out, you were kicked out. He didn't have to like you and you didn't have to like him, he just did his job and that was how he worked.'

In November 1978, Phillips was sold to Swansea City and became one of the early casualties of Saunders' final revolution. With Evans and McNaught's central defensive partnership flourishing, the Welshman was no longer required; Saunders was never one to rely on experienced figures in reserve, always preferring young and hungry rookies on the sidelines preparing to grasp their chance, such as Brendan Ormsby and Noel Blake.

Phillips had an inkling his days at Villa were numbered when the manager called him into his office and asked him to be captain following the departure of Chris Nicholl. Although stating what a privilege it would be, he pointed out that Ian Ross had been captain shortly before being sold to Peterborough and Nicholl had led the side before he was shipped out to Southampton. He laid down his concerns about meeting the same fate, having just bought a five-bedroomed house in the salubrious suburb of Sutton Coldfield, where his children were settled in school.

'Saunders said to me, "Haven't you just signed a new three-year contract with Mr Kartz?" I said, "Yes," and he replied, "There you are then, you'll be here for another three seasons." But still I was gone soon after,' recalled Phillips with a chuckle. 'Villa bought me for £100,000 and sold me for £70,000 so I only cost them thirty grand. I have no idea why I was sold but Giddy, Andy Gray, Brian Little, myself, Budgie John Burridge, nearly everyone had their differences with the manager at some point. I'm just proud I was there at the start of the journey in that Villa team. I had the time of my life.' Chelsea inquired with Villa about Phillips first but they were in disarray then and had no money to offer, which was of no interest to an Aston Villa desperately seeking to reduce their own overdraft.

Days after Phillips left for his native South Wales, Saunders attended a board meeting and informed the directors his squad needed strengthening, notifying them that England striker Trevor Francis, the terrace hero of fierce rivals Birmingham City, was available for a transfer. It was a move Francis might well have rejected for fear of ruining his legacy at City, but still demonstrated Saunders' determination to improve his team. The board advised Saunders in no uncertain terms he needed to sell before he could recruit any more players, but they still penned the option of buying Francis in their boardroom minutes. It read: 'Francis had asked for a transfer that morning and a full discussion took place on the club's possible action should the transfer request be granted. The manager agreed to inquire from Birmingham City's manager [Jim Smith] the situation the following day. The board felt that the club had about reached its maximum commitment.' That Francis subsequently broke the British transfer record by signing for Nottingham Forest for a million pounds was enough evidence that Villa could never then have afforded him, given their budget restraints.

Saunders, motivated to raise cash for new players, quickly offloaded goalkeeper Jake Findlay to Luton Town for £100,000 after he had slipped to number three in the keeper rankings behind Jimmy Rimmer and Nigel Spink. Chelsea tried to sign Findlay and Saunders actually worked on an exchange deal with the aim of bringing Clive Walker to Villa but that never transpired. Life under Saunders' regime had been a slow, painful suffering for Findlay, but in Hatters boss David Pleat he found someone who finally believed in him and appreciated his abilities. The transfer only went ahead after Pleat succumbed to a canny trick by Saunders.

'I remember going to see Ron at his office at the training ground,' Pleat recalled. 'Ron said, "Sit down there, I'll be back in a minute." While he was gone I noticed this list on his desk that was titled 'Players to sell'. Jake was one of them. I suspect Ron wanted me to see that list and I certainly couldn't help noticing it. I was happy to sign Jake because he was a bloody good goalkeeper. He was big, strong, had huge hands and he commanded the box. Jake was terrific for me.'

In the same month, John Gidman submitted a second transfer request, which was rejected by the board. Gordon Smith also requested a transfer after rookies Colin Gibson and Gary Williams were increasingly preferred in the left-back role. Smith, in fact, was fined two weeks' wages for complaining in the media about his lack of first-team opportunities. He started just six league games that season.

Saunders was becoming ever more frustrated by his team's casualty list and wasted no time in reinvesting all of the £100,000 he earned for Findlay on Chelsea winger Kenny Swain, who had impressed him during the *Daily Express* five-a-side event at Wembley Arena. Swain's move was completed while Chelsea were managerless following the sacking of Ken Shellito. Indeed the Londoners would be relegated from the top flight that season after finishing bottom.

Swain met Saunders at Bodymoor Heath and was sold the Villa dream. That same week, Villa beat Chelsea 1–0 as Swain watched the match from the stands. Afterwards, he confirmed to the Villa boss that he would be joining. Swain was initially bought as a right-sided forward who could fill the hole Ray Graydon had left over a year earlier, but those plans would change the following season.

In the New Year, Doug Ellis continued to caution the board against Saunders' overspending, which led to what was effectively the board's first acknowledgement of financial mismanagement. Ellis exploited their rare agreement with his concerns and proposed there be no more player purchases until Villa's bank overdraft was significantly reduced.

Saunders was still under pressure to offload players before adding further to his squad and he advised the board in February 1979 that he was receiving 'continual enquiries' to sell Gordon Cowans, Gary Shaw and Gary Williams, though there was no enthusiasm to part with any of those starlets, destined to be the future of the club. He told the board he would instead seek to transfer Ian Hendry sold to Hereford for £5,000, Tommy Craig sold to Swansea City in the summer, Ivor Linton went unsold, Gordon Smith bought by Tottenham for £150,000 and, surprisingly, John Deehan who eventually joined local rivals West Bromwich Albion for £400,000 after bids of £250,000 and then £300,000 were rejected from Queens Park Rangers.

'We had a few quid available and I was looking round,' West Brom manager Ron Atkinson said of signing Deehan. 'I wasn't sure if we could get him; I don't know why, but Saunders didn't seem to fancy him so we took him.'

Saunders tried to buy Wolverhampton Wanderers' winger Steve Daley to give his team more bite and pace in wide positions. The enquiry was not especially encouraged by Wolves manager John Barnwell, who craftily blocked Villa's overtures for his star man by demanding that either Andy Gray or Dennis Mortimer move in the opposite direction in return. Saunders was initially deterred, but came back with a second approach. Barnwell demanded £650,000 for Daley but with Villa's escalating debt it was never going to be a doable transfer.

Saunders' financial frustrations were compounded by more injury news in April 1979 when Ken McNaught suffered ankle ligament damage, while John Gidman needed eight stitches in his wrist following what was termed a 'dressing-room accident'. In May, Gordon Cowans sustained a fractured cheekbone and Andy Gray required surgery on his persistent knee injury.

Further shock waves came in the form of Brian Little's verbal transfer request, which the board advised he put in writing. The board then told Saunders to reject the subsequent request, but while doing so to also listen to suitable offers. Curiously, the one club who eventually made an offer that was acceptable to Villa – reported to be £600,000 – was Birmingham City. Little agreed to the cross-city switch and only did not sign because of a failed medical. Although his career faltered soon after this time because of knee problems, on this occasion it was the condition of his back that concerned Birmingham's medical staff. Little was happy to remain at his beloved Villa, albeit playing under a manager he never liked, but was disappointed nonetheless his career change did not work out.

'I didn't mind going to Blues too much because I never got along with Ron anyway and I quite liked Jim Smith as a bloke and thought it would be good to be part of what he was doing at Birmingham,' Little admitted.

'He was putting a decent side together with the likes of Frank Worthington, Colin Todd and Archie Gemmill and I thought it would be a good move for me. But that's when my injury was discovered.'

To cap a challenging few months, another of Saunders' rocky relationships, with John Gregory, culminated with the player's exit shortly after he was fined two weeks' wages for not making the team's end-of-season trip to Mallorca, boardroom minutes stated. Saunders used the misdemeanour as the catalyst to offload him and raise more money for his rebuilding project. Brighton & Hove Albion manager Alan Mullery paid £300,000 for the utility man, who went on to play with a much-improved Brighton side that contained Mark Lawrenson, Michael Robinson both later sold to Liverpool and other future England players like Gary Stevens and Steve Foster, so it was a scenario that suited all parties.

With the income Saunders managed to scramble together, the club's debt with the Midland Bank came down to a more respectable £436,437 by the summer of 1979, so the board were happy to then sanction more signings, especially after the manager had advised that two of the club's prize assets, John Gidman and Andy Gray, were unhappy. Saunders' key signings that summer were Tony Morley from Burnley for £200,000 and Scotland's once-capped international Des Bremner from Hibernian for £275,000 in a deal which included Villa's £55,000-rated Joe Ward. Supporters would not see the best of either Morley or Bremner for another season, but they added the width, creativity and industry the manager had unsuccessfully tried to bring in with Steve Daley. Middlesbrough's David Armstrong and the West Ham United duo of Geoff Pike and Alan Curbishley were other wide midfielders Saunders enquired about, without success. Hammers boss John Lyall proposed a swap deal between Curbishley and Villa full-back Gordon Smith, which Saunders rejected. The manager also spoke with St Mirren about forward Frank McGarvey, who headed instead to Liverpool for £270,000, and with Derby County about Gerry Daly but was deterred by the £200,000 price tag.

Morley had started his career at Preston North End, playing two seasons under Bobby Charlton's management. He impressed Villa scout Tony Barton in a match for Burnley against Villa's reserves while coming back from injury. He played on the right wing in that game and soon learned Villa were interested in buying him – Morley did not have to think twice about making the switch when an approach came.

'The salary was a bit bigger but not by much, as Burnley had not long been relegated from the First Division,' Morley said. 'I'd always felt a connection with Villa from playing against them for Preston's youth team and playing at Villa Park for England Youth.

'Even when driving past the stadium I would see the "AV" painted in the seats – everything about the place made a lasting impression on me and I couldn't wait to join them; at night when the lights were on, the place looked incredible.'

Morley was comfortable with either foot but mostly operated on the left flank for Villa, crossing naturally with his left to aid opportunities for the strikers from wide positions. He scored on his home debut against Brighton with a free-kick and in only his fourth league game for Villa he scored again, this time at Everton –

the club he supported as a boy.

In the same week that Morley signed, Saunders added to his pool of strikers, knowing John Deehan and Andy Gray, and possibly Brian Little, would soon be out of the club. Terry Donovan had impressed Tony Barton with his goalscoring exploits for Grimsby Town, who he had helped to promotion from the Fourth to the Third Division. He was set to sign a new three-year contract to stay at Blundell Park when his manager, John Newman, advised him of an offer. He would subsequently sign and remain at Villa for four years.

'John wouldn't tell me on the phone who the club was and I had to go round his house before he told me it was Aston Villa,' recalled Donovan. 'I was only twenty then and probably needed another year or two in the lower divisions to properly learn my trade. I wasn't good enough or experienced enough to play at that level then. When I walked into the dressing room there was Andy Gray, John Deehan, Brian Little, while Gary Shaw was also coming through. But in no time Andy had gone to Wolves, John moved to West Brom and Brian was lost to injury. It was a club in the midst of change.'

Donovan, who would go on to represent the Republic of Ireland in two internationals, scored on his debut against Coventry City on 19 December 1979, but was rarely more than an effective fringe player at Villa.

Meanwhile, the right of midfield had been taken care of by Frank Carrodus since he arrived in 1974. His worsening knee condition, though, led Saunders to replace him with Bremner, who was a similarly industrious player but with often unheralded creativity.

Bremner's formative years would have influenced the way he played, as his tireless, selfless work aided any team he represented. He was raised in the remote village of Aberchirder in Aberdeenshire where his father Sandy was a farmer. Shifts on the farm for Des and his three brothers were non-negotiable, so carrying bales of hay on their backs uphill to the cattle – sometimes in deep snow – prepared him well for Saunders' pre-season routines in later life. He had also been a right-back as a junior so was accustomed to the defensive side of his role. Saunders had initially bought Gary Shelton from Walsall to play that position but he judged pretty quickly that he would not be the right fit for the long term. Like Morley, Bremner had earned his stripes in the game the hard way by the time Villa came along. Aberdeen were his boyhood club and he played for their nursery side, before impressing enough for the Scottish amateur team to earn an invitation to train with Aberdeen's first-team squad on a Thursday night, on a gravel car park in front of the Pittodrie stadium. The Dons, though, allowed him to slip through their net as he ended up at Hibernian. It was at Easter Road where he made his name, played for his country and, ultimately, alerted the attention of other clubs' scouts.

Bremner was initially 'tapped up' by Celtic and Rangers as the respective managers Billy McNeil and John Greig advised him to ask for a transfer. Hibs boss Eddie Turnbull was not naive to such tactics and was fiercely opposed to selling his midfielder to Glasgow's powerbrokers. So when Bremner knocked on his manager's door and sheepishly inquired about a move, Turnbull was delighted to be able to offer an alternative club that allowed him to profit from any subsequent sale. Bremner was the last to find out the club's identity, though. Even when turning up at Edinburgh Airport for a morning flight, he had no idea where he was going.

'It wasn't until I spoke to the chairman at the airport that I learned we were going to Aston Villa,' Bremner recalled. 'I had heard about them in the lower divisions when they were getting capacity crowds but if I was being honest I didn't even know they were based in Birmingham!

'Ron Saunders picked us up from Birmingham Airport. I then learned that big Ken McNaught had mentioned my name to Saunders as I had played against him for Scotland's amateur youth team. We went to the training ground where the two managers and chairmen met and Saunders said he wanted me to train with the lads rather than hanging about. He ended with the words, "But don't worry, you won't be going back, you'll be signing."

'By that time I was twenty-seven and I felt my time for a big move had passed me by. The Villa move meant my wages tripled and I was given a club car. I thought, "Fucking hell, Christmas has come early!"'

With the wide areas settled, Saunders did not stop there with his rebuilding. He had been blighted by an ongoing curse with regards to the left-back position and attempted to rectify that issue. Historically, he inherited Charlie Aitken before mercilessly banishing him in 1976. He flirted with the idea of Bobby McDonald, who he also inherited, but they never saw eye-to-eye. John Robson was a Vic Crowe signing also there when he arrived; Saunders actually admired Robson's qualities but his illness meant a replacement was needed. Tony Barton then recommended the signing of Gordon Smith from St Johnstone and McDonald was sold to Coventry to accommodate his fellow Scotsman. Saunders eventually banished Smith too and so in the summer of 1979 signed former England defender Mike Pejic from Everton at a time when he still had reservations about permanently using rookies Gary Williams and Colin Gibson, who both played in the 1978 FA Youth Cup final defeat to Crystal Palace.

Saunders did not know it then but that jinxed position would continue as Pejic's two-year stay would amount to just ten games, due to a mysterious pelvic injury.

'The good times had gone at Everton and I was delighted when Ron rang me and even offered me a pay rise from what I was on at Everton,' he reflected of his move. 'I saw Villa as a big club so I was excited.'

Saunders' motivation for shaking up his squad was mostly about improving the strength in depth, but there was another significant reason why he was determined to change things. Put simply, the dressing-room culture and atmosphere. Although the players generally got along well, there was evidence of splinter groups among his squad that the manager felt was caused by club politics. Pointedly, he felt not all players were behind him and that some were too sympathetic towards, and aligned with, his chief boardroom adversary Doug Ellis.

Certainly, John Gidman and Brian Little had never been comfortable disciples of the Saunders Way. Andy Gray was not so much in Ellis's camp but just not in Saunders' camp after their fallout emanating from the UEFA Cup quarter-final tie with Barcelona. So, a gradual 'them and us' gulf opened up in the squad, which was not obvious to every player but was there nonetheless.

Saunders judged this worsening atmosphere as making it the right time to sell his star names – viewed as heroes by the fans and headline-grabbers to the media, but trouble-making agitators to him. The manager disliked the term 'star' and wanted no such characters in his team any longer, if they felt they deserved more money than their teammates. He felt that for Villa to move on to the next level he required a close-knit team where politics and splinter groups were no more and where every player bought into his 'all for one and one for all' mentality.

'Before I left, I detected a split in the dressing room which came from the Doug Ellis–Ron Saunders battle,' Frank Carrodus said. 'There were people in the boardroom who were backing Saunders. I felt there was maybe two camps with the likes of Andy Gray, John Gidman and maybe John Gregory and Brian Little on one side Ellis's and Dennis Mortimer and more on the other Saunders'. I myself liked Doug *and* Ron. Whatever you say about Doug, he loves Aston Villa and he did want the best for the club. But Aston Villa wasn't big enough for the two of them.'

The most extreme clash was between fellow Merseysiders Gidman and captain Dennis Mortimer. While it would be expected the captain would have a healthy relationship with the manager, Gidman and some other players considered Mortimer too close to Saunders and felt he confused his loyalties. Gidman, when interviewed for this book, berated a former Villa team-mate and described him as 'the snitch'. Although he never revealed the identity of that player, it seemed clear he was referring to Mortimer.

Jim Cumbes said: 'I was at an event when we were being called up on stage and as soon as Dennis Mortimer's name was read out, Giddy left the stage, which I thought was very obvious. I think Giddy always felt that Dennis was too close to Ron, though that is just my feeling from afar and from what I heard.'

Gidman openly admits he was 'always with Doug' as far as his loyalties lay in the Saunders–Ellis political tug-of-war, and claims that he and Little were Ellis's babies, from the days when the then chairman dedicated so much emphasis towards youth. Gidman went as far to describe Ellis as 'like a second dad'.

Allan Evans knew 'there was something going on' in the dressing room but reflects now that he was too naive to appreciate it at the time. 'I didn't get involved in anything like that,' Evans said. 'I married young, had two kids by the time I was twenty, so when I came to Villa I did my work and went home. I didn't take sides but I was aware of a split, certainly with Gray and Gidman on one side – they were causing problems. I've never had a bad word to say about either of them but as people they were different animals to me. There's nothing wrong with that, we're all different.'

The facts are, on 13 August 1979, Saunders told the board that Gray had officially requested a move away as he felt his career had come to a standstill at Villa. Two subsequent written transfer requests were turned down but Gray maintained in the media he wanted away. In the same board meeting the directors heard that Gidman had requested more money but the manager rejected his demands, so Gidman asked to meet with Ellis and another director as he knew Saunders would not help him. The board then asked Saunders to leave the room while they debated the two transfer requests from Gray and Gidman, knowing Saunders was not popular with either player. Ellis requested a deferment on any decision, suggesting the team could ill-afford to lose two such quality players. A majority board decision came down in favour of the manager that both players be made 'open to offers'.

In his 1980 end-of-season chairman's statement, Harry Kartz openly reflected the mood of the board and support for Saunders, with the obvious exception of Ellis: 'The turmoil in the boardroom was preceded by unrest in the dressing room and it was inevitable, and necessary, that these were ironed out with a minimum of fuss and the maximum of resolve. Your board was well aware that the departure of Andy Gray and John Gidman was hardly likely to increase its popularity with the public but they were determined to act in the best long-term interests of the club and on the advice of Mr Saunders. Consequently, both Gray and Gidman were transferred for fees which reflected their obvious playing ability.'

Curiously, Gray does not recall a bad dressing-room atmosphere. He openly admits he had an ongoing feud with Saunders at that time, but never had any problems with the team. 'I don't get involved in politics anywhere,' insisted Gray. 'Was I having my disagreements with Saunders? Yes. But would I be part of an anti-Saunders group? No. If I had been part of an anti-Saunders group I would have got him sacked when I was offered the opportunity to do so by Doug Ellis, but would have nothing to do with it. There were people like Dennis Mortimer who were a little too close to Saunders and some of us felt they took too many stories from the dressing room into the manager's office. There's no doubt that as captain of the side Dennis felt it was his job to tell Ron Saunders about various things that may or may not have been going on in the dressing room, and he shouldn't have done. That caused a few problems, not only between John Gidman, myself and the others, but lots of people. There was never a clique in training where we couldn't train with each other – that would have been a nonsense.' For the record, Dennis Mortimer refutes all suggestions, especially from Gray and John Gidman, that he relayed any dressing room talk or gossip to the manager. He said: 'I was always one hundred per cent behind the manager, yes, but I was also one hundred per cent behind my team-mates. I always took a civil tongue when discussing my fellow players with the manager. I would never "snitch" on any player, as has been suggested.'

Gray's subsequent sale covered extensively in the next chapter was inevitable, as was Gidman's exit shortly after. Ellis was just about still at the club then but his executive powers were now far weaker than in years gone by and he was not able to resist the transfers – though in Gray's case he was glad to be out of Villa Park. Those departures coincided with a blip in Villa's form and they slumped to seventeenth in the league after a goalless draw at home to West Bromwich Albion on 13 October. However, that match was the start of a turnaround in results as Villa lost just three matches in the next twenty-five, and they were against that season's league champions Liverpool, European champions Nottingham Forest and European Cup Winners' Cup finalists Arsenal.

Gidman soon followed Gray out of the Villa door. Although Gidman submitted transfer requests, mainly to earn a pay hike, he felt he was forced out of Villa. When his exit became inevitable, he met with the board and they asked him if he thought he would be leaving Villa had Saunders not been manager and he answered with an unequivocal 'No!' The next day he was on the M6 heading towards to Everton.

'That situation should never have occurred,' a still dismayed Gidman said. 'Most Villa fans at that time thought we must be trouble-makers, me and Andy. But we weren't. We were the victims of a certain snitch – or I was. I was heartbroken.' That was another reference by Gidman towards Dennis Mortimer, who he and Andy Gray felt conveyed too much talk from the dressing room to the manager's office. He was also bitter that Mortimer was on more money than he was yet hadn't been at Villa as long or even had an England cap like he did. Gidman ultimately reserves most of his anger at his Villa departure towards Saunders.

'He couldn't handle me and Andy because of our personalities in the dressing room – I always said what I thought and he didn't like it – fine,' Gidman revealed. 'He wanted me out and he wanted Andy out. I don't think he was a [good] man-manager. I shouldn't be having a go like I am because he was successful, but I still have a few bitter memories about how my Villa career ended. I never wanted to leave Villa; I wanted to finish my career there. But other doors opened and I went on to play for Man United, one of the biggest clubs in the world.'

Gidman's career eventually prospered again under Ron Atkinson at Old Trafford, where he was able to claim an FA Cup winners' medal in 1985 – against Everton. Atkinson's easy-going culture – that tolerated or even encouraged dressing-room 'banter' and the boozy nights out that were seen as positive in terms of team bonding – suited Gidman. Before United came calling, though, he endured a difficult eighteen months at Goodison Park. From the time Everton manager Gordon Lee identified Gidman as the perfect solution to boost his attacking options on the right flank, through to the time Lee's successor Howard Kendall came in and left him out of an end-of-season trip to Tokyo, his Everton days were uncomfortable. Gidman believes he was never able to fully focus on Everton because he was still so bitter at his exit from Villa. On the day Gidman cleared his locker at the training ground when his move was all but finalised, he could not resist one last dig at Saunders.

'I went to Bodymoor Heath to pick up my boots, after I had to train on my own for ten days as that's how much he pushed me out,' Gidman recalled. 'I wasn't even playing in the reserves. It was terrible to be treated like that. Anyway, Saunders had told the lads I was on my way. But before I left I saw him and I said, "I may not fuckin' sign for 'em yet!" His face dropped. I just wanted to give him a fright.'

Everton rookie Pat Heard moved to Villa Park as part of the £650,000 package. If Gidman had refused his personal terms the deal would have been off but he knew his decade at Villa was now at an end. For Heard, it was an exciting and surprising development after he had been spotted by Tony Barton while playing for Everton reserves. Toffees manager Gordon Lee never really wanted to offload Heard but felt his need for an attacking right-back was more important.

'His fee was worth about six times more than mine and we still wind each other up now,' Heard recalled with a smile. 'I tell him that he earned all my money!'

There was a feeling of shock among the squad that first Andy Gray was sold and then Gidman. Players, like supporters, did wonder what the masterplan was because these were Villa's two biggest stars, talisman performers, inspirational on their day. No one could be blamed for doubting whether Saunders had got these decisions right. Was he allowing his own agenda to disrupt Villa's ambitions?

Soon enough, Saunders was to be proven correct. Not that those players deserved to be sold. But no one could question his transfer policy when Villa went on to win the league championship and European Cup in subsequent years. Hindsight has led players of the day to reflect positively on Saunders's decision-making.

'They were two big sales but Ron had built up some decent trust with the supporters so they seemed to accept what he was doing,' Kenny Swain reasoned. 'It was classic Alex Ferguson and Brian Clough-style management – "there's no player bigger than the club, I'm the manager and I will do what is best for the football club". That was Ron's way.'

Colin Gibson understood why the manager wanted to move Gidman on from Villa Park: 'Giddy was a fantastic right-back and was he good enough to get into our team that won the league? Yes, he was. But was he the kind of character Ron

Saunders wanted in his dressing room? Probably not. He was possibly too much of a maverick for Ron, who wanted everybody to be similar, not exactly the same, but similar.'

Des Bremner, who had only rubbed shoulders at Villa with both Gray and Gidman for a matter of weeks, had been there long enough to still detect that both players were not the kind of characters Saunders wanted in his new-look team.

'Moving those two out of Villa just showed the strength of the manager,' Bremner insisted. 'He wanted team players and he obviously thought that Andy and Giddy weren't team players, maybe Andy to a lesser extent. But we weren't full of our own importance.

'Don't get me wrong, Giddy was my favourite player, he was great. But my first introduction to him at Bodymoor Heath told me a bit about his character. We were playing a practice match against the reserves. He was obviously used to playing with Frank [Carrodus], who'd just give him the ball, as Giddy liked to be the main outlet on the right. Well, early on I went down the right and crossed and I can't remember who it was but we scored. Giddy came running back to me, after I didn't pass to him, and said, "Oi, you bastard, just give me the fucking ball, don't do anything else with it." That was my intro to Giddy.'

Gidman was gone, his former deputy in that position John Gregory was gone, and while rookies Gary Williams and Ivor Linton could play there, Saunders was yet to trust them enough as first-team regulars; in the same way he was unable to yet trust Williams and Colin Gibson enough at left-back then, which is why he recruited Pejic from Everton.

Few knew it at the time, but when Gidman was sold, Saunders already had his replacement in mind. Kenny Swain, a right winger-cum-striker, first played at right-back at the start of the 1979/80 season when Gidman was out injured. When Gidman came back, Swain shifted back into attack. But in that time, during those three games, Saunders had seen enough from the former Chelsea player to decide he could 'do a job' at at right-back while he found Gidman's permanent replacement. History shows, though, that when Swain was eventually given an extended run in the position, he adjusted seamlessly and never returned to attack.

Swain still remembers the moment when Saunders approached him to fill Gidman's boots.

'Ron told me he needed to find a right-back and had not done so yet, so he was going to give me a run in that position for six games – win, lose or draw – to buy him some more time,' Swain remembered. 'You were rarely guaranteed anything in those days so a six-match commitment was really something.

'The first of those games was a 0–0 at home to West Brom, so a clean sheet was a good start. Next match we won 3–1 at Derby. When we were coming home on the coach he came and sat next to me and said, "You did well tonight, son, you're hand and glove in that position and I think you could make that position your own. What you think?"

'I told him I was happy and he said, "Good, so I'm looking for a striker now then, not a right-back!"'

In the event, Saunders made do with strikers Gary Shaw, Brian Little, David Geddis and Terry Donovan before target man Peter Withe arrived in summer 1980. But a right-back was now the least of Saunders' priorities. 'Ron always knew what he was planning – he was always one step ahead,' Little said. 'He knew he was going to replace Giddy with Kenny Swain. As a footballer, you don't see it, and none of us saw it.'

There was evidence, before the season concluded, that the future might just be brighter than the pessimists predicted with such a volatile turnover in playing personnel. On 5 April 1980, weeks before Nottingham Forest retained the European Cup, Villa recorded a rare 3–2 victory at home over Brian Clough's team. It was a full-strength Forest team against a Villa side missing Gary Shaw, Dennis Mortimer, Tony Morley and Ken McNaught. Instead, Saunders began to test the depth of his new-look squad, with Brendan Ormsby, Pat Heard, David Geddis, Terry Donovan and Ivor Linton all starting. The rookies also featured at Liverpool on the last weekend of that 1979/80 season, which was a challenge too many, as they lost 4–1.

'The funny thing about that game,' the Hull-born Heard revealed, 'was that Hull Kingston Rovers were playing Hull FC at Wembley Stadium in the [Rugby League] Challenge Cup final on the same day, which was a massive thing for our city.

'A journalist asked me beforehand how I felt about playing at Anfield. I said that I'd played there before and that my mind was more on Wembley ... Liverpool battered us that day when they won the championship.'

Villa finished seventh. And very soon, that mediocrity would be a thing of the past as Saunders' newly designed team moved on to a level that had not been seen at Villa Park.

'Wolves a Move
I *Had* to Make'
– Hero Gray

*'I did not see Wolves as a step down from Aston Villa.
I saw Wolves as a club who had some fantastic footballers.'* – **Andy Gray**

IT WAS CLEAR THAT BY THE SUMMER OF 1979, ASTON VILLA HAD MUCH work to do just to regain their reputation as the best team in the Midlands, never mind the country. Brian Clough's ever-improving Nottingham Forest had won the European Cup courtesy of a goal from their new million-pound striker, the player Villa could not afford, Trevor Francis. Forest were not done there and would soon add a second consecutive European crown. Meanwhile, West Bromwich Albion had finished third in the English top flight and were ruing a weather-inflicted fixture backlog that, they felt, had denied them a genuine shot at the title. Even Birmingham City responded to their relegation from the First Division by ambitiously recruiting two inspirational figures in Frank Worthington and Archie Gemmill. Scotland international Gemmill had been a driver of Forest's success under Clough and scored arguably the best goal of the World Cup only a year earlier. Further afield, Arsenal had reached a second straight FA Cup final, winning this time, Liverpool had won another league title, and Everton, Leeds and Ipswich had also finished higher than eighth-placed Villa.

Against this backdrop, Aston Villa's willingness to sell star striker Andy Gray to West Midlands rivals Wolverhampton Wanderers would come as a shock. It was not so much that Gray had left, especially after his transfer demand to Saunders eighteen months earlier following their falling out after the Barcelona UEFA

Cup tie. The surprise had more to do with his destination, as Wolves had escaped relegation by just two places only months earlier. The transfer surprised the Villa players, the Wolves players and both sets of fans, with Villa's faithful distraught at losing their powerful, heroic frontman and those from Molineux stunned their club was able to secure the services of one of the most respected goalscorers in the English game.

'I was surprised Villa let him go but John Barnwell was quite ambitious, so it was one hell of a coup for us to sign a player like that,' Wolves' legendary goalscorer John Richards commented. 'Lots of clubs were after him and rightly so as Andy was the best striker I played with. We would have got more out of him if we had better service from wide areas. He was so brave and that's the reason why he picked up injuries. He was fearless. He gave everyone a boost, as did the arrival of Emlyn Hughes.'

Gray's signing even surprised both managers and chairmen. Ron Saunders' surprise stemmed from the fact it was Wolves of all clubs who made the most serious approach for his greatest asset. Equally, Gray's signing was the one Wolves manager John Barnwell craved most but did not honestly expect to complete due to Wolves' moderate financial position and an anticipation that Villa would not sell anyway.

Barnwell's summer review of the previous season with his assistant Richie Barker had identified three key areas for strengthening. Inspirational central defender Emlyn Hughes ticked one box after he signed from Liverpool, following an endorsement from Bill Shankly. Roy McFarland had been approached on more than one occasion to fill that role but his indecision ultimately discouraged the manager. Another former England international, Dave Thomas, arrived from Everton to provide the width he also felt was lacking. The third requirement centred on their offensive tip, as Barnwell and Barker desired a more direct style, preferring to move the ball to the strikers more quickly and play their football from there. Gray was, therefore, the perfect number nine who also added the will to win, leadership and attacking bite they sought. He strengthened an attacking force consisting of veteran Richards, Norman Bell and Billy Rafferty – Mel Eves was yet to establish himself.

'I was surprised we were able to sign Gray,' Barnwell reflected. 'But while I didn't know Ron well, I knew him well enough to realise that if he wanted to do the deal, he would make sure he did it – and his way. It was clear from the stuff

TICKET TO THE MOON

coming out in the press he wanted rid of Gray and fortunately we were able to get our man.

'I was interested in Gray as soon as the journalist Hugh Jamieson asked me if I was aware Andy was uncomfortable at Villa. I wasn't in the business of tapping up players but at the same time I wasn't naive enough to think it never went on, so I was keen to stay in touch with his situation. Realistically, though, I knew he would be out of our price range.'

Wolves' bargaining position altered significantly when Manchester City manager Malcolm Allison made a phone call to Barnwell to lodge his interest in signing their wide-man Steve Daley. Barnwell was not actively trying to offload Daley, but once that call was made he knew it was his one big opportunity to generate the funds he needed to sign Gray. He had an agreement with his chairman Harry Marshall that he could retain whatever transfer income he was able to accrue for reinvestment in new players. Therefore, Barnwell played the Daley move craftily so he could somehow engineer the once unthinkable signing of Gray.

Barnwell knew he could afford to wait for the right offer on Daley as he was already aware of interest elsewhere. Brian Clough attempted to take Daley to Nottingham Forest before Barnwell had joined Wolves and there was still a feeling Clough might return with an improved offer. But that option became less important once Manchester City chairman Peter Swales advised Barnwell, who was calling all the shots at Wolves in a deal he manipulated single-handedly, that City would be prepared to pay at least one million pounds. That was the first time the Wolves boss knew he had an outside chance of scrambling enough funds together to buy Gray, and he wasted little time in testing the water at Villa by calling Saunders up.

Barnwell: *Hello, Ron, it's Barney. I want to buy Andy Gray. How much?*
Saunders: *He's not available!*
Barnwell: *Come on, Ron, every player has his value. Name a price.*
Saunders: *You can't afford him. Two million pounds.*

Barnwell was shrewd enough to detect Saunders' enthusiasm to agree a deal and knew that he would negotiate from his original standpoint of a then unprecedented £2 million – double the record British transfer fee. Gray, though, felt Saunders' tactic was an effort to price him out of the market. It didn't work, as Barnwell was determined to get his man.

'We ended up agreeing on £1.5 million,' recalled Barnwell. 'Half of the money was to be paid up front with the rest drip-fed over two years. I didn't tell Richie Barker or my chairman about the deals because I had learned the more people you tell, the more chance there is of a deal breaking down. We ended up agreeing £1,175,000 for Daley plus the league's fee, plus the player's fee, plus VAT, which came to a total of £1,475,000, so I was £25,000 short to buy Gray …'

Daley was told to report to Barnwell's office at eight-thirty on the Monday morning and it was there that he spoke to Manchester City for the first time by phone. He was then sent on his way to Manchester to meet Malcolm Allison, his assistant Tony Book, and Peter Swales. He nearly didn't go and it was his wife who finally persuaded him, much to Barnwell's relief, as he had arranged for Gray to travel to Molineux on that same morning. If the Daley deal had collapsed, there would have been no Gray transfer.

Even at this advanced stage, Wolves owner Harry Marshall knew absolutely nothing about it all, which is slightly ironic given how Ron Saunders was always held to account so tightly over transfer activity by former chairman Doug Ellis. This was an era when managers ran clubs and certainly dominated transfer dealings, but not at Villa under Ellis. By this time, though, Ellis was close to the Villa Park exit and Saunders was free to cajole his squad and transfer fees as he saw fit. The new board would not dare resist him.

Harry Marshall's euphoria at the pending record transfer fee for Daley was short-lived when Barnwell interrupted him with the words, 'Chairman, there's a small hitch, I need another £25,000,' leaving Marshall dumbstruck. 'What for?' To which Barnwell replied, 'Because I have just signed Andy Gray …'

Barnwell's personal opinion is that Marshall, in an effort to retain the Daley fee and not reinvest it, then attempted to scupper the Gray deal by manipulating a false medical report that suggested Gray had a dodgy knee.

'He used the services of a surgeon I had fallen out with a couple of weeks before,' revealed Barnwell. 'The Andy Gray deal was almost off because of it, but I took Andy off to have tests at a neutral, local hospital and his knee was deemed OK. The deal was back on.'

Although Wolves were committed to the Gray transfer, they were still £25,000 short on the fee, so Barnwell devised a plan whereby the player would sign his contract on the pitch before the game so the fans could share in the moment. More, though, for commercial reasons so Wolves could generate advertising revenue from the event. They brought in £15,000 from a brewery and managed to get the remaining money from the bank interest on the Daley fee as that money was filtering into the club account quicker than the Gray money was going out. It all fitted into place.

'It was a shame to lose Daley as he was a nice lad and a good player,' said Barnwell, 'but with Gray we had a leader on the pitch and, more importantly, someone who could score us a lot of goals. We would never have won the League Cup or finished top six without Andy and Emlyn.'

Gray benefitted in more ways than one from this move as he not only left a manager that he no longer had any respect for, but was also able to secure much-needed funds for his struggling nightclub, Holy City Zoo. Wolves were keen to ensure their new prize asset had no external pressures affecting his on-field displays. The nightclub's financial challenges meant there were some payments that Gray had to meet personally. 'Wolves loaned me that money and I paid it back in instalments as and when through my salary,' Gray admitted. 'We're not talking five hundred grand or anything like that, it was just a few grand.'

Sections of Villa supporters, who were probably unaware of Gray's non-relationship with Saunders by that stage, believed Gray had left for the money. They questioned why he would wish to sign for a club who were far from established as a top-flight force. But Gray did not share that view.

'It was a move I *had* to make and, besides, I did not see Wolves as a step down from Aston Villa,' Gray reflected. 'I saw Wolves as a club who had some fantastic footballers like Kenny Hibbitt, Willie Carr and John Richards to name only three. They were terrific players. Then they took Emlyn Hughes from Liverpool and Dave Thomas from Everton.' In fairness to Gray, no one then could foresee the financial problems Wolves would be facing within a couple of years when bankruptcy beckoned. In the short term it looked a positive switch as they won the League Cup in his first season and finished sixth in the First Division – crucially, one point and one place ahead of Villa.

Willie Carr acknowledged Wolves were 'too quiet and timid as a group' before the arrival of Gray and Hughes, and that the Scottish striker particularly added an edge that had been missing. Brian Little had no hesitation in naming Gray the best he ever worked with during his playing days. He appreciated how he could play an errant pass towards Gray between a defender and an opposition goalkeeper and Gray would still, somehow, find his way to the ball first out of pure bravery and whole-hearted fearlessness and commitment. 'There was so much to him,' Little said. 'He loved every minute of every game, he was never beaten or down, he was always angry if he was losing and high as a kite when he was winning. Andy was an inspiration in many respects and was a great player.'

Furthermore, Leighton Phillips considered both Gray and Little as the best strike combination he played with throughout his career and has particular admiration for the way Gray converted himself from a rough diamond into one of the most polished strikers in Europe. 'Andy's touch wasn't the best when he came to the club and he would admit to that,' Phillips said, 'but boy did he come back in the afternoon and work on his game. He squeezed every ounce of ability out of himself.'

The simple way of viewing the situation would have been to suggest Gray's signing had improved Wolves so much and hurt Villa that there was no longer a gulf in quality between the two clubs. Wolves' superior league finish, however marginal, plus a cup win added further weight to that argument. However, the optimists would say Villa were still building and heading in the right direction and that Saunders had offloaded key players previously like Chris Nicholl, Phillips and Charlie Aitken yet never to Villa's detriment. Frank Carrodus, who was also sold in that volatile year of 1979, felt Saunders was 'totally ruthless' in agreeing to sell Gray, but that was never an area he struggled with.

Colin Gibson, whose breakthrough season of 1978/79 was also Gray's final complete campaign at Villa Park, reflected on Gray's departure from a different angle, with a more sympathetic view of Saunders' aim of trying to mould his perfect combination. His squad reshaping, after all, was only possible because of the funds that Gray's transfer generated. 'It did look a strange transfer at the time going to a club like Wolves from Villa,' said Gibson, 'but given the way everything fitted into place you can't question what Saunders was doing.

'There's no doubt Andy was a fantastic player, but he was also a very individual player and Ron was trying to build a team. When Andy was at Villa he was almost bigger than the team. Everything was about Andy Gray – that wasn't Andy's fault. That was merely a result of his success. But if you were Ron Saunders and you're offered £1.5 million in 1979, I don't think it would have taken him too long to decide.'

However generous the fee Villa received, and despite Saunders' favoured philosophy that the 'team is always greater than the individual', the immediate impact of Gray's exit in September 1979 was painful and results suggested he would be difficult to replace. In fact, Villa endured six consecutive league and cup games without a single goal scored in the rest of the month. This sequence even included a 2–0 home defeat to Colchester United from the Third Division, with Villa bailing themselves out of that particular tie 9–8 on penalties after a 2–2 aggregate score over two legs. In comparsion, Gray's Wolves career in that time began with four goals in five games, including goals against title candidates Manchester United and Arsenal. Flickers of hope came in other ways: the three straight 0–0 scorelines showed Villa were at least solid defensively if not at all potent in attack. And teenage striker Gary Shaw was given an extended run in the team and his second-half hat-trick at Bristol City over the Christmas programme showed there could be life beyond Gray after all. One other curiosity was a 3–1 home loss to Liverpool, almost three years to the day after they had demolished the Reds 5–1; goalscorer Brian Little was the only remaining Villa player from that game involved in the match, while Liverpool had six survivors present to ensure they did not suffer like that again. Villa captain and boyhood Liverpool fan Dennis Mortimer would have played had he not been sent off in the previous game against Norwich and was therefore serving a suspension.

By the end of 1979, Doug Ellis was out of the way, Andy Gray was gone, John Gidman was gone and Little would also have been gone if it were not for a failed medical. Saunders now had total power at Villa without any dissenting voices or personality clashes inside the dressing room or boardroom. The all-powerful manager proudly told director Harry Kartz shortly after those departures, 'I have no stars in my team – it's not about individuals, it's about building a team. I don't want stars!' And that's how it was.

Saunders soon managed to exploit his newfound freedom with the board by successfully negotiating himself a lucrative testimonial match against Birmingham City on 7 May 1980. The honour is traditionally reserved for players who have given ten years' service. Saunders had completed six as manager.

'Give Me 60 Points and We'll Win the League'

'Ron Saunders asked me if I was able to go out and train with the lads.
I said, "No." I would have loved to but my injury didn't allow me to.
I will never forget driving back on the M6. I pulled over and just broke down.
I couldn't drive. So many little things had snowballed until
I couldn't cope any longer … I just didn't feel part of it and never connected
with their success at all.' – **Mike Pejic**

PRIOR TO THE 1980/81 SEASON THE LAST TIME ASTON VILLA WERE English league champions, in May 1910, the First World War had not started, the *Titanic* disaster was a couple of years away, cricket great Donald Bradman was not even two years old, while future Wimbledon tennis champion Fred Perry was just one.

Villa's first league triumph in 71 years was far from obvious, even though there was clear evidence that brighter times looked to be on the horizon under Ron Saunders' management.

Villa finished fourteen points behind champions Liverpool in the 1979/80 season and did not appear to be championship contenders-in-waiting. There was a slew of other clubs, seemingly, far more likely to challenge Bob Paisley's dominant Liverpool team. One of them was Manchester United, who had trailed the Reds by just two points under boss Dave Sexton the previous year.

Ipswich Town were third and becoming a consistently competitive force under future England manager Bobby Robson, having won the FA Cup in 1978 and notched eight top-six finishes in the last nine seasons. Fourth-placed Arsenal also made the FA Cup and European Cup Winners Cup finals that summer, to firmly showcase their strength domestically and on the continent. Terry Neill's team was laced with quality, notably their Irish group of skilful midfielder Liam Brady, veteran goalkeeper Pat Jennings, rock-steady defenders Pat Rice, David O'Leary and Sammy Nelson, and powerhouse centre-forward Frank Stapleton. That the Gunners overcame Liverpool after a marathon three semi-final replays before advancing to the 1980 FA Cup final against West Ham United said much of their resilience.

Fifth-placed Nottingham Forest retained the European Cup that year with a slender 1–0 victory over Hamburg. With the proven brilliance of manager Brian Clough and players such as England internationals Peter Shilton, Viv Anderson, Tony Woodcock, Garry Birtles and Trevor Francis, and the added experience of Martin O'Neill, John Robertson and John McGovern, their star did not look as if it was ready to fade.

Villa were not even second in the Midlands at this point as Wolverhampton Wanderers not only finished a place above them in the league in sixth in 1979/80 but had also managed to edge Forest in the 1980 League Cup final at Wembley. Even West Bromwich Albion had managed two top-six finishes in the past three years and looked better equipped for a title challenge than their more decorated neighbours Aston Villa.

While Villa were admired and respected for their workmanlike collective, they were not expected to achieve anything other than a respectable league position and possibly a successful cup campaign. The British footballing public's opinion of Villa was seemingly reflected by a media that had scant faith in their title aspirations. Forest, who also were not in any way viewed among the elite of English football when they embarked on their own remarkable title-winning campaign in 1977, had previously belied national scepticism, as would another Midlands club, Leicester City, in 2016. But here and now, it was Aston Villa's opportunity to turn the form book on its head and steamroll their way to glory, motivated by an inferiority complex that Ron Saunders used to fuel his team's will to win. Villa never had the big-name line-up that would attract the Fleet Street hacks as happened at more fashionable venues like Highbury, Anfield or White Hart Lane; they never had a quotable manager like the effervescent maverick Clough. But they had a shrewd manager who did not care what anyone outside the club thought, and players who believed in his mantra.

Saunders first completed the final piece of his team jigsaw when he recruited forward Peter Withe in the summer of 1980, as Brian Little's knee injury showed no sign of improvement. Withe arrived from Newcastle United for what was then a club-record fee of £500,000. Withe was to become a Holte End hero imminently – but he may never have been signed had Saunders listened to the proven, trustworthy advice of his assistant, Tony Barton, who instead had identified a striker with eighteen goals in the 1979/80 season for Third Division outfit Chester City. His name was Ian Rush; a prolific centre-forward who, of course, went on to become Liverpool's all-time leading goalscorer, wining five league titles in the 1980s, as well as three FA Cups, five League Cups and two European Cups, before signing for Juventus. He might have been snapped up by Villa first, at a time when Everton manager Gordon Lee was also scouting him.

'I was with Tony when he spotted Ian Rush at Chester,' remembered Tony's wife, Rose. 'On some scouting trips I would go along with him. He'd drop me off at the shops and he would go to the game. But on this particular day I went to the match with him. What I know about football you can write on a postage stamp but I will never forget that day. Tony said to me, "See that lad there, he's going to be a big star." He then went back and told Ron to sign Ian Rush but it never materialised.'

Saunders did actually try to sign him for £40,000 but it later transpired Liverpool had first option on him. Tony's eldest son, Chris, added: 'Dad was never interested in big names; his forte was going to the lower divisions on a rainy Tuesday or Wednesday night and saying, "Him. That lad's going to be a star," and getting him signed for peanuts.'

Despite interest from Manchester City – the Chester manager then was former City midfielder Alan Oakes – and in spite of Rush being a boyhood Everton fan, Liverpool won the race to sign him in April 1980, though he had to remain at Chester until the end of the season as the transfer deadline of 27 March had passed. Bob Paisley paid a record fee for a teenager of £300,000, which remains Chester's record sale. Withe was not Saunders' first-choice signing. He picked the phone up to Coventry City manager Gordon Milne and offered £750,000 for their target man Mick Ferguson, who had struck up a potent strike force with Ian Wallace. Saunders, a manager who always preferred to control his own transfer business, clearly felt that Villa could afford such an outlay having raised more than £2 million from the sales of Gray and Gidman. Wrong! A controversial investment of more than £900,000 on the North Stand affected his budget and this explains why his offer for Ferguson was withdrawn by the board. It would have meant

Villa's overdraft with the Midland Bank ballooning to £1.25 Had Ferguson joined, Peter Withe would never have played for Aston Villa, as they were the same player type. Ferguson ended up at Everton a year later in a £250,000 deal, though Saunders and Ferguson were united in 1982 when he signed the striker on loan for Birmingham City.

Everton tried to beat Villa to Withe's signature but were unable to compete financially. 'I hoped to bring in Withe from Newcastle, but after selling Andy Gray and John Gidman to me at Everton, Villa had cash to spend and we couldn't compete with them,' then Toffees boss Gordon Lee explained. 'I liked Withe as a commanding target man but in hindsight if I had signed him, I wouldn't then have opted for Graeme Sharp so it all worked out well in the end, for us and him!' Saunders was looking at Sharp, too, but favoured the experience of Withe.

Saunders had tried to recruit Austria strike legend Hans Krankl, but could not pull the deal off.

As one avenue closed, another opened. Villa may not have pursued Barton's recommendation of Rush or been successful in buying Ferguson, but youngster Gary Shaw instead flourished in a new strike partnership with Withe, whose headed flick-ons and chest-downs often created goalscoring opportunities for Shaw. Equally, the teenager's deft touches and vision around the goal area complemented Withe's all-over power and aerial strength. The team was complete. 'Ron built a team with good balance and players who showed great appreciation for each other and with great mental strength,' observed Gordon Lee.

Tony Morley remembered how Saunders always used Liverpool as a benchmark for where they needed to be, to expect any success. 'He would always say to us, "If we finish above Liverpool we will have done well," which was his way of trying to guide us to the top. And he thought the team was strong enough to do that.' Not only was the first team shaping up well, the youngsters had won the FA Youth Cup against Manchester City in 1979/80 with the likes of Mark Walters, Paul Birch and Noel Blake, while the reserves were also in good order. So much so, the future Celtic and Manchester United player Brian McClair could not even make the team. Reserve striker Terry Donovan commented: 'The first team picked itself and never changed much but we had a cracking reserve team with Nigel Spink, Pat Heard, Terry Bullivant, Gary Shelton, myself, Dave Geddis, Mark Walters, Ivor Linton, Robert Hopkins and Noel Blake. I'd say we were that good that, while our first team won the league, we could have come halfway in the same division.'

Des Bremner felt that it was a Villa team that knew their strengths and stuck to them with discipline. 'We could stop the opposition from playing, get hold of the ball and then express ourselves when we had possession. But when we weren't in possession everyone had to work their bollocks off to win it back.'

The latter was not a quality Morley was especially known for. Jimmy Rimmer said the players would often 'have a go at him' for not working hard enough or tackling back. And though he would learn to adapt to expectations, there was still the odd occasion when Morley would slip back into his old ways. He was once walking off a muddy pitch at half-time and Gordon 'Sid' Cowans noticed how clean his white socks and shorts were. 'If I were you, I'd smear some mud on myself quick,' Cowans teased, so Morley would not attract a Saunders rocket for not working hard enough. Fast-forward five minutes, the winger was sitting innocently in the dressing room looking like he had been breakdancing in cowpats. Ken McNaught, who was well aware of Morley's immaculate kit, took one look at his new appearance in the dressing room and fired off an even bigger rocket than Saunders was capable of. 'Tony being Tony looked at me and said, "He's talking to you, Sid!"'

That was how disciplined this Villa team was; it policed itself and Saunders was very much in favour of his senior players working as his lieutenants.

Much of what Villa achieved that season stemmed from a solid defence. Goalkeeper Jimmy Rimmer had already proven himself a terrific signing, even though Saunders told a board meeting on 14 April 1980 that Rimmer was seeking a free transfer at the season's end. His request was rejected in favour of a new deal whereby Rimmer would be paid £25,000 loyalty money when he was 35 and a £5,000-a-year loyalty payment. Villa raised £15,000 from their pre-season trip to Germany after they turned down an offer to tour Australia for 25 days. Rookies Colin Gibson and Gary Williams shared the troublesome left-back position successfully, while Kenny Swain continued to improve at right-back after replacing John Gidman. The partnership at the centre of defence, though, between McNaught and Allan Evans, typified Saunders' ethos. The team was actually full of partnerships, with Swain and Bremner on the right-hand side, Morley and either Williams or Gibson on the left, Withe and Shaw up front and then there was Evans and McNaught at the back. They all worked as efficient 'teams within a team', but that defensive combination gave Villa the backbone they needed to keep clean sheets, of which there were fifteen in the league. 'For me the organisational captain of that back four was Ken [McNaught],' Colin Gibson said. 'He was not as quick as Allan but he was quick enough, he was hard and he was brilliant in the air. He had the entire back line on a string almost. Al was like a battering ram. If you need[ed] him to go and win a header he never missed. He would get a few cuts and bruises but that's what it took in those days to be a good, hard centre-half.'

The success of the partnership between Ken McNaught and Allan Evans was no fluke. They were two of the most reliable 'stoppers' in the division and were complemented by tough-tackling, athletic full-backs who were equally comfortable in attack and delivering crosses. The combination of Evans and McNaught was conceived in 1978 but that partnership was never prone to complacency and they perfected their understanding of playing alongside one another in countless training sessions, despite the 42 league games they would always play, fitness permitting.

'After training when we were done as a squad, we did drills together as Saunders used to pull us aside and have us defending against some young legs like Paul Kerr and Mark Walters attacking us, with a couple of young midfielders running from deep as well,' McNaught recalled. 'Me and Evo would already be breathing out of our backsides but Saunders wanted to see how we defended as a pair while our legs were like jelly. It was only now and again but he had a habit of picking up on any complacency if he felt things became a bit easy for us.'

The job-share between Williams and Gibson was another Saunders masterstroke from what started out as a disappointment in losing left-back Mike Pejic to injury. At the end of the 1979/80 campaign, the manager called Williams into his office and strongly advised him to have a good pre-season because he would be the number-one left-back for the coming season. Williams walked out feeling ten feet tall and was raring to carry out his boss's instructions. Later in the year, Williams and Gibson realised that Saunders had said exactly the same to both of them. Not that the manager was lying, because they ended up playing the same amount of league games in that campaign, 21 each. 'Saunders was ahead of his time in terms of psychology,' said Williams. 'There was never any rhyme or reason to Ron's alternating of us. We never knew who was going to play from one game to the next. The only clue we tended to get was in training on a Thursday, if he threw you a yellow bib to take your place with the first team it generally meant you were in the team for Saturday. But while me and Gibbo both badly wanted the shirt, we were never too competitive with one another personally as we first met at sixteen in the youth hostel where the club used to put us up, so we never fell out.'

None of the players really believed they were genuine title contenders until Saunders sat them down at a training session just before the season started and gave them an uncharacteristic pep talk. The manager was routinely one to keep focusing on the next match and the one after that. But on this occasion, he allowed his players the rare luxury of looking into the future and seeing what could lie ahead if they played to their potential.

'Very rarely did Saunders sit us down in the changing room for a big talk – that stuff was always done on the training pitch,' recalled McNaught. 'He only did that a handful of times over the years I played for him. But on this day he gave us a target to aim for and said if we could give him sixty points we would win the league.'

Gary Williams also revealed how new signing Peter Withe shared with him a comment from Saunders that he was his final piece of the jigsaw and he thought Villa were now equipped to be English league champions. 'That comment from Peter was probably the first time I even considered the prospect,' admitted Williams. 'So while Saunders thought so highly of the team and was happy to share his thoughts privately with Peter, he would never put that pressure onto us as players and would instead just make sure we did our jobs from one game to the next.'

The season began as everyone had hoped, with five wins from the first six games. The squad was tested immediately when Allan Evans was unavailable for the season-opener at Elland Road and Irishman Eamonn Deacy came in at left-back as Gary Williams slotted into the centre of defence alongside McNaught. Despite these occasional challenges they managed to use only fourteen players all season, and seven were ever-presents in their 46 league and cup games: Rimmer, McNaught, Morley, Bremner, Swain, Cowans and captain Dennis Mortimer. Pat Heard one game, Terry Donovan two, Gary Shelton three and Brendan Ormsby one were unused substitutes at various times.

''How the hell did we manage with fourteen players?' Allan Evans asked. 'The answer is because we were the fittest team there was – Saunders worked us so hard. I used to start training on my own for two weeks before we went back for pre-season because I knew how hard Saunders was going to work us. I had to prepare myself for that so I was ready. It didn't matter because you still felt rubbish afterwards and were still heaving with the workload, but at least I was better than I would otherwise have been.'

Just as everything seemed to be going so well early into that campaign, almost too well, Villa hit a sticky patch that presented an early test of their mettle. They lost 1–0 at Ipswich – the first of three defeats to the team who would be their nearest rivals for the title that season. Then John Gidman came back to Villa Park, in the same Everton team that included a future Villain Steve McMahon, and left with a shock 2–0 victory. The worst, though, was yet to come.

A Tuesday night on 23 September saw any early promise that Villa had shown over the first six matches of the campaign drifting from memory. A 2–1 loss at second-tier Cambridge United at their Abbey Stadium was a sharp reality check as Villa even fielded their strongest team, with the exception of David Geddis who was selected instead of Gary Shaw.

'I don't know what happened that day,' Cowans reflected. 'Subconsciously we probably felt it was going to be easy, but it was a kick up the arse and was something we talked about as players. We felt that was a game we shouldn't be losing and we needed to kick on and start winning games.'

Allan Evans remembers target man and future Watford star George Reilly winning every ball in the air that night, and said that while Saunders would have hated to lose the match, he never allowed himself to become too depressed by a poor result in the same way he rarely delighted over an unexpectedly pleasing win. 'Ron was the master of keeping an equilibrium,' said Evans. 'Whether we won or lost he never got too up or down about anything.'

Villa erased their mini-blip from memory by constructing a sequence of performances that saw them win eight of their next ten league matches, and the other two were admirable draws – 3–3 at Manchester United and a goalless affair at the Hawthorns against Ron Atkinson's West Bromwich Albion side that included Bryan Robson, Cyrille Regis and Peter Barnes. The 4–1 demolition of Brighton at Villa Park, having gone 1–0 down to a goal by former Villain John Gregory, meant Villa soared to the summit of England's top league for the first time in 48 years. Players were starting to believe in themselves much more, though the occasional humbling defeat eroded any cockiness at their lofty prospects they lost three further games before the turn of the year after their winning run, against Liverpool, Middlesbrough and Brighton. Even so, from the day they beat Tottenham Hotspur on 18 October, Villa were either first or

Tommy Docherty, the new manager of Aston Villa in 1968, with a new board of directors in Harry Kartz, Pat Matthews, Doug Ellis, Bob McKay, Harry Parkes. (Getty)

Charlie Aitkin becomes Aston Villa's all-time record appearance holder. (Getty)

Ron Saunders dozing off amongst members of the Villa board. (Getty)

Saunders, a fitness fanatic, putting the Villa squad through their paces in pre-season. (Getty)

Saunders lifts the League Cup at Wembley in 1975 having beaten Norwich City. (Getty)

Andy Gray with his Player of the Year and Young Player of the Year awards in 1977, after his manager refused to allow him to attend the awards dinner in London. (Getty)

John Gregory and Johan Cruyff in the Nou Camp. (Getty)

The potent forward line of Peter Withe and local boy, Gary Shaw. (Getty)

Winning the league at Highbury in 1981. (Mirrorpix)

Ken McNaught, disgusted by the defeat at Highbury, was already wearing a suit when news of Ipswich's result confirmed Villa as champions. (Getty)

Ron Saunders before his public. (Mirrorpix)

The team that went to Rotterdam. (Getty)

Rookie Nigel Spink replacing the experienced Jimmy Rimmer in De Kuip. (Getty)

Take me to the moon…Villa are European champions… (Getty)

Tony Barton enjoying a glass of wine... (Getty)

Tony Morley would feature in England's World Cup song for 1982, though he – and other fine Villa players – would not make the squad. (Getty)

Battering Barcelona at Villa Park in the European Super Cup. (Getty)

Steve McMahon and Gordon Cowans providing steel and silk in the Villa midfield. (Getty)

Local boy Mark Walters emerges in the new-look Villa. (Offside)

Graham Turner in happier times with Doug Ellis and his pain in the neck… (Getty)

Celtic hero Billy McNeill would take Aston Villa into the Second Division. (Offside)

Graham Taylor arrives! (Mirrorpix)

David Platt,
he came
from Crewe
Alexandra and
he left for Italy.
(Offside)

Promotion! Featuring Garry Thompson. (Getty)

Taylor wheels and deals, bringing in Paul McGrath and Kent Nielsen. (Mirrorpix)

Dr. Josef Venglos becomes Doug Ellis's new fancy…but not for long. (Mirrorpix)

second in the league for the remainder of the season.

Despite the buoyant mood at the club then, one or two elements behind the scenes gave less cause for celebration. Brian Little sat through the entire campaign nursing a knee injury that would eventually bring about an early retirement. But more sinister was the disposition of defender Mike Pejic. Nobody knew it then, but the former Stoke and England player was in such a bad place mentally that he considered taking his own life. His last match for Villa had been the home game against Liverpool in the previous season. Villa were kicking towards the Holte End and, with no one near him, he felt a click in his groin. That was Pejic's career over, though he never knew it at the time and tried in vain to regain his fitness for the next eighteen months.

'It was horrific, having treatment every day,' recalled Pejic, who revealed the eventual hernia diagnosis did not arrive for eight years such was the paucity of the the medical expertise available to him. 'I felt completely alone. The longer it went on I was forgotten. Even your mates start to walk past and don't even notice you. What made it worse was that I was travelling from Wales and staying at various hotels in the area, so I couldn't settle. You become a lonely figure sitting in the stand watching the matches week after week. I just didn't feel part of it and never connected with their success at all.'

Worse was to come when, during a reserve game in which he was testing his injury, a supporter shouted from the stand, 'Pejic, you cheat!' in reference to his extended injury layoff while picking up his not insignificant wages. 'That hurt me deeply. I will never forget that. It was just one man but I was so low at the time that was all it took to knock me. I wasn't in a good place and I had a breakdown towards the end of my two-year contract.

'I was driving back from the Villa after a meeting with Ron Saunders at Bodymoor Heath. He asked if I was able to go out and train with the lads. I said no. I would have loved to but my injury didn't allow me to. I will never forget driving back on the M6, before the Stoke turn-off at Junction 15. I pulled over and just broke down. I couldn't drive. So many little things had just snowballed until I couldn't cope any longer. Some of it was harmless banter to the lads but to me it was like a dagger going in and I was hurting deeply.

'I would be in the office claiming my expenses and a couple of the lads would take the piss, because I was claiming my money but wasn't playing. I know they were only joking but at that time I took the slightest comment very personally.

I felt people thought I was a liar and a cheat. It took me two years to recover from this breakdown. I was in a black hole, my own world, and nothing comes in there with you. I don't know how my wife coped with me. I was gone and I thought many times about doing something stupid. It was only my daughter being into show-jumping that kept my head above water, as I drove her around the country to competitions. My other saviour was a teacher at my kids' school in Wales asking me to help out with the sports. I was shaking the first time I taught them, but over time that was the beginning of my way back to sanity and normality.'

'Do You Want to Bet Against Us?'

'Ipswich gave it large in the dressing room afterwards and were so loud with their celebrations it felt as though they were trying to wind us up. They were too overzealous and they acted like the league was done and dusted.' – **Gary Williams**

IT WAS CHRISTMAS 1980. VILLA WERE SECOND IN THE LEAGUE TABLE but Ron Saunders detected an atmosphere on the training pitches that he felt was not quite right. Tackles were going in that were over the top and players were kicking each other a little bit harder than usual. The frustration among the squad was tangible. Saunders was a great believer – as were the players – that you trained at the tempo that you played. Yet something was up and he aimed to put a stop to it there and then before any dent in morale derailed Villa's title bid.

'He sat us down and said, "What's going on? Something isn't right,"' explained Ken McNaught. 'I told him that we were grinding out results but we weren't playing as well as we could. We were pissed off because we all knew we could play a lot better. He asked us how many points we had and we answered and Ron then managed to get us to see that we were doing enough to carry out his target at the start of the season and our mood suddenly lifted. We started to think, "We can't be playing that badly then, can we?" That was the mentality we left with.'

On Saturday, 3 January 1981, there was an all-too-familiar tale for Villa, who suffered the second of their three defeats to Ipswich Town that season. On this occasion, it wasn't the league championship at stake but the FA Cup as the teams met in the third round. England striker Paul Mariner settled this tightly fought

139

contest at Portman Road with the game's only goal in the fourteenth minute, against a Villa team at full strength.

The East Anglian club had been building for success throughout the 1970s, culminating with an FA Cup final win in 1978 over a strong Arsenal team. Their line-up had more so-called stars – or internationals at least – than Villa's with England players like Terry Butcher, Mick Mills, Russell Osman, Mariner, Kevin Beattie and Eric Gates; Scottish trio John Wark, George Burley and Alan Brazil; and the classy Dutch duo of midfielders Frans Thijssen and Arnold Muhren. Their goalkeeper Paul Cooper, too, was one of the best in the league but, like Villa's Jimmy Rimmer, suffered a lack of international recognition due to the plethora of quality available to England at the time.

'The one regret we all probably have is not getting a result over Ipswich that season,' Colin Gibson admitted. 'I know they beat us three times but it would be hard for me to say they were better than us. Man for man they had more flair than us. If they played well and we played well, they might win. But if they played well and we didn't play so well, we were still capable of grinding out a draw. Whereas if they had an off-day and we didn't we would beat them. We were more resilient.

'In the end, did we have their flair? No. They had a team of internationals. Maybe only their goalkeeper Paul Cooper was not an international but he was a fantastic keeper. We had no regular internationals. But ultimately, winning the league is about a marathon not a sprint and we were worthy winners.'

Terry Butcher agrees with Gibson's analysis and insisted that he and his Ipswich teammates had a great respect for that Villa team, despite the three wins they earned over them that season. 'When both teams were at their best, they really went for it,' Butcher commented. 'Villa were hard-working and honest like us and it is a compliment to both teams that we fought it out for the title that season while Liverpool and Nottingham Forest were still in their pomp.'

Villa's FA Cup exit was their fourth loss in eight matches and led some sceptics to suggest their bubble had burst. However, they rebounded from that reverse with a seven-match winning streak that began the following week with a 2–0 triumph over that season's European Cup winners, Liverpool. The all-powerful Reds were without key central defensive pair Alan Hansen and Phil Thompson and midfield warrior Jimmy Case but, nonetheless, still had enough quality in the likes of Kenny Dalglish, Graeme Souness, Terry McDermott and Ray Clemence to avoid any need for excuses.

The most significant outcome of this result was the belief the Villa players took from it. If they did not contemplate that they were genuine title contenders beforehand, they did now. Goals either side of half-time, coincidentally scored by Scousers Peter Withe and Dennis Mortimer, gave Villa a surprisingly comfortable victory. Mortimer's goal, eight minutes from time, exemplified Villa's free-flowing football. The rampaging Kenny Swain back-heeled the ball to Gary Shaw and he then threaded it between the middle of Liverpool's defence for the skipper to run on to and slot home. Even Graeme Souness was impressed by Villa's championship credentials, especially the midfield trio. Reflecting on that season, he revealed: 'They were a nice mix as a combination, especially in the midfield. Bremner was a workaholic, Cowans added a bit of extra quality and flair, and the captain was a very good player, too. In fact, I first came up against Dennis Mortimer as a boy in the FA Youth Cup final between Tottenham and Coventry and I got sent off in a final that went to a second replay. So Dennis and I go back a long, long time. They were a particularly strong midfield then at Villa and a match for anyone.'

Jimmy Rimmer regarded Villa's midfield as the best in the country and Colin Gibson was equally complimentary about the variation of characters, styles and abilities available. 'Dennis had great legs and could run all day, up and down, box to box,' Gibson explained. 'Des was the same and more that he often wasn't given credit for, while Gordon could land a ball on a sixpence. Even Tony Morley could be up and down but it only took one spark from him and we could create a goal.'

It was the Liverpool result more than any that convinced the Villa players they were good enough to dethrone the Reds as English league champions, and their confidence and self-belief reflected such a mindset thereafter. The manager, though, would never think too much about the big prize ahead, a first league title in 71 years, so his focus on the next game and the game after meant the players rarely lost concentration.

'Liverpool were the team of that day and if you managed to beat them you were on the right track,' said Allan Evans. 'Similarly, Forest were the European Cup champions and if you're beating those teams you know you're doing well. That's how we gauged ourselves, but that thought process came from the players because Saunders would never show too much respect for any team – not in front of us anyway. He would approach a game against Liverpool the same as Norwich or Stoke. He was very good at keeping a level head.'

Gordon Cowans thought Villa beat Liverpool 'pretty comfortably' despite a scoreline that was far from emphatic. Jimmy Rimmer was experienced by then and had been a substitute when Manchester United won the European Cup in 1968; he was not as likely to be carried away by a few good results as more impressionable youngsters in the team might have been. He still sensed the magnitude of the Liverpool win though.

'They were the best club side in the world then, they were invincible and we not only beat them in that game but finished nine points ahead of them at the end of the season,' Rimmer beamed. 'We knew it was a significant result but for Ron, it was just another good result. He said afterwards, "Enjoy this one for a few hours, lads, but don't forget, it's Coventry away next week." He had that knack of bringing us back down to earth.'

But for those few hours, the Villa players did enjoy the moment and allowed themselves to briefly consider the special prize ahead of them. They never approached that season thinking they would win the league. They were getting nosebleeds, as it were, because they had not threatened the top of the league for some time. But after the Liverpool game they began to think the unthinkable. Colin Gibson was not even 21 at the time and had no clue as to whether Villa were good enough to last the pace. But in the bath after the match, when chatting to Peter Withe who had seen it all before at Forest, he asked him if he thought they could do it. 'If we keep doing the right things and stay together, you bet we can,' came the reply. The same message came from skipper Dennis Mortimer.

Saunders later reflected that the victory over Bob Paisley's team laid down a significant marker on the title race, but also demonstrated the value in the team ethic he had worked so hard to achieve. 'The experts may criticise expressions like work-rate, effort, running and teamwork; they may drool over words like natural ability, balance, skill and class. But without the work-rate, the effort, the teamwork and the will to win, players as individuals will never begin to show their ability and their class. For me, Liverpool had been the great exponent of such qualities through the years, and I felt when we got the better of them at Villa Park we were ready to look them straight in the eye, as it were.'

Also in that seven-match winning run came a champagne moment that is still talked about as one of the best goals in the league's history – when Tony Morley scored what would become *Match of the Day's* goal of the season at Goodison Park. After Gary Williams and Gary Shaw's interplay, Morley attacked the Everton defence with pace, cut inside onto his right foot and thundered the ball into the

Everton goal from twenty yards. It was the first Villa goal after just three minutes in a comprehensive 3–1 win. The moment had all supporters purring and even Everton manager Gordon Lee appreciated his ability to produce magic. 'Morley was the kind of player that all teams needed,' said Lee, 'with the ability to keep the ball and contribute a good number of goals from wide positions.'

Morley did not even expect to be playing on the day, but in the event his doubts were unfounded and only came from some master mind games played by his manager. The day before in training, Morley was not handed a bib, which generally indicated being out of the team in the following game. Saunders even followed up that tactic by advising Morley later that day, 'I don't think I'm going to play you tomorrow, you're too flash and you'll be trying all your fancy flicks. I need twelve players I can rely on and not trying to show off to everybody.' Saunders knew Everton away was the biggest game of the season to Morley, as he was an Everton supporter in his youth and all of his family would be there. The reality, though, was Saunders was merely ensuring Morley was doubly committed and would go all out to prove him wrong, a tactic he also used on numerous occasions with Brian Little to good effect. That was how he extracted an extra ten per cent out of players who he regarded as 'luxury players' but match-winners nonetheless.

'I kept quiet but I was gutted,' Morley recalled. 'It wasn't until we were in the dressing room before the game when he came to me and said, "Pat [Heard] is a bit young for this game against his old club, so you're playing." In hindsight, I was always going to play, though I never knew it at the time. It was typical Saunders kidology and I happened to have a good game and scored that goal. I knew as soon as I hit it, it was a screamer. Thankfully it went in. Shooting from distance is like playing a golf shot, you're never too sure where it's going to go. But that time I knew it was in. I gave Saunders the V sign as I celebrated. He never said anything to me afterwards like "well played" or "great goal", he just congratulated all the lads. Then on the Monday morning he called me into his office and said, "You did alright on Saturday, son. But that sign you gave me? That's going to cost you a hundred pounds."'

Saunders' harsh but shrewd treatment towards Morley did not go unnoticed by his teammates but they all realised the manager knew how to unlock Morley's best football. And when he was at his best there were few better wingers in Europe.

'So many times he would haul Tony off towards the end of a game and it wasn't because he was playing badly, it was to wind Tony up so that he would be guessing all week whether he would play the next game and so he would be fired up to prove him wrong,' Gary Williams said. 'He manipulated situations expertly and you can't argue with his results.'

Either side of that Everton win came away-day victories at Coventry City 2–1 and Wolverhampton Wanderers 1–0. In fact, they were two of an incredible eleven wins Villa recorded in Midlands derbies that season, with three drawn to Stoke, West Brom and Forest away and no defeats. Saunders regarded derby matches as being twice as difficult to win, because of the inevitable distraction the local rivalry brought, so making it especially challenging for a Midlands club at the time to finish up as champions. Ipswich, in comparison, had just the two league matches with East Anglian rivals Norwich to contend with.

West Brom defender Ally Robertson summed up just how closely contested those Midland derby games were when he suggested: 'We weren't all that far behind Villa when they won the league in '81 – eight points. In the closing weeks of the season, we beat Ipswich 3–1 and then four days later gifted Villa both points through a bad back pass.'

Villa's juggernaut-style success that season disguised various worrying situations behind the scenes, with Mike Pejic and Brian Little's injuries two examples. Reserve midfielder Pat Heard, too, suffered a health scare in the March, just two months before Villa's title win was sealed. It was a serious enough complaint to have threatened his life and he was in intensive care for a week after collapsing in training.

'I had a heart complaint diagnosed and never actually received the all-clear until six months later,' Heard revealed. 'It was a virus on my heart passed on by my newly born son. It's called pericarditis and was very serious. Luckily I was OK but I had to go through all kinds of tests. I was just twenty-one and for some time there was definitely a doubt about whether my career was over or not.'

Meanwhile, as Heard began his recovery, Villa entertained title rivals Ipswich at home on 14 April, a Tuesday night, which was hyped as a winner-takes-all game to settle the Championship. Alan Brazil gave Bobby Robson's men an early lead in the fourth minute and Eric Gates doubled their advantage in the 79th, and though a goal from Gary Shaw three minutes later set up a pulsating finale, Villa were unable to prevent an Ipswich win. Seemingly, the majority of the media – and perhaps Ipswich themselves – then considered the title race to be over. Ipswich were bidding to win only their second English league championship in their history. Until that week they had been in the midst of chasing an unprecedented treble, but had lost an FA Cup semi-final 1–0 against Manchester City. That left the league and UEFA Cup. The Villa win at least gave them considerable hope that one of these targets would be attainable.

But few reckoned on Ron Saunders' ability to manufacture enough motivation from a seemingly hopeless situation to spark a whole-hearted end-of-season rally. Saunders showcased his fighting talk in a post-match, pitchside television interview with commentator Brian Moore that inspired his players, who on that night were left shattered with disappointment.

Saunders: Although we've only got four and they've got five games left, that's a long way to go at this stage of the season.
Moore: So it's all to play for still?
Saunders: I think so. Do you want to bet against us?

Saunders later explained why he was so confident that Villa were still firmly in the title race. 'Unfortunately, on the night we were by no means at our best and conceded two sloppy goals. Immediately everybody assumed the title belonged to Ipswich. But even though we had played badly by our standards, I felt even more convinced that Aston Villa would finish up as champions. Indeed, at the after-match press conference I suggested to the media that I would stand any bets they cared to place against us. There wasn't one taker.'

Saunders was proven right as Villa won two, drew one and lost one of their remaining four games. Ipswich, in contrast, lost four of their last five league games. Some would suggest Ipswich's UEFA Cup involvement and the two-legged semi-final against Cologne presented an awkward distraction and drained their energy for the league games. Certainly the statistics are difficult to challenge. Villa had seven players that season who appeared in all 46 of their league and cup games. However, Ipswich defender Russell Osman played in 66 matches, Butcher played in 64 games, while a further eight Ipswich players appeared in more games than those Villa ever-presents in that campaign, with six of them in total playing at least 60 matches.

As Butcher pointed out: 'Villa didn't play in Europe that season, unlike us, and they exited both of the domestic cups early so they only had the league to focus on, which would have helped their cause hugely. Towards the end of that campaign fatigue and the pressure of going for the triple clearly took its toll on us. We have seen various teams over the years going for a treble only to fall short somewhere. It is a draining challenge.'

Allan Evans told of how his mood was instantly buoyed by Saunders' outspoken optimism. 'After I heard Ron say that, I really thought we could do it.' Gary Williams, who deputised in the centre of defence for the absent Evans in that clash against Ipswich, also felt that as soon as the manager made his bold statement, the title race was back on. However, he's honest enough to admit that on the final whistle he thought Villa 'had blown it' and considered Ipswich as good as the newly crowned champions after they moved to within a point of Villa with a game in hand.

Ipswich, though, then unwittingly committed a mistake that might have cost them dearly. For that night there was one other major factor as well as Saunders' words that spurred Villa's renaissance. The Ipswich players celebrated their victory extravagantly and raucously and Villa's players to a man were adamant their cheers and highly vocal dressing room songs of triumph were intentionally aimed at them, twisting the knife further when they were already hurting.

'They gave it large in the dressing room afterwards and were so loud with their celebrations it felt as though they were trying to wind us up,' Williams recalled. 'They were too overzealous and they acted like the league was done and dusted. If the boot was on the other foot Ron Saunders would never have allowed us to behave like that, as he respected the opposition and he would have reminded us that we hadn't won anything yet.'

Kenny Swain believed they also attempted to tease Villa with their cocky behaviour at the Professional Footballers' Association awards dinner. John Wark claimed the top prize that evening, with his teammates Frans Thijssen and Paul Mariner joining him in the top three for the Player of the Year contest. Dennis Mortimer was Villa's only candidate, so it seemed everything was going in Ipswich's favour.

Swain, who was one of three Villa players voted into the PFA's Team of the Year along with Allan Evans and Gary Shaw, remembered: 'Their table was not far from ours and hearing them celebrate after our match and then at the dinner, it was clear they felt the title was all over.

'While I wouldn't say they were arrogant or smug, they were certainly confident, maybe even cock-a-hoop. While it was frustrating that we couldn't play them again to settle the score, we definitely took some motivation from the way they behaved. I think, whether you're a footballer, cricketer, boxer or whatever, if you think you have won long before a competition is finished, that's a weakness in your make-up. As their opponent we gained a lot from the way they conducted themselves.'

The match – and especially the aftermath – certainly made for a pulsating run-in to the season finale.

Terry Butcher understands Villa's reaction to their celebrations but insists his team were not in any way trying to 'wind up' the Villa players and were instead letting off steam after a difficult few days.

'I saw Tony Morley after the game and he was as low as anything as he thought they had blown it, so there's no way any of us would take any satisfaction in their defeat like that,' Butcher said. 'We were loud, yes, but it was more out of relief and elation as we had been at the same ground only three days earlier and lost an FA Cup semi-final when we were going for the treble. So to have to drive back to Birmingham two days later to play this game, we were steeling ourselves to get up for it again. Our celebrations were purely about putting things right from the Saturday.'

Villa rebounded by defeating Nottingham Forest 2–0 at home courtesy of a Gordon Cowans penalty and another goal from Peter Withe. Conversely, Ipswich began to crack when they needed to retain their winning streak more than ever to hold on to their advantage. On the same day they lost 2–0 to Arsenal, as Villa went to 57 points with three games left. Ipswich remained on 54 points with four games to play.

Two days later on the Easter Bank Holiday Monday, Villa had yet another Midlands derby to negotiate, this time at the Victoria Ground against Stoke City. Another Withe goal earned them a hard-fought 1–1 draw. Crucially, an under-strength Ipswich without Frans Thijssen, Paul Mariner, Eric Gates and George Burley did not fare so well in their only derby against Norwich, as they went down to a Justin Fashanu goal to slip to another defeat. The standings now saw Villa with 58 points after 40 games, with two to play, and Ipswich with 54 points after 39 games.

That Stoke match came less than two days after Tony Morley's house had burned down, but it never stopped him from playing the full ninety minutes, having travelled up on the team coach wearing hoPeléssly outdated clothes borrowed from his girlfriend's father. 'I went into training the day before,' Morley recalled, 'and the gaffer wasn't all that sympathetic. He said, "I don't care about your house, get your kit on and train." That was Saunders for you. And the lads gave me a fair bit of stick for the gear I was wearing, so I had to get on with it.'

On Saturday 25 April, both Villa and Ipswich registered victories to keep the title race open, though Villa's slick 3–0 demolition of Middlesbrough was more convincing than the 1–0 win Ipswich chalked up against Manchester City at Portman Road. Gary Shaw, with his twentieth goal of the campaign, Withe again and Allan Evans kept Villa in pole position for the title on sixty points with one game remaining, while Ipswich were four points adrift with a game in hand, meaning they had to win their final two games against Middlesbrough and Southampton, both away from home, and hope Villa slipped up.

Kenny Swain felt that performance against 'Boro really tightened the screw on Ipswich and showed they were well past their own mini-wobble. 'The way we played against Middlesbrough, who had always been a bogey team of ours, was a good example of just how fired up we were,' Swain said. 'We were at their throats from the first minute till the last. It was a very aggressive 3–0 win.'

Villa had the opportunity to seal a historic league title triumph in the presence of special guest Pelé at Highbury on Saturday, 2 May. It was all quite anticlimactic as they suffered a meek 2–0 defeat to Arsenal in a game where goalkeeper Jimmy Rimmer felt he had his worst game for the club. Fortunately for Villa, Yugoslav striker Bosko Jankovic scored twice for Middlesbrough as they beat Ipswich 2–1 at Ayresome Park, where 'Boro manager and ex-Villa League Cup winner John Neal was able to share in the glory.

'The Arsenal game was a horrible match for us, we just didn't perform,' admitted Colin Gibson. 'I don't know if the occasion got to us or if we were too hyped up. We got stuck in traffic beforehand and arrived late but we can't use that as an excuse. Coming off, we were disappointed with our own performances and upset we might have lost the league. But hearing our fans' cheers, it didn't take us long to realise Ipswich were losing. In normal circumstances we would have received an almighty rollicking from Saunders. He wasn't happy with us but he soon changed because we hadn't won the league for seventy-one years and by the time we got in the dressing room we knew we had won it. It was about putting this game into perspective and overall we had won the most points over a nine-month period and deserved our success.'

Gibson's fellow defender Ken McNaught initially struggled to accept the performance and result as readily as his teammates and had no interest in hanging around for radio reports about Ipswich.

'I was so disgusted that while everyone was waiting for the Ipswich result I had a shower and got changed,' McNaught recalled. 'We never turned up. We performed so badly that I had a pop in the dressing room. I had a go at one or two and went straight in the shower. I told everyone they were shite and said we should be ashamed of ourselves. That's why, when the celebration champagne pictures came out, I was the only one who had his clothes on, because I was so pissed off.'

Those results meant, despite a game in hand, Ipswich could no longer catch Villa, who finished on 60 points with Ipswich closing on 56 following yet another defeat at home to Southampton eleven days later. The 3-2 scoreline sounds close, but Saints were 3-0 up after 21 minutes in that season-ender to emphasise how far Bobby Robson's team's had fallen.

Swain bumped into Villa's unlikely hero Jankovic some years later before the Yugoslav's untimely death in 1993. 'His English wasn't great,' Swain recalled, 'but I reminded him of what he did for us. He didn't see it like that and was quite nonplussed. He just felt he was doing his job.'

Meanwhile, those Ipswich players who were thought to have sewn up the title at Villa Park three weeks prior were now on the floor having had their league title aspirations shattered on the back of an FA Cup exit too.

'Not winning the league when we had such a great opportunity did get under my skin and still does,' Butcher added. 'We ended up winning the UEFA Cup, which was the cup we probably least wanted to win out of the three. But fair play to Villa. They had a terrific team and were worthy winners, as the times we beat them that season is ultimately irrelevant as the league is decided over a season.

'I roomed with Peter Withe at the World Cup in 1982 and became mates with him and a few Villa players – there were no hard feelings. But the pain will always be there for Ipswich because we will probably never have another season like that.'

At Villa, there was also sadness mixed with the elation of the league triumph. Against the backdrop of Villa's subsequent title-winning celebrations, club great Brian Little was forced into retirement at the age of 27 after medics ruled that his long-standing knee injury could not be remedied adequately enough for him to carry on playing at the top level. 'Brian was one of the best players I have ever seen for Villa – he was so graceful,' Allan Evans reflected. 'I was close to Brian and I was gutted for him that he was in the treatment room while we won the league.' Fellow casualty Mike Pejic travelled down to London on the train with Little as their playing careers were both officially written off by specialists for insurance purposes. Later that day, on returning to the house he had purchased from Kevin Keegan in North Wales while he was an Everton player, Pejic broke down in tears at the realisation it was all over. Not even the joy of his club-mates could lighten his mood; it only made him hurt more.

'I hadn't played a single game in that season yet here I was, celebrating with the boys on an open-top bus through Birmingham city centre; I felt like a fraud,' Pejic admitted. 'I was happy for the lads because they were a great bunch of guys but inside I was hurting. It was like a dagger going through me because I knew while Villa were on the up in a big way, my career was over.'

Saunders had made a huge statement in English football and surprised many observers from various sectors of the game. Wolves manager John Barnwell acknowledged: 'I was surprised Villa won the league after they lost Gray, Gidman and Little in such a close timeframe. But Peter Withe was a fantastic signing for them because he could link people into play as well as being a good target man. They had pace with Morley, strength of passing with Cowans and were solid at the back. Ron seemed to have a good grip of what was going on and knew he could succeed by doing things his way.'

The club treated the players and their wives to an end-of-season holiday in Long Beach, California. They had fun driving out to various places like Newport Beach, Huntington Beach, Hollywood, Beverly Hills, and generally savouring a week with no training or the need for cautionary behaviour with management watching over them. 'I hired a shooting brake [car],' recalls Kenny Swain, 'and along with my wife and kids and Des Bremner, Dennis and Evo, I drove to Bel Air to admire the Hollywood movie stars' homes and the views over the Hills. This car pulled up and an old man got out and he said, "Can I help you?" I told him we were just admiring the sights. When he realised we were from England and not local he invited us through into his garden so we could take a proper look at the valley. While his wife made us homemade lemonade he pointed out Charlie Chaplin's house, and said his next-door neighbour was Paul Michael Glaser from *Starsky and Hutch*. Apparently, he'd had a chip-pan fire at his house and it was being renovated at the time otherwise he'd have introduced us. We told them who we were but they were more impressed that we were English tourists.'

On his return to England, Gordon Cowans received a message that Nottingham Forest wanted to sign him; it was a basic case of a player being tapped up. Cowans did not believe his manager was aware of it – but he was wrong. Saunders explained to the Villa directors in a board meeting that his league-winning players were now being tapped up left, right and centre and therefore they needed to be looked after – or, simply, paid more. In Cowans' case, in 1981, Forest were a head-turning proposition as a career move having won the European Cup in 1979 and 1980. Out of curiosity, Cowans agreed to speak to them. He was collected from his home in Tamworth and driven to East Midlands Airport. There, he met with Clough's assistant Peter Taylor and the two casually chatted in Taylor's car in the car park.

'It was all under the radar and Ron Saunders wasn't supposed to know about it as far as I was aware. I didn't want to leave Villa anyway as we had just won the league, and that is what I told him. Peter told me what a good player I was and how Cloughie wants to sign me but I didn't spend much time with him as I explained to him that I was happy where I was. That was the end of that.' For another two years, at least.

The league championship meant a great deal in a historical sense to Aston Villa and the local area as it was the first time Villa had made it into the top three of England's highest league since they were runners-up in 1932/33. It was also a significant event for the city of Birmingham. Unlike Liverpool, Manchester and London, which have enjoyed multiple league title wins before and since, Birmingham can only lay claim on seven, all for Villa, and this triumph in 1981 was the first in 71 years, adding to the previous six Villa had won before the First World War. The league title was also meaningful for the West Midlands region as a whole, as it had not had enjoyed such a victory since Wolverhampton Wanderers achieved the third of their three title victories in 1958/59. Wolves actually registered as many as ten top-three finishes between 1946/47 and 1960/61. Thereafter, the West Midlands only had sporadic cup wins to boast from Villa, West Bromwich Albion, Birmingham City, Wolves and Coventry City. So at this moment, given such a success-starved landscape, Villa were now the kings of the region. And their reputation would soon grow further afield as they embarked on a maiden European Cup voyage.

The 'José Mourinho of his Time' Quits as Barton Steps Up

'Ron Saunders leaving Aston Villa was even bigger than Brian Clough's exit from Forest, because it happened during our golden era, which never happened at Forest. They held on to him.' – **Colin Gibson**

THE 1981/82 SEASON WAS AS BITTERSWEET FOR ASTON VILLA AND their supporters as could be imagined, with euphoria packaged with failure, frustration, anger and administrational turmoil.

The club's first foray into the continent's most prestigious club competition culminated in a shock final triumph against European heavyweights Bayern Munich. It remains one of the most unexpected European Cup victories since the tournament's inception in 1955. However, this success came at a cost. Villa's league form that had been so consistently good the season prior tailed off to such an extent they failed to make the top ten in the league championship, falling painfully from the high standards that had been set and met in the 1980/81 campaign. Ultimately, the strength in depth of Villa's squad was desperately found wanting, as manager Ron Saunders knew would be the case if he was forced to continue with the same small group. Villa were able to survive those shortcomings in 1980/81 and use just fourteen players all season because none of their key players suffered any serious injury, which was now not the case. And despite the league title win, Saunders had a hard time persuading the board to release sufficient funds to aid his ambitious vision for the 1980s.

This, along with serious distrust and widespread suspicion between the manager and chairman, led not only to results in the First Division suffering but also to the devastating resignation of the inspirational manager. The no-nonsense boss had hoped to spend the rest of his managerial career at Villa, which was the pinnacle of his life's work in football. He had taken them from the middle of the second tier to the brink of being European champions. He even spurned two informal approaches from the Football Association – one such effort made by Jimmy Hill – to be the heir apparent to Ron Greenwood as the manager of the England team. According to his family, he simply did not want the job as it never came close to giving him the pride and enjoyment he found at Aston Villa. Around that time Manchester United also courted him, when seeking to replace Dave Sexton. He had several conversations on the telephone with then United chairman Martin Edwards. They offered him a transfer kitty that dwarfed the one he had to work with at Villa, but he chose to stay in the West Midlands where his team were champions and where his family were happy. Southampton manager Lawrie McMenemy also rejected United, before West Bromwich Albion's Ron Atkinson took on the role. Saunders was sounded out for several other jobs too, according to his son Ron Jr.

Not that Saunders' loyalty was appreciated by the Villa hierarchy, quite the opposite, which was why he never worried about joining Villa's fierce rivals Birmingham City. That controversial cross-city move doubled his salary, but any cynical observer suggesting he left Villa for the money at St Andrew's should note he could have done that with England, United or other clubs beforehand, and with greater prospects of success. But he had chosen to stay. While the Villa board took pride in Saunders' team's achievements on the field, they were not prepared to back their manager with more funds to strengthen the squad. That Coventry City's promising midfielder Andy Blair was Villa's only signing in the summer of 1981, after they had just become champions of England and were preparing for their first European Cup campaign, summed up the struggle Saunders was having upstairs in the boardroom. He failed to persuade the directors to release more money to add quality to what was a strong team but not necessarily a strong squad ready to handle the challenges of a European Cup campaign and a bid to retain their English crown.

'I wanted and needed to sign many new players,' Saunders said. 'I wanted to put pressure on every position in the team. There was more money coming into the club than ever, but it was being eaten up. Some players were now champions and were getting tapped up for big money. I needed a bigger squad. The fact we worked wonders with fourteen players worked against me as the those in the boardroom thought we would do it again.'

His reference to the funds 'being eaten up' was a barb at then owner Ronald Bendall. Indeed, Bendall did admit in the summer of 1982 in his chairman's report that income had increased by £546,173 due to European football, while they received an insurance pay-out of £450,000 for Brian Little's premature retirement to injury. However, they still recorded £3,673 less profit than the previous year. These were the kind of curiosities Saunders had suspected and failed to understand.

Following the departure of Doug Ellis as a director in 1979, Saunders had initially enjoyed a fruitful relationship with the board. In those early post-Ellis months, he was actually delighted with the atmosphere at the club. Whereas Ellis could not stop himself from interfering in football matters, new owner Ron Bendall kept out of sight and allowed Saunders to run his team and set player wages and bonuses as he wished. Eventually this changed, and Saunders' gradual frustration at the club's lack of support for his transfer plans boiled over. Saunders was highly suspicious of financial mismanagement behind the scenes and was aware of large amounts of money coming in but somehow that money was not finding its way to his transfer kitty or wage budget, but to other areas that ultimately attracted the attention of the West Midlands Police, which came as little surprise to the manager.

'Bendall left my dad to do his job and never tried to interfere with the players,' Ron Saunders Jr said. 'Bendall was a very shrewd businessman. However, when extra money started to flow in, their relationship deteriorated as that money was not going to where it was meant to go – the squad.'

He added: 'In those days the club did things that made no sense other than to just make money. The friendly against Glasgow Rangers would be one example. There was always going to be violence that day but still they went ahead with the game to make money. When Dad saw already-rich people trying to do things to make themselves richer rather than help the club he could never understand it. Dad was sticking his nose in to find out what was going on with all the money. He was always more of a general manager anyway.'

Saunders had a casual Villa-supporting friend who was also a senior police officer. When the police were tipped off about alleged financial misappropriation, he asked Saunders to help the police with their enquiries, which of course he was happy to agree to – he was adamant wrongdoing was going on but he had no proof.

But there was enough suspicion to interest the police.

Saunders' growing discontent at Villa finally bubbled over on 2 February 1982 at an explosive board meeting. It began with Saunders expressing his exasperation at the lack of funds available to him to strengthen his team. He then proposed, knowing it would cause a stir among the directors, that Tony Morley and Gary Shaw be made available to offers. Morley was by then a full England international and one of the best players in Europe, while Shaw was not far away from being a full international either with the world at his feet. The board reacted with surprise and counter-suggested that 'lesser players' such as David Geddis be sold instead, as Geddis had just attracted an offer from Stoke City.

Saunders then expressed his annoyance that players should have to be sold at all when Terry Rutter, the stadium manager, was 'taking money out of the club'. The minutes from that board meeting say 'the manager went on to state cases when he felt Rutter had deceived the club by pointing out that he brought this matter, of which he was very concerned, to the board's attention on previous occasions'. Rutter was later convicted in court along with North Stand architect Harry Marsden for their part in fraudulent activity surrounding building and maintenance work on that same stand, while Bendall Sr would have joined them had he not passed away before he could answer to the police. The actual description of the case that is currently filed privately at The National Archive says, "Terence John Rutter and Harry Marsden: inciting to obtain by deception, conspiracy to obtain by deception and false accounting in connection with Aston Villa Football Club and other football ground contracts between August 1980 and May 1983." In January 2018, Saunders' son said his dad 'had no real problems with Terry Rutter when he realised he was only the fall guy'.

In that same board meeting, rather than investigate the manager's claims or offer him extra transfer funds, Ron Bendall served the three years' notice on Saunders' job, effectively trying to extricate the club from the lengthy rolling contract they had previously handed him.

It had been around this time that Saunders started to feel he was being watched, too. Saunders had a healthy relationship with most of the Villa directors and saw club secretary Steve Stride like another son – he liked Stride for his honesty, but in Ron Bendall he had a chairman who grew to vehemently resent Saunders' penchant for wanting to know what was happening with the finances of the club. Saunders found out around this time a shocking revelation. He was being spied on, like a suspect in the Cold War.

'In that [1981/82] season, just before Dad resigned, he discovered he was being followed,' Ron Saunders Jr revealed. 'He noticed there was a dark Ford Corsair always behind his car or parked outside the house [in the affluent Solihull village of Copt Heath]. Dad being Dad, he went to confront the driver one day but the guy pulled away and I don't blame him because Dad could be a horrible piece of work when he was pissed off. He took the registration number, though, and gave it to his police contact who subsequently found out the car was registered to a private detective company. Someone around that time also advised us to check our phones because there was a weird delay on the line, and we found that the home phone and Dad's private lines were both tapped.

'Whoever had arranged the investigator was wasting their time and money because Dad wasn't doing anything he shouldn't have been or having an affair or anything like that. They couldn't get anything on him. He just did his job and went home to his family. Not long after, the club effectively tore up his three-year rolling contract by issuing him three years' notice that his contract was being terminated, stopping short of sacking him but trying to reduce their long-term financial commitment to him.'

Today this process would surely be termed 'constructive dismissal'.

'Dad was always one to look to the future and he liked to know that if they got rid of him he would have been paid ninety grand compensation . But when they cancelled his rollover that was when Dad walked out as he was so pissed off with everything going on behind the scenes. Quite simply, I know Bendall felt Dad was getting too big for his boots and made things as hard for him as he could until he left, and I guess he got what he wanted in the end. He walked away with absolutely zilch [£5,000 to be precise, but only if he returned his club car in good condition, with the keys]. Dad could have gone to the courts for some justice but he couldn't be bothered with all that. He left on principle. When Villa fans are aware of what Dad went through they might then understand why he was happy to go across and manage Birmingham City.'

This, remember, was at a time when Villa were through to the quarter-finals of the European Cup. Boardroom minutes then state, 'The manager appeared extremely annoyed at the board's decision and his reply to a question from [vice-chairman] Donald Bendall stated that he did not trust any board of directors of football clubs.'

When Saunders' official resignation came through on 9 February 1982, he advised the Villa board in a letter via his solicitor that he was considering issuing a writ against them, for the way his contract situation had been handled. The club, in retaliation, said they would consider issuing a writ against Saunders for leaving before the end of his term. Neither sued in the event.

Saunders' previous suspicions were later vindicated when Steve Stride wrote in a directors' report on 14 September 1982 that, 'The directors have been informed that the West Midlands Police, acting in conjunction with the Director of Public Prosecutions, have made certain enquiries in relation to building works carried out at Villa Park. It is further understood that the Director of Public Prosecutions is currently considering whether further enquiries are necessary. The directors' have received no details from the West Midlands Police regarding the nature or subject of their enquiries and the directors' offer to make all information and documents in the possession of the club available to the police ...'

There were no winners from the Villa–Saunders spat, maybe with the exception of Birmingham City, whose board had tried to entice Saunders for months, though then he was not interested in moving. Until, that is, he felt his role at Villa became untenable.

Birmingham City chairman Keith Coombs would often joke, 'How much, Ron? What would it take for us to bring you here?' But many other chairmen wanted him too and would often sound him out. Mike Wiseman, the son of Blues director Jack Wiseman, recalls the Saunders switch vividly and insists it was not a decision the City board made on the spur of the moment. 'Keith Coombs was literally obsessed by the idea of taking Ron Saunders off the Villa and maybe that is why they were prepared to pay him so handsomely for coming across.'

In most cases each set of supporters would be in uproar for different reasons. One might have expected the Birmingham fans to reject him for his nine-year allegiance to Villa, yet they felt a smug pride that their supposedly inferior, less successful club historically was able to go one better than Manchester United and England had done and lure Saunders with a pay packet that doubled his salary and seemingly improved the club's footballing prospects. Villa supporters might have been forgiven for venting their angst against Saunders for what appeared to be a clear betrayal, turning up at their most unpopular neighbours. Yet they instead directed their anger towards the Villa board and even, though somewhat more twistedly, towards Saunders' successor Tony Barton, his assistant who never campaigned for the role but who was happy to accept it when it came along – first as caretaker manager and then permanently on 1 April 1982, when he signed a two-year contract. Although Barton was promoted to arguably the most important role inside the football club, he was previously on the low wage of £7,250 a year around £33,000 in 2018 terms, according to club board room minutes. He was actually earning one thousand pounds a year less than the physiotherapist Jim Williams.

'It was tough for Dad because the Villa fans were chanting they wanted Saunders back as he was a bit of a god there after what he had achieved,' Tony Barton's son, Chris, recalled. 'The fans' fury was aimed at Dad but he was caught up in it indirectly.'

Barton had no idea that Saunders' resignation was going to happen, according to his wife, Rose. She remembers how Tony was out scouting one night, as usual, and Bendall phoned their house and left a message for Tony to call him as soon as he came in, 'no matter how late it was'.

'He was subsequently told, "Saunders has gone, you're in charge for the next game." That was it,' Rose said. 'I'm certain Tony didn't know. The first I had heard of it was when Mr Bendall rang up that evening. When the surprise had faded, Tony was in no way fazed by the job. He just carried on doing what he had already been doing in the background, so it wasn't as though he had been thrown in at the deep end.'

There was no contact between Barton and Saunders in the aftermath of the resignation.

The Villa players – and those who knew him well around the club – were stunned that their boss, the man who had guided them so forcefully, shrewdly and professionally towards the top in England and Europe, was no longer their manager. The general theme of the players' reflections demonstrates their surprise at the time and also their frustration at what might have been achieved had Saunders been 'allowed' to stay on and run the team the way he wanted to instead of feeling the need to leave.

'I never saw the writing on the wall,' said Kenny Swain. 'Someone called to tell me the news, I think it was Dennis [Mortimer], and I was shocked because he had been my manager for the best part of five years. I thought, "What the hell has gone on?" A lot of people were asking a lot of questions and not many answers were coming back.

'Saunders was just like Sir Alex Ferguson. They were both terrific man-managers with totally different personalities. The common denominator in both was their 110 per cent conviction that what they're doing was always right. It's so easy to wobble or waver from your preferred path and allow outside pressures to shake your belief, but these managers never did.

'I was out for a meal and a few drinks a couple of days after Ron walked out. On the way back I stopped off at his house and left a bottle of brandy on his doorstep with a note saying, "Thanks for everything". I did something similar when I left Forest for Portsmouth. I bought Cloughie a box-set of Frank Sinatra albums because I knew he was a big fan of his; he had a picture with him in his lounge after he'd met him. It's nice to say thanks when someone has been a good influence on you, as Ron and Cloughie both were on my career.'

'Ron talked to me more than any player but he would keep those kinds of secrets to himself,' commented Jimmy Rimmer. 'He would not have told me if he was going to leave tomorrow or the day after. Ultimately, he did his own thing as he was the manager. But I do think he expected to go on and on at Villa.

'He could see the potential of our team and felt that we could be successful year in and year out – as long as he could bring in the players he wanted. That would have made the difference, but it didn't work out.'

Tony Morley added: 'I can't remember who it was who phoned me but they said, "Have you heard about Ron?" I thought he was going to say he's died. It was a hell of a shock because although we weren't having a great [league] campaign – we were about mid-table – we were in the last eight of the European Cup. We still had a lot to play for.

'If Villa had just given him a five-year contract and left him alone to do his job, we would have had another three or four trophies in the cabinet, easy. Of course, he would have gotten rid of us all eventually but at least we would have been part of a dynasty, rather than something that was far too brief.'

'I was devastated,' Colin Gibson said, 'that this man who had been there right through my career was suddenly gone. The mantle was picked up well by Tony Barton, who was a lovely man, a really good coach and a good spotter of players, but he didn't quite have the ruthlessness of Ron Saunders, though it didn't make him a bad manager. Tony was nicer to us face to face, but as a manager Ron Saunders got the best out of you.

'I am sure Ron Saunders was difficult for the owners to get along with but so was Brian Clough. I know Cloughie didn't last long at Leeds but he didn't do a bad job at Derby or Nottingham Forest. Ron Saunders leaving Aston Villa was even bigger than Brian Clough's exit from Forest because it happened during our golden era, which never happened at Forest. They held on to him.

'Ron was right to want to strengthen his squad. Liverpool and Forest had way deeper squads than we had back then. We depended too much on a small core of players. If you didn't have any or many injuries one season there was a good chance they would come in the following season, as it proved.'

'Without Ron, none of our success would have happened,' insisted Dennis Mortimer. 'He built a team and built resilience into us and when he left we went into overdrive. We might have lost our manager but we didn't lose our focus.'

'I was totally shocked, and for him to turn up at Blues, that was an even bigger shock,' Gordon Cowans said. 'The feeling between the clubs then on and off the pitch was brutal. I was disappointed that he had left and for him to go to Blues was a strange one.

'Ron was a big loss; he didn't take any shit from anyone. Tony Barton was such a lovely fella and he knew he didn't have to change anything, which was a skill in itself. He got us through to winning the European Cup, of course.'

Gary Williams said: 'Fergie used to control everything at Man United and Ron was no different with us. He controlled which players came in and out, their wages, he was on the training ground leading the way, he spoke to the media. He ran the show and that is how he liked it. So, when he left, there was a huge void.'

'What he gave us was irreplaceable,' said Ken McNaught. 'Saunders was the Jose Mourinho of his time because he could get inside players' heads, and if you can do that you can then motivate them and manage them. I could be a moody bastard and Ron would sometimes come up and put his arm around me and say, "What's the problem with you ... what do I have to do to motivate you?" I told him I wasn't enjoying the football. He said, "Listen, Ken, if you want to enjoy your football, you go back to being an amateur and play in the parks. When you're a professional you don't always enjoy what you're doing." He was right. I had forgotten that football was my trade. And to him it was about getting results.'

'I was Ron's last signing for Villa and in the brief time I spent with him I could see what a great psychologist he was and how he got players playing for him,' recalled Andy Blair. 'Before I signed I was in Saunders' house and I asked him, "Where am I going to play as you already have a very good midfield?" His answer was: "Have you not got any confidence in yourself, son?" Of course, my natural instinct was to say yes and sign!'

'I chatted to Ron after he quit and I don't think he left for the money,' said former secretary Alan Bennett. 'He just didn't like the atmosphere in the boardroom any more and he had enough and wanted out. Villa has never paid ridiculously high wages. I wasn't at the club when Ron left but as long as I worked with him he always felt he was worth more. Ron did think about his own personal terms a lot, but only when his contract was under review. Equally, he always tried to look after his players. If he could give them a better contract, he would.'

'The timing was terrible considering we were in the quarter-finals of the European Cup,' said Steve Stride. 'And I think the players lost some respect for him over that. But to this day they still call him "Boss" so there is still a lot of respect for what he did for the club. Tony Barton was a lovely man who played a key role in the European Cup win but probably not cut out for being a manager, not at this level anyway. He took over Ron's team and kept things going nicely but the players were used to being kicked and bollocked.'

'It was a shock,' former chairman Harry Kartz said. 'Keith Coombs at Birmingham City made him an offer he couldn't refuse. Manchester United wanted to speak to him but Bendall wouldn't let them. So, Blues managed to do what even the great Manchester United could not and woo Ron. He never got the credit he deserved at Villa. He was a top manager but he rarely gets mentioned. If you look at that European Cup-winning team, he bought nearly all of those players and for not very much.'

Two people who knew Saunders away from Villa Park were Birmingham City striker Wayne Clarke and Terry Neill, who played against him for Tottenham before they were rival managers in the top flight, with Neill in charge of Arsenal between 1976 and 1983. Both of them regard Saunders to have been a different character in actuality than how he was perceived during most of his tenure at Aston Villa.

'Ron was a mate of mine and although he had this rough, tough reputation, he was a big softy underneath all the bravado,' Neill revealed, smiling. 'I used to say to him, "I don't believe all this tough-guy crap, you're a big softy really." He would say, "I know, but don't tell anyone, otherwise I won't get these fellas to play for me any more!" He had a good sense of humour. But honestly, he was a tough guy as a player, Ron could handle himself.'

Wayne Clarke added: 'He was good for me and toughened me up. Unless you know him, people think he is dour, miserable and depressing, and he has this preconceived image of being a hard man and tough on players. He wasn't at all. In training, he was a laugh a minute. He was funny and would take the mickey out of players but not in a nasty way. I enjoyed playing for him and he knew how I liked to play.'

Many Villa players from Saunders' era would no doubt be thinking Clarke is referring to someone different. However, Frank Carrodus knew Saunders at Villa and then briefly at Birmingham City and he also felt the manager had mellowed after the bitterness of his fall-out with Villa. 'He wasn't the same man at the Blues. It was clear to me that by then his spark had gone. I think he cared so deeply about the Villa and what he had built up there that he was never the same man once he left Villa Park.'

The last word on the walk-out and his Villa career goes to Ron Saunders himself.

'If the conditions were right I wanted to stay at Villa until I retired. In retrospect, if someone like the ex-Norwich City chairman Geoffrey Watling – who was my all-time favourite chairman to work with – if he was the chairman at Villa, we would have gone on to win so much more and everyone connected with the club would have enjoyed the fruits of this success. Geoffrey left me and the players to get on with our jobs and I rarely had that freedom at Villa, sadly. As Villa's demise worsened after my time, I felt very sad for the Villa supporters and the people that worked very hard there through the bad times.'

Saunders' final season at Villa began with a Wembley spectacle attended by 92,500 for the Charity Shield, as English League champions Villa took on Keith Burkinshaw's FA Cup winners Tottenham Hotspur. The Shield was shared after a 2–2 draw, after two goals from Peter Withe and a Mark Falco brace for Spurs.

Villa were without striker Gary Shaw after he sustained a foot injury in training and was unable to shake it off, despite fitness tests the day before and on the morning of the match. David Geddis replaced him and partnered Withe in attack. 'I can barely remember it, it was like a non-event,' Allan Evans reflected. 'I remember going to Wembley and Withey and Mark Falco each scoring twice, but it was crap that it was shared. I would rather have won or lost it on penalties.'

Villa lost their opening two league games, at home to Notts County and away at Sunderland. Despite an impressive 3–1 win at Tottenham, they did not register a victory at home in the league until they beat West Ham 3–2 on 17 October. Saunders' fears about squad depth were vindicated. Defensive rock Ken McNaught missed the whole of October, November, December and January due to a blood clot in his left calf an injury that would mean he was never the same again and full-back Colin Gibson missed the last four months of the season. McNaught's position was taken up by a combination of rookie Brendan Ormsby, midfielder Des Bremner and full-back Gary Williams, exposing the squad's deficiencies.

Progress in the European Cup would make up for the disappointing performances in the league. Villa conceded just two goals in the competition, one at home and one away to East Germany's Dynamo Berlin in the second round. Des Bremner says Europe suited Villa's way of playing.

'The interesting thing is, the recipe for doing well in Europe hasn't changed all that much over the years and the way we played would still be successful now,' Bremner said. 'Pep Guardiola's philosophy is when you have the ball, be creative and play football, but when you haven't got the ball stop the opposition from playing and win it back. That's exactly what we did in our glory days: closing down from front to back to win possession and then playing our own game in attack, trying to score goals.'

Their European campaign started with a comfortable 5–0 win over Icelandic side FC Valur. Terry Donovan made the most of a rare outing by scoring two goals, as did strike partner Peter Withe, after Tony Morley had opened the scoring. Donovan was only playing because Gary Shaw and David Geddis were injured. 'I should have scored a hat-trick as we created quite a few chances,' said Donovan. 'We didn't realise then it was the start of a big occasion that culminated in Rotterdam the following May.' Donovan was unlucky not to play more often and demonstrated his scoring knack by notching 24 goals in 27 games in that 1981/82 season in the Central League for Villa's reserve team.

For the away leg, Villa took a charter flight on Aer Lingus to Iceland. Reykjavik was bitterly cold and Valur's ground, with a 3,500 capacity, was sighted next to a fish factory, which expelled an overpowering stench around the ground. 'It's one of the weirdest places we ever played at because of the smell,' recalled Allan Evans. 'It made you heave. We went abroad a lot and people think it's great but we never went anywhere. We trained, rested, played and travelled. It was work. We never saw anything.'

Evans was a teetotaller so he was not speaking for every player. Secretary Steve

Stride saw some of the players in the local nightclub on the night before the game in Iceland. Coach and Ron Saunders' eyes and ears Roy McLaren was waiting for them at the team hotel and gave them a dressing down on their return.

One man who did sightsee but who later regretted it was the physiotherapist Jim Williams, who accepted an invitation for an aerial tour of the city and was subsequently late for afternoon training. Saunders was seething. Fortunately, there were no injuries during the session but the dry-humoured manager was determined to have his revenge on the physio. He roped in a few players to strap both of reserve full-back Mark Jones's legs together to give the impression he had broken them both. For added effect the players poured brandy all over Jones's legs. When a frantic Williams finally arrived at the hotel and was ushered into the patient's room, he found the rookie playing his part like a *Coronation Street* audition, screaming in agony. Williams smelled the liquor and asked, 'Has he been drinking?' The quick-witted Saunders replied, 'Of course he has, it was the only way we could kill the pain!' Eventually the many onlookers could no longer keep their laughter in and the ruse was out. But Williams never missed another training session.

Ken McNaught was by now struggling with his blood clot and Saunders was forced to introduce 21-year-old Brendan Ormsby in games where he would have preferred more experience. Around that time, Saunders inadvertently met Arsenal's centre-back Willie Young at a Midlands golf course and told him he would like to bring him to Villa. He was a powerful, fearless, tough-tackling McNaught-type player – and Scottish too. Young was keen as he was not 'being looked after' at Highbury, but Saunders could not raise the fee. Instead, Young headed to Nottingham Forest in December 1981 for just £50,000.

Saunders' final influence on Villa's European Cup campaign was what many of the players considered the toughest round, against Dynamo Berlin, both away at the JahnSportspark Stadium and at home. They were the powerhouses of East German football, pre-unification, winning their domestic league ten times between 1979 and 1988. Tony Morley's goals either side of half-time in East Germany, as well as Jimmy Rimmer's penalty save, were enough to see Villa through despite a 1–0 loss at home in the second leg. Morley's second goal was a breakaway solo effort and was followed by another celebratory two-fingered gesture to his disciplinarian manager, who opted not to sanction his maverick winger this time, unlike when he fined Morley £100 after his wonder-goal at Goodison Park a year earlier. The aggregate win created history, as Villa joined reigning champions Liverpool in the last eight and it was the first time that two English clubs had reached that stage since the inception of the European Cup.

'I found playing in the European Cup very easy; easier than in our league,' Morley said. 'Here they instructed midfielders to cut the service off to me in the wide positions. But in Europe they had man-to-man marking and I never had a problem with that. I always backed myself to beat my man. I must say, though, Berlin were better technically than even Bayern Munich.'

Morley added: 'It was the first time behind the "Iron Curtain" for most of us and it was an eye-opener. You would see old ladies in the street pulling carts with old rotten fruit in. It made you realise how lucky we were.'

The poverty and greyness in the Communist-led East Berlin made for a bleak but fascinating trip for the players. Their hotel was a short distance from Brandenburg Gate and a tourist visit to Hitler's bunker was one excursion on a trip that the players otherwise viewed as being quite boring.

'It was a tough game but not just because of the football, the whole experience was a challenge,' remembered Rimmer. 'It was one of those places where you wanted to get in, play the match, and get out straight afterwards. Everywhere looked dull, drab and miserable. We would go to training and we could see the Berlin Wall with soldiers walking dogs next to it. We used to give teams five-star hotels but when we ventured to Eastern Europe they'd give us the worst hotel available.'

Villa were in the last eight of the European Cup, but Saunders would soon be gone and it would be up to rookie manager Tony Barton to improve their league position and steer them on towards the final.

'Who the Bloody Hell Are Aston Villa?'

'Reaching the final gave me a bigger buzz than playing in it.' – **Allan Evans**

IN THE EARLY 1980s IT WAS A MONUMENTAL ACHIEVEMENT FOR A club like Aston Villa to qualify for the European Cup because, unlike in recent years when fourth place in the Premier League is enough to qualify, clubs had to have won their own domestic league to make this most exclusive of competitions. The traditionally unfancied, unheralded, underrated team from Birmingham were now ready to rub shoulders with the elite. So, they really went for it.

This additional drain on their limited playing resources, though, meant their league form suffered terribly. A 1–0 defeat at home to Notts County on the first day of the league campaign set the tone. But would any of those Villa players swap what was to come in that topsy-turvy season? Not at all, when you consider they ended with a European Cup winners' medal.

The disappointment of their inconsistent league results and the obvious jolt of losing Ron Saunders could easily have dented morale and subsequently the belief that they were good enough to progress further in the European Cup, but it did not in any way derail their momentum in Europe.

Next up was Dynamo Kiev, a powerhouse of Soviet football. This challenging quarter-final tie presented caretaker manager Tony Barton with a stern test of his managerial skills, though taking over such a well-drilled, highly disciplined side would have made his task easier than it might have been. Barton showed his football intelligence and shrewd man-management skills by opting not to stamp his own authority on the team as many new managers do. He realised it was already a successful team that merited little alteration. The modest and humble Barton was in terms of personality and style the polar opposite to Ron Saunders. The fearsome Saunders was always 'Boss' to the players whereas the mild-mannered Barton, even after stepping up to become the new manager, was 'Tony'.

'The biggest accolade I can give to Tony Barton is he didn't mess with a formula that was working,' said Colin Gibson.

Tony Morley agreed with that sentiment, adding: 'Tony Barton did not receive enough credit for us winning the European Cup. He knew we were a well-oiled machine and nothing much needed to be changed so he did well to let us roll as we were going. He could have changed things straight away but he didn't.'

The first leg was away and Dynamo officials were initially refusing to reveal the match venue. This was almost certainly part of a mind game. They reasoned that their pitch in Kiev was likely to be frozen due to sub-zero temperatures and the game might have to take place in either Tashkent now the capital of Uzbekistan or Sevastopol, a major port on the Black Sea. Villa needed to make logistical arrangements yet were unable to and were aghast when the Kiev officials informed them the venue might not actually be known until the day of the match. In terms of hotels, flights, fan travel etc. it was proving a nightmare scenario and was clearly a tactic to unsettle Villa's preparations. Villa appealed to UEFA for assistance and Kiev were subsequently given until 22 February to name the venue, just eleven days before the game, which was subsequently played at Simferopol about 50 miles inland from Sevastopol, some 450 miles south of Kiev.

Villa did not trust local food hygiene so took their own chef and loaded the plane with 150 steaks, 72 eggs, multiple bags of potatoes, plus cereal, bread, tea and coffee. Dynamo Kiev and the local hosts went out of their way to make life as difficult as possible for Villa's travelling party. It was a UEFA rule that the home team had to provide the away side with a hotel of a good standard. This hotel, though, was situated in a bleak industrial area, clearly not intended for tourists. The beds were also substandard and many of the senior players were not shy to protest about the conditions and general hospitality afforded them. 'As soon as we walked out of the hotel we were followed, by people we were told were KGB,' recalled Ken McNaught. 'So, each day we would go a different way to training, though maybe they were looking after our interests?'

Even inside the hotel, life was not much better, as their first-team dinner demonstrated. They opted to trust the hotel catering on the first evening because there was insufficient time to unload their food skip that was still tightly sealed from the flight over. 'We started with soup,' recalled Gordon Cowans, 'and as I broke open my bread roll to dip it in my soup there was a huge cockroach in the middle of it. Then all of the lads threw down their spoons and said, "I'm not eating that!"'

It was a difficult few days before the match, with little to keep the players occupied in the remote city of Simferopol. The players instead made their own entertainment and sat around the hotel playing three-card brag in their bedrooms. At least it buoyed camaraderie. Training was another bizarre experience.

'We trained in the grounds of a mental home,' recalled Jimmy Rimmer. 'There would be people walking round in their pyjamas watching us.'

Ken McNaught remembers half-dressed children hanging out of windows with bars in, watching the team train. 'The whole experience was a bit weird,' Cowans concluded.

On match day, they knew their main threat would be Oleg Blokhin, the greatest Soviet footballer of his generation and a Dynamo legend. A clever and speedy forward, he played at Dynamo from his youth until near his retirement in 1988, winning the Ballon D'Or in 1975. Villa managed to battle through to a goalless draw before they faced Dynamo at Villa Park a fortnight later. There, in front of an atmospheric crowd of almost 39,000, Villa triumphed over a physically robust Dynamo, courtesy of first-half goals by Gary Shaw and McNaught, to earn a two-legged semi-final with Belgian outfit Anderlecht. Surprisingly, Liverpool were eliminated by CSKA Sofia in the last eight, which meant if the European Cup was to be won by an English club for a sixth consecutive season, it was all down to Villa.

By the time of the semi-final, Tony Barton had been appointed as the permanent manager on a two-year contract, with his assistant Roy McLaren also contracted for the same period. The home leg was his first game in charge, officially, and he was thankful for a Tony Morley goal that gave Villa a 1–0 advantage going into the second leg in Brussels. That goal summed Villa up at that time. They won the ball back through hard work in defence, and after a back-pass Jimmy Rimmer rolled the ball out to set up a break of some speed and fluency. Cowans attacked on the left flank and played a ball into Gary Shaw, who had dropped deep to link up play as he often did so well. Shaw played a first-time ball back to Cowans and he then played a defence-splitting ball to Morley, who held off a defender to finish in style. Villa would progress to the final after a goalless draw in Belgium, but crowd violence marred what should have been a jubilant occasion.

'Anderlecht was a really pressurised game,' right-back Kenny Swain remembered. 'We were really organised in those games, so compact and were really hard to get behind. It summed up our defensive performances throughout that campaign. A lot of our play was based on being hard to beat.'

He added: 'I remember the pitch invasion vividly. Police dogs were on the field, supporters were on the field. It was all so bad that it looked like it might get replayed.'

A lengthy pitch invasion was not helped by substandard anti-hooliganism methods undertaken by the Belgian club, according to Villa's then secretary, Steve Stride. The game was held up for six minutes as police battled to restore order. Villa escaped any major sanctions courtesy of help from local MP Dennis Howell, a former sports minister and also a Villa fan, who presented the club's case eloquently at a UEFA tribunal in Zurich. Villa were content to accept a fine and be ordered to play their next European home tie behind closed doors, as Anderlecht had appealed for the semi-final to be replayed on the basis they might have scored had it not been for the pitch invasion.

'The crowd trouble ruined the occasion a little,' defender Allan Evans said. 'It was a shame that got all the headlines. That was the one game, after we had qualified at the final whistle, when the hairs stood up on the back of my neck. I get goose bumps thinking about it. Reaching the final gave me a bigger buzz than playing in it.'

In the other semi-final, Bayern Munich overcame CSKA Sofia, despite losing the first leg 4–3. As was so often the case, they had their West Germany internationals Karl-Heinz Rummenigge and Paul Breitner to thank for two goals apiece in their 4–0 second-leg demolition job that sent them through to the final in Rotterdam.

Barton's side won just two of their last seven league matches leading into the showpiece at Feyenoord's De Kuip stadium. It was hardly the kind of form to create nervousness among their German opponents, who were also in something of a slump by their standards, having finished third in the Bundesliga. It was just one season, though, in an era when Bayern won the league five times in eight years.

Bayern had a galaxy of international stars. There was not only 1974 World Cup winner Breitner and 1980 European champion Rummenigge, but also Klaus Augenthaler, Dieter Hoeness and Wolfgang Dremmler, who all subsequently went on to win the World Cup or play in a World Cup final. And while defender Udo Horsmann did not actually represent his country, he had already claimed a European Cup winners' medal in 1976, after Bayern defeated Saint-Étienne. Similarly, Bernd Durnberger never made the full West Germany team but was part of three consecutive European Cup final wins from 1974 to 1976 against Atletico Madrid, Leeds United and Saint-Étienne.

Villa, in comparison, had few players with European experience, never mind established internationals. Although Peter Withe and Tony Morley had by then made their England debuts they were not in Ron Greenwood's starting XI regularly and their total international caps did not reach double figures. Captain Dennis Mortimer's previous success over Bayern as an eighteen-year-old rookie was a straw-clutching consolation. That was when he played for Coventry City in the second leg of the second round of the Fairs Cup in 1970. The Sky Blues won 2–1 – but this was after a chastening 6–1 defeat in Munich. At least Mortimer was able to say he had played against Sepp Maier, Franz Beckenbauer, Uli Hoeness and Gerd Muller – and won. Equally, Des Bremner's brief foray into European football at Hibernian in the Cup Winners' Cup was hardly going to make Villa fans feel more comfortable about the challenge ahead.

It was one of the most one-sided European Cup final match-ups on paper. Yet silverware is never won on paper. Gary Williams revealed how the underdog feeling motivated Villa throughout the competition. 'Apart from the first game against FC Valur we were expected to get beat in every game. All the hype leading up to all the other games gave us the impression we were not going to last long in that competition. But we just kept going.

'Tony [Morley] was red-hot and scored some great goals. We knew we had a chance but everybody else wrote us off. The lack of expectation probably kept the pressure off us and it motivated us also to show people how good we were. Nobody gave us a prayer from the start through to the final. I remember that most in Russia when we played Kiev. They thought we were just turning up, to get slaughtered.'

Bayern's players were on a win bonus of £10,000 a man; Villa's were on a fraction of that at £2,500. Villa were dwarfed in every way, it seemed, but not in spirit or belief. And certainly not in support thanks to 10,000 travelling fans who made the trip from Birmingham. Kenny Swain took comfort from the fact so many legendary clubs had entered the competition such as Juventus, Liverpool, Benfica, Celtic, Red Star Belgrade and Olympiacos – yet little old Aston Villa were still standing.

'There was no pressure on us because nobody expected us to be there so Bayern Munich had to carry all the expectancy,' said Swain. 'There was a quiet resilience about us. If it's possible I felt we were half a goal up before the match because no matter how great Bayern were, they would have known English clubs had won this competition for the last five years, through Liverpool [1977, 1978 and 1981] and then Forest [1979 and 1980]. They must have thought, "Who the bloody hell are Aston Villa?" That gave me an inner confidence.'

There was a carnival atmosphere around the Dutch city of Rotterdam despite a high police presence after the crowd violence in Brussels for the semi-final. The Rotterdam police played their part as they asked to play football with the Villa fans in true 'jumpers for goalposts' style. One of Tony Barton's sons, Chris, travelled with his brother Gary and Vince Cowans, brother of Gordon, on the coach and ferry. That relaxed feeling of just enjoying the occasion applied to the team also and most if not all of the Villa players left their hotel to explore the bars of Rotterdam on the afternoon before the biggest day of their football lives. 'The older lads went out in a group, like Ken [McNaught], Dennis, who didn't drink anyway, Jimmy, Withey and probably Swainy and Allan Evans [who also never drank],' Cowans recalled. 'The other group would have included me, Tony, Shawry, Gibbo and Gary Williams. There was nothing over the top, we just had three or four pints to help us to relax and to get to sleep later on.'

Team selection was very clear – every position was almost guaranteed by now, with the exception of the left-back. Gary Williams and Colin Gibson had shared the number-three shirt for the previous two seasons but all of a sudden, the game of their lives was upon them and both desperately wanted to play. Williams got the nod in the event, though even Gibson magnanimously concedes Tony Barton made the right choice because 'Willo' was the man in possession while he had been out injured.

Villa took their relaxed attitude into the match day. Nottingham Forest manager Brian Clough, who was at the final as a co-commentator for ITV, remarked beforehand to Tony Barton that he could not believe how relaxed the team were. Villa's players were taking photos like they were tourists, while the Bayern players looked studious and nervous. Villa were such overwhelming underdogs that there was very little pressure in their dressing room. Which is why, then, Tony Morley was loitering outside the ground waiting for a couple of his friends so he could pass on the complimentary match tickets that he had obtained for them. 'That was just fifteen minutes before the kick-off,' Gordon Cowans remembers disbelievingly. 'Tony was more stressed about that than taking on Bayern Munich in a European Cup final. The lads were all very composed in the dressing room and there was a feeling that we were all in it together and we'd be OK.'

That feeling of ease soon transformed to panic when the game started. Not only did Bayern assume early control with their pressing game and extra quality, but Villa were dealt the cruellest blow possible when their experienced goalkeeper Jimmy Rimmer signalled to the bench after nine minutes that he was injured. He was replaced by the 23-year-old Nigel Spink, who had been at Villa for five years but had played just one first-team game previously.

Rimmer had been struggling with a muscle injury to his neck and shoulder before the match but was encouraged to play, though the manager ultimately gave Rimmer the chance to make the final decision. Rimmer, Barton, physio Jim Williams and club medic Dr Targett all committed to keep the issue private. Rimmer did not even confide in his best friend, Ken McNaught, as none of them wanted the team to needlessly worry that Spink, might have to play in the most important game in all of their lives. And, especially, they did not want Spink worrying about that prospect. Having started the game, Rimmer soon knew he was in trouble.

'I knew I had to come off when Rummenigge had a shot that flew past me and I wasn't getting near it,' recalled Rimmer. 'What was worse, I couldn't even get my arm up as it went past the post. I thought, "I've got no chance here." Fortunately, Nigel had one of those games where everything came off for him. But personally, it was sickening. I'd played every minute of every game and then had to miss all but nine minutes of the final. I couldn't let the lads down and knew I had to do the right thing. You can sometimes carry an outfield player, but you can't carry a goalkeeper. I would have let them down if I had stayed on. The fact my medal says "Winners" tells me I did the right thing.'

Spink was in the thick of the action immediately, with a dominant Bayern frequently keeping him busy. One attack culminated in a Rummenigge bicycle kick that narrowly evaded Villa's goal. Gordon Cowans collected the ball for the goal kick when Spink smiled at him and asked, "What am I doing here, Sid?" It was a significant step-up for a player who was once told by West Ham United manager John Lyall that he would never be good enough to have a career in the game, when he was with the Hammers as a youth.

'It was an incredible fantasy night to the extreme,' Spink reflected. 'I was just delighted to be going to the European Cup final and sitting on the bench for the best seat in the house. My adrenaline was flowing just being there. I had played one game in five years, as Jimmy was always fit and so consistent, so I never expected to get a sniff of being on the pitch apart from the warm-up. The first I knew about going on was when Gary Newbon, who was sitting on our bench working for ITV, digged me in the ribs and said, "Spinksy, you're on." Even when Jimmy was walking off I thought, "Who's going to go in goal now then?" I didn't have time to worry about it so it was the perfect scenario. I thought to myself, "I've played loads of reserve games for Villa, treat it like another reserve game."'

Kenny Swain was in awe of some of Bayern's play, and he was not alone among his teammates in that view. That Villa were able to stay on level terms for so long said much about their resilience and ability to keep the ball. 'When Rummenigge put that bicycle kick narrowly wide after a right-wing cross I was slightly in awe of what a great goal it would have been,' Swain conceded with a smile. 'I thought, "Fucking hell, when did I last see an effort that good? Probably Pelé ..."'

Then, on 67 minutes, Villa shocked their opponents and probably the vast majority of the football-watching world when Peter Withe tapped home a left-wing cross from Tony Morley, via the inside of the post. It was a move that was started by Gary Shaw, who cleverly played in Morley, who turned Bayern's right-back inside and then out before his cross to Withe. Co-commentator Brian Clough suggested Villa could have been 3–0 down by then – but they were not and they managed to see out the rest of the match despite many nervous moments, including a Bayern goal disallowed for offside.

'It was a magnificent performance,' substitute Colin Gibson remembered. 'They were on top for most of the game but we could have been 2–0 up in the first half-hour. They had quality, experienced internationals through their team but we were not the slightest bit frightened of them. We all had a hell of a lot of belief in each other.'

Des Bremner was possibly Villa's best performer on the night with a characteristically tireless display showing his ability to keep finding his own man time after time, when keeping possession was paramount.

'Des didn't get enough credit, which is wrong,' Cowans commented. 'Everyone called him a workhorse, which he was, but he was so much better than that. He was everywhere in that match against Bayern. He wasn't the best player in the team, but like Tony Morley says, he was so athletic getting around the pitch and he had so much desire putting himself about that he did embody the Ron Saunders spirit and was exactly what that team needed.'

Allan Evans said at the final whistle he was simply drained, having used up so much nervous energy on a warm and clammy evening. 'I always used to chew gum during games and it was stuck to the roof of my mouth,' said Evans. 'It was that dry. I felt uncomfortable and the pressure we were under probably made me feel even more uncomfortable. We were up against it and had to grind it out. Withey got the glory, as is the nature of the game for the strikers to grab the headlines, but it was a great team effort. I don't think Peter was any more important than anyone at the back or midfield, like Kenny Swain or Des Bremner. All the successful teams over the years have a player who does all the graft, keeps things simple, works his bollocks off, helps people out and never gets the credit for what they did. Des was in that category. Des was our engine room up and down the pitch.'

Evans also claimed a Bayern player's shirt after the match, grabbing the prized shirt of Rummenigge, who he regarded as a great player in the mould of Kenny Dalglish. 'My son now has that shirt framed in his house. Karl-Heinz even sent me a letter of authentication to accompany it, which was a nice touch from what was probably a forgettable game for him.'

Ron Saunders watched the game from his home in Copt Heath with the family and 'he was made up' for the team he had moulded, according to his son.

The celebrations were memorable. But for match-winner Peter Withe and defender Ken McNaught the champagne-swilling and beer-swigging was temporarily delayed when they were literally collared after the lap of honour by a UEFA official who requested they both submit a urine sample for a random anti-doping test. The Villa duo were detained for an hour while they waited to pass urine. The UEFA representative did his best to be helpful by offering them each a bottle of Pepsi or 7-Up. They looked at one another and promptly snubbed what was on offer.

Says McNaught, 'I told him, "Chief, we've just won the best club competition in the world, there's no way I'm drinking Pepsi or lemonade!"'

At that moment, there just happened to be a man carrying three crates of beer to the storeroom from the bar.

'Withey shouted out of the window, "Bring them over here, mate!" We asked the UEFA guy if we could drink a few beers to help us pee and he gave his blessing and Withey managed his first and then I eventually followed. By the time I got to the dressing room it was just me and the kit man. The other lads were on the bus. I missed out on about ninety minutes of celebrations.'

The team then had to be driven from Rotterdam to Amsterdam, where they met their wives and girlfriends at the Apollo Hotel. Strangely, while they all did their best to celebrate, the general consensus was that the night was a bit of a mess that started with the doping test. Then there was the mood-sapping one-hour drive to the capital and by the time they reached the hotel Gary Williams was not in a drinking mood and went to bed early because he felt exhausted. Allan Evans and Andy Blair were teetotal anyway, while skipper Dennis Mortimer was not a big drinker either, though they all tasted some champagne that night.

Jimmy Rimmer was also not in the best of spirits after his forced premature substitution. He tried to enjoy himself but was inwardly upset by his withdrawal after nine minutes. He has two European Cup winners' medals – having also been a substitute to Alex Stepney at the 1968 final when Manchester United overcame Eusebio's Benfica. 'I just could not enjoy the evening celebrations at all,' Rimmer conceded. 'When you played all those minutes home and away and then have to go off so early in the final, it was just sickening. I was there celebrating with the boys afterwards and was so happy, but I couldn't laugh and joke. I wasn't my bubbly self. The lads tried to keep my spirits up by saying things like, "You got us to the final," but I was so gutted it ended that way, though I was pleased for Nigel.'

Even the normally jovial Kenny Swain couldn't help feeling dejected with the way they had played, even though they'd won the Cup. 'I was disappointed with our performance on the night,' Swain admitted. 'We were not good enough in possession and should have used the ball much better. It felt the same as when we won the league at Arsenal, so bittersweet. But winning a European Cup is not just about one game. We deserved it because of what we had achieved throughout that tournament.'

Gordon Cowans bumped into Paul Breitner at a Swiss ground years later when scouting Xherdan Shaqiri for Villa, before he was signed by Stoke City. 'I spotted Paul Breitner at half-time so I went over to him and said, "Hello, Mr Breitner.

Do you remember me?" He said: "Remember?" I said, "Yes, the European Cup final …?" And he did remember and said, "Oh yes. You were lucky!" I said, "We *were* lucky. But we won!" I shook his hand and we went our own way. It was clear he didn't really want to speak too much about the game.'

At the celebrations in Amsterdam, there were still enough lively characters around to maintain an upbeat mood. The pranks were in full swing and after calling Tony Barton's room and waking him up saying it was an 'early morning call' at 3 a.m., Colin Gibson was the victim of a ruse the following morning. Chris Barton remembered: 'The lads wound Gibbo up the morning after the night before, saying, "Gibbo, we can't find the cup and you were last seen with it around by the pool …" All along it was safe in Dad's room but they put Gibbo through the mill first.'

Poor 'Gibbo' 'used to get wound up a lot', Gary Williams said, 'but not because he wasn't popular, far from it – he used to bite so he got wound up frequently'.

The wives flew back to Birmingham the morning after the match, while the team had to wait until the afternoon to fly into East Midlands Airport, one hour away from Birmingham. 'How did that happen?' asked Ken McNaught. 'Surely it should have been the players going back first to Birmingham? So, we had a few more drinks and watched a recording of the game in the hotel bar.'

For Andy Blair, who made three appearances in the European Cup, it was a remarkable first season at his new club having transferred from Coventry City the previous summer. Although he was never likely to play if everyone was fit – captain Dennis Mortimer, Gordon Cowans and Des Bremner commanded automatic selection for the three midfield places – he was still able to appreciate being part of not only the success but the camaraderie. He never realised how great Villa's team spirit was then until he moved on to Sheffield Wednesday in 1984.

'When I joined, Howard Wilkinson had this saying, "It's amazing what can be achieved if no one minds who takes the credit and you all play your part,"' Blair explained. 'That perfectly summed up the team ethos at Villa then. They were good players, but the spirit was unbreakable, which carried them through in Rotterdam.'

When the players did finally touch down at East Midlands, they were warned that as they climbed down the airplane steps there would be a photo opportunity for the media, who wanted to snap them posing with the European Cup and their medals. That news provoked a frightening twenty minutes for Gordon Cowans.

'Just as we were about to leave the plane, I thought, "Where's my medal?" I looked everywhere and was frantic. By now all the lads were on the steps of the plane having a team photograph as the victorious team returns home. But at that time, I was crawling around the floor of the plane searching for my medal. I was fuming, was in tears almost as I left the plane. But as I walked onto the bus, Morley was laughing his bollocks off with my medal around his neck. I can't repeat what I called him!'

That was not Cowans' only experience of loss after the Rotterdam showpiece. A few days after returning home as a hero, he was in The Fox public house, in the village of Hopwas near Tamworth, for a game of darts and a few beers with team-mate Colin Gibson and, as was allowed to happen in those days, the gleaming European Cup. The left-back's language was apparently 'colourful' and this led to a confrontation that they later lived to regret.

'This bloke came over to ask Gibbo if he would mind his language,' explained Cowans. 'Gibbo advised him we were in a darts area, they had a few words that ended with Gibbo telling the bloke to eff off. About five minutes later this same bloke came over again and said, "Lads, do you mind if I borrow the European Cup for a few moments for a photo or two?" We said it was fine, carried on playing, before someone remembered, "Where did that chap go with the cup?" He had cleared off and took the European Cup with him. We later heard he drove up to Sheffield, had some fun with it with his mates and it was later handed into a police station up there. That was his way of getting us back. It was crazy the way we were able to have that kind of access to the European Cup.'

Fortunately for UEFA, when it was Tony Barton's turn to look after the cup, he took much better care of it, though he was not shy in allowing his entire neighbourhood to be seen with it. 'That cup toured round everywhere,' Chris Barton recalled. 'It was at our house for a week and I slept with it in my bedroom for one night.'

Tony even instructed his wife, Rose, to put the cup on show in their front window so if any schoolchildren walking past wanted to see it, they could. She said, 'Tony would happily welcome kids into the house to have their photo [taken] with the cup. He said it was a once-in-a-lifetime opportunity. I would be waiting to cook the dinner and had a house full of kids touching the European Cup in my front room.'

Around that time, the Villa manager received a telegram from Liverpool's manager supreme Bob Paisley, and it read, 'Welcome to the club'.

The Barton family, who tragically lost Tony to a heart attack in 1993 when he was just 56, have felt for a long time that he was never afforded the credit he deserved. The common perception is that he took on Ron Saunders' team and was lucky to walk away with a European Cup winners' medal. But as his son Chris explains, that is not how they see it.

'If anyone wants to rile the Barton family they will say the European Cup-winning side was Ron Saunders' side. In truth, it wasn't really Tony Barton's side either, even though he helped scout half the team. It really was a joint effort, but Ron ultimately decided to quit halfway through that campaign.'

Frank Carrodus was one of Saunders' favourites during his five years at Villa Park from 1974 to 1979 but he feels that Barton deserved more adulation than generally came his way. 'Although it was essentially Ron Saunders' team that won the European Cup, many people forget the part that Tony Barton played in the development of that side along the way,' Carrodus said. 'Ron relied on Tony Barton, who brought some great players to the club. It is interesting to know what that team could have gone on to achieve under Ron or Tony, had they remained together for longer.'

Barton was not the only figure at Villa feeling underappreciated. The players did too. One might have thought the hype and media coverage that a European Cup win brings would have attracted headline pressure on the England and Scotland managers to select more Aston Villa players for the World Cup that summer in Spain. Instead, Scotland manager Jock Stein selected only Allan Evans in his 22-man squad, while Des Bremner might have been deserving of a second cap at least but he made only the initial forty-man squad that was later cut down.

That was more recognition than Evans' central defensive partner Ken McNaught received, who did not even make the forty. This went against advice he had been told earlier in the season. 'I was gutted never to play for Scotland but there was a time when I thought I was on the plane to the 1982 World Cup,' he recalled. 'I came back from injury that season to play against Dynamo Kiev, came up against Oleg Blokhin, who had been a European Player of the Year, and I managed to keep him quiet for a couple of games and also scored in the home leg. I met Jock Stein afterwards and he told me, "Don't book any holidays for the summer, because you will be coming with me to Spain." I thought, "Great!" But unfortunately, I never heard any more.

'What made it worse was that he told me in front of my father, Willie, who played against Jock many times in his career. My father was proud as punch but it never came to fruition. In those days, though, there were some great players around like Willie Miller, Alex McLeish, Alan Hansen, Evo and Gordon McQueen. It just wasn't to be.'

Right-back Kenny Swain remembered how Villa's English players were always on the fringes of the England squad, like when he and Mortimer were called up once without making an appearance, but he felt it was almost like a courtesy call than a genuine effort to give them an opportunity. 'Jimmy [Rimmer] was especially unlucky with Peter Shilton, Ray Clemence and Joe Corrigan around at the same time. And in my position, we had Phil Neal and Viv Anderson who were two bloody good full-backs, so I had my hands full.'

Perhaps the unluckiest of all not to earn a single full England cap was striker Gary Shaw. His form during the European Cup-winning season was such that he won the coveted Bravo Award before it became known as the European Young Player of the Year. Those who he shares that honour with reads like a who's who of football's greatest ever – with Lionel Messi, Cristiano Ronaldo, Paolo Maldini, Marco van Basten, Eden Hazard, Wayne Rooney, Paul Pogba and more – but Shaw's name stands with them as an oddity in that he never played international football. He was on an England tour party to Australia in 1983 when Bobby Robson indicated he would be making his debut but he pulled his hamstring in training. Shaw, though, expected to be involved long before then.

'When I went to Italy to collect my award they couldn't understand why I wasn't in the England team,' Shaw revealed. 'I think I was regarded higher in Italy than I was in England. It was ridiculous that only two of us went to Spain with England in '82 – Peter [Withe] and Allan Evans. Tony [Morley] should definitely have gone but they took Graham Rix instead, probably because of the [England and Arsenal coach] Don Howe influence.'

Saunders never helped the players' cause in terms of their international aspirations, as he would be known to say to Morley or others, "You've got an injury, haven't you, and can't play for England next week?" Morley, for one, always opposed Saunders in that regard and never missed an international call-up, despite the manager's best efforts to preserve his players' fitness for the next Villa match. Some might view this cynical approach as being too ruthless but others would acknowledge how Saunders was only interested in obtaining the best results for Aston Villa. Highly respected captain Dennis Mortimer was surprisingly overlooked by England's various managers and that shocked a few observers in the game. Don Masson, Notts County's Scottish midfield general in the 1970s and 80s, could not comprehend how Mortimer failed to earn a single cap. 'I would consider Dennis as one of my most difficult opponents,' Masson insisted. 'He was very under-rated and never received the opportunities he deserved. But like Andy Gray before him with Scotland, look at the players England had then in Mortimer's position: Bryan Robson, Ray Wilkins, Trevor Brooking, Terry McDermott and Glenn Hoddle. It was tough on a lot of players.'

Andy Gray maintains he was omitted from the 1978 World Cup on the opinion of Scotland manager Ally MacLeod and not because of his club. But he does consider the English players of that era unlucky to not have been capped or played more internationals, due to not being at a flagship club.

'Some of Villa's English boys suffered from the late 70s through to the mid-80s,' Gray said. 'Players like Peter Withe, Gary Shaw, Gordon Cowans, Tony Morley – all these guys had unbelievable skills. They would have had a few more caps if they'd have played at Liverpool, Manchester United or Arsenal in those days. There's no doubt about that.'

Allan Evans, who missed Villa's photoshoot with the European Cup when landing back into the UK as he had to fly to Glasgow for a Scotland game, takes a different view on international football. While he would accept he is one of the lucky ones, even though his four caps were way below what his ability would have merited, he does not reflect on his Scotland career favourably.

'I was proud to play for Scotland and it was great for my family, but I didn't get the experience I expected or wanted it to be,' Evans revealed. 'Jock Stein didn't know his best defensive pairing and the problem he had was that Alan Hansen had to play and then there was Willie Miller and Alex McLeish.

'I shouldn't say this, but the 1982 World Cup was a very negative experience for me. The World Cup should be the pinnacle of a footballer's career but for me it wasn't.' Evans' sentiments were influenced strongly by a highly political campaign he was well aware of to ban English-based Scots from playing in the Scotland team. That was ridiculous when you consider Kenny Dalglish, Alan Hansen and Graeme Souness were at Liverpool and others like Steve Archibald, John Wark and Alan Brazil were south of the border.

The last word on a season of mixed emotions goes to Gordon Cowans, widely regarded as the most stylish midfield player in Aston Villa's history. He remains as dejected about how Villa's league form dipped so suddenly – from champions to eleventh place – as much as he will forever be ecstatic about being a European Cup winner.

'It was really disappointing,' he reflected. 'I don't understand how we deteriorated as much as we did. I honestly thought that team had plenty more in it. You would have thought we would have had a better chance to sign talent when we were champions but it never happened. Eleventh doesn't look good on paper but that's the way things can go. The squad wasn't big enough and we could have done with reinforcements but I would say there were some good young lads coming through like Brendan Ormsby and Mark Walters. It's disappointing we didn't keep it going, though, like Forest managed to do.'

He added: 'But I don't think our drastic dip in 1981/82 necessarily means we overachieved the season before. We deserved to win the league. The season after is the season after and there's no doubt the European Cup run was a massive distraction as we were preparing for huge games. There was probably an element of players and the staff prioritising the European Cup at the expense of some league games. As much as we wanted to do well in the league, when you have something as big and prestigious as the European Cup to go for, there might subconsciously have been some loss of focus along the line.'

Improbably, then, Aston Villa were the champions of Europe. Villa made the claret and blue section of the West Midlands proud. The morning after their unlikely win over Bayern, Villa fans were able to clock in for a shift at the local Austin Rover or Jaguar assembly line, the Cadbury's factory or any other given job, with an inflated chest, raised jaw and be as infuriatingly cheery as they had ever been. It was a time for justifiable smugness; not only then but long into the future. Villa's decline in the years since have been frustrating for supporters but they always have 26 May 1982 as a fallback whenever the success or stature of their club is called into question. That fans must reflect back so many years ago now in modern times amuses rival supporters, but the European Cup victory will always be Aston Villa's proudest achievement.

It was felt by players and fans alike that Villa did not exploit the status of being European champions enough. Logic would suggest that a club has a fighting chance of attracting some of the world's best talent when they have just been crowned kings of Europe. But like the summer before on winning the league, they failed to leverage their newfound lofty status. When they were champions of England, 21-year-old Coventry City midfielder Andy Blair was their only signing of note before they embarked on their first European Cup campaign. Similarly, after conquering Bayern Munich to stand atop of the contininet's football pecking order, if only briefly, Villa did not sign a single player in that 1982 summer. And this was before Doug Ellis returned to power later that year. When Ellis did come back, Villa signed Alan Curbishley from bitter rivals Birmingham City.

Tony Morley and other players wanted to see more ambition from Villa – a familiar tale that has been the case long before and after those heady days. In fact, Morley asked why Villa were not looking to buy England internationals such as Ray Wilkins. Wilkins transferred from Chelsea to Manchester United in 1979, was part of their runners-up finish in the 1979/80 season and neutrals may wonder whether players of that ilk actually viewed Aston Villa as a realistic club to sign for where they could be successful.

Classy defender Mark Lawrenson, who signed for Liverpool from Brighton in 1981, said he regarded Villa as a big club and he would certainly have been interested in signing for them before Liverpool made their interest known. Wilkins, though, speaking just before he passed away in April 2018, took a different view and said he would never have contemplated leaving Manchester United for Villa at that time, despite Villa being champions of Europe.

'The investment was always there at United,' Wilkins said. 'That investment was clear to the players, that the club was building up to what it later became in the years to come. Players like myself were just part of that journey. United put the money in and got the rewards. It's just so sad that an enormous club in the Midlands like Villa were not kept at the top level.

'The Villa side that won the European Cup were so workmanlike it was almost embarrassing [to the rest of us]. Mortimer in the middle of the park was box to box like a thoroughbred race horse, while Gary Shaw and Peter Withe up front as a big and small duo were a real handful. It was so sad what happened to Gary with his knees because he was one hell of a player. I trained with him for England and it was clear he was very special.

'But, like all clubs who are very successful, if you do not put money into the club year in and year out, you will suffer. And that's what happened to Aston Villa. It was a travesty to see the way the club deteriorated after their great success. If you do not invest enough, your club will not push forward.'

Ellis Returns, and Champions of Europe Face Pay Cut

'I was desperate to go because I could see the changes Tony Barton was making …
Things had changed quite dramatically, with the new manager
and with Doug Ellis trying to get back into Villa. From my perspective,
I thought I'd try my luck elsewhere.' – **Kenny Swain**

THAT VILLA WERE IN AS MANY AS SIX COMPETITIONS IN THE 1982/83 season was a reflection of their success; silverware from the league championship, the FA Cup, the Football League Cup, the defence of the European Cup, the World Club Championship and the European Super Cup was all up for grabs. You wouldn't have believed they had a chance of winning anything after their opening three matches – all humiliating league defeats.

Villa's first competitive match after winning the European Cup was a lacklustre 3–1 home defeat to Sunderland, an underwhelming celebration of their summer high with the home fans. The next match was considerably worse, losing 5–0 at Everton, before a 1–0 loss to Southampton at The Dell. So that was one goal scored and nine against after just three matches. The fact they won their next four league games, shortly before a 4–0 demolition of a talented Tottenham Hotspur side, demonstrated an inconsistency that frustrated the manager, players, supporters and all who cared for Aston Villa. They finished sixth at the end of the season, which would be respectable enough most years for Villa and a significant improvement on the previous season, but it was nonetheless a disappointing finish for the defending champions of Europe, even though they were just three points behind runners-up Watford. Further exasperation lay in the fact their seventeen league wins from twenty-one at home was superior to any other club in the First Division; unfortunately, this was not complemented by their away form, that witnessed just four wins in twenty-one. Perhaps the strongest example of Villa's decline came with a trio of defeats to Notts County in October, with a 4–1 hammering at Meadow Lane sandwiched by 2–1 and 1–0 defeats in the League Cup. County avoided relegation by just five points that season.

'They were terrible results, no doubt,' conceded Allan Evans. 'Maybe we weren't fit enough, maybe we didn't work hard enough. Ron Saunders would have hammered us but Tony Barton wasn't like that, that wasn't his demeanour. He didn't have a nasty side – there was a massive difference. Tony was almost like a mate you got to know. Tony knew the game really well, but he wasn't a tough character and didn't push footballers like Saunders did. That is a fact of life. But those results were not all Tony's fault, of course, the players have to take a lot of responsibility.'

Goalkeeper Jimmy Rimmer conceded the squad was not strong enough to continue being successful without further investment in some added quality. 'We needed strengthening or needed to be pushed a bit more. Nigel Spink was pushing me, but there were a few positions where it might have been getting a bit easy for some people. Perhaps we were still celebrating and feeling pleased with ourselves after the final?'

In response to the claims that Barton was too soft on his players, his son Chris insists his father was no pushover and that he knew how to handle players and felt that to earn respect you had to give respect. 'He wasn't a teacup thrower like Fergie and wouldn't round on a team; he preferred a calm, one-on-one approach.'

The patchy league form was, at least, offset by continued success in the European Cup as Villa progressed into the quarter-finals after overcoming Besiktas with a home tie behind closed doors as a punishment for the crowd violence in Brussels in the semi-final of the previous season followed by Dinamo Bucharest. Gary Shaw was in particularly good form, scoring both goals in a 2–0 win in Bucharest before netting a hat-trick in a 4–2 win at home. They were five goals towards a stunning return of 24 that season.

The stinging 5–0 loss at Goodison Park proved to be Kenny Swain's final game for Villa before he signed for Nottingham Forest for £35,000. His departure was the first from the league and European Cup-winning squad; Doug Ellis is widely criticised for ripping apart that team yet Ellis was still not back at Villa when the right-back was initially loaned to Forest. The player was advised by new manager Tony Barton he was probably going to make way for Mark Jones or Gary Williams. Swain, still only thirty, was happy to explore a new environment after almost five seasons at Villa and subsequently found new manager Brian Clough a pleasure to work with. Swain regards his three seasons at Forest as the happiest of his career, though his Villa days were his most successful.

'We got tonked at Goodison,' Swain said, 'but it wasn't just the Everton game that was a worry as that result had been building from pre-season [Villa toured Germany and lost all three games, to Kaiserslautern (5–1), Werder Bremen (2–0) and Schalke (4–2), and then even lost a home friendly to Dukla Prague]. There was a wind of change with Tony Barton coming in from the latter part of the previous season and then taking that team on. This new season was his first major challenge and he needed to decide whether to carry on with the same side or make a few changes – and I was his first major change. Considering they paid only £100,000 for me they got their money's worth in five seasons, but they still haggled over thirty grand. I nearly didn't go in the end.

'I was desperate to go because I could see the changes Tony was making. Things had changed quite dramatically with the new manager and with Doug Ellis trying to get back into Villa. From my perspective, I thought I'd try my luck elsewhere.' Swain, who made his Forest debut six weeks later at Ron Saunders' Birmingham City, was paid £12,500 ex gratia and was allowed to keep his BMW car that was valued at £5,000, according to boardroom minutes.

Swain was right about Ellis, who had never given up hope that one day he would walk back into the club as its new owner. Ellis had a deal with Ron Bendall that should he sell his shares he would be given first refusal; when that did in fact occur there was no way Ellis was going to give up on the opportunity. Bendall was feeling the strain of health issues and the ongoing police investigation into financial irregularities at the club, and was glad to relieve himself of Aston Villa. He passed away before the end of that season.

Before Ellis took over the reins again at Villa, some significant business had taken place. For, on 10 June 1982, Ellis became chairman of Wolverhampton Wanderers after being persuaded by friends linked to Lloyds Bank to lead their recovery from near insolvency. A new stand at Wolves had helped to saddle the club with a debt of around £2.5 million, according to Ellis, which was £500,000 more than he had initially been advised. He chose to place the club into receivership after just ten days in charge, considering the debt irretrievable. He reflects that this ruthless decision saved Wolves from ultimately going out of business, because a new consortium, headed by Derek Dougan, was able to take over the wreckage and begin work on the club's recovery. That was as far as his spell with Wolves went during his three-year hiatus away from Villa Park. This brief dalliance with the Molineux club certainly focused Ellis's mind even more on the importance of the balance sheet once he regained power at Villa.

His repurchasing of Villa only occurred after Ellis reminded Bendall of their gentlemen's agreement on his ousting in 1979 that, should he sell up, Ellis would be offered first refusal and at the same price. In the event, former player-turned-businessman Harry Parkes made an offer to buy the club and it took a newspaper headline saying as much to alert Ellis to this fact. Ellis immediately flew out to Bendall's home on the Isle of Man to secure the purchase after Bendall agreed to honour the gentlemen's agreement, albeit after changing the goalposts somewhat by advising Ellis if he paid the same as what Parkes had offered the club was his. Bendall still managed to pull a fast one on Ellis. After subsequent conversations between Ellis and Parkes, it turned out that Bendall overquoted Parkes' offer by £80,000. Initially, Ellis was smug in offering to buy Villa for £1 more than what Parkes had offered. But in actuality he paid £80,001 more.

The official changing of the guard occurred on 30 November 1982 when vice-chairman Donald Bendall proposed that Ellis not only be co-opted onto the board but was also elected chairman. The board unanimously agreed. Ellis wasted no time and entered the boardroom and took the rest of the meeting that same day. 'Doug was lucky because he bought Villa for a quarter of a million and sold it for £64 million,' said Harry Kartz, who was still a board member at the time even though he knew Ellis had his number. 'He wanted me off the board as soon as he came back because I helped get him out the club. Doug ran the show from then on and I had no say in what went on.'

Almost immediately in his first full month back at the helm, Ellis asked the board for their view on the reports in the media regarding overpayments on work carried out on the North Stand, work that had attracted the attention of the local police. He was told the club had been overcharged. Ellis set about cleaning up the mess from then on and made cost-cutting his number-one priority. He claims Villa were £1.8 million in debt, though Steve Stride does not consider this view an accurate one. 'That is a bone of contention because, as Doug always said himself, you can make what you want of figures,' Stride said. 'There was a fair amount of debt but I don't think it was anywhere near that figure.'

Stride's predecessor as secretary, Alan Bennett, also denies the overcharging claims against the North Stand work and feels that if any financial irregularities went on it was after he left the club in 1979, when Ron Bendall ran Villa with more autonomy.

'If Doug believed the North Stand saddled the club with debts, he is completely wrong – I can promise anyone that,' Bennett said. 'It was signed off about 1977 and it was carefully costed along with an architect by the name of Harry Marsden from Manchester. It was budgeted at around one million pounds. We designed corporate boxes in it and Sir William [Dugdale – the chairman] wanted to have the debt paid off within five years but we had to tell him that we would be left short of money with the design the way it was with that repayment plan, so Sir William came up with the idea of doubling the number of boxes to shrink the repayment period. By the time Doug came back to Villa in 1982, that debt was clear, certainly as far as the North Stand went.'

Whatever free-spending had gone on during the Bendall years, mostly on improved player salaries and bonuses than transfer fees, it was about to stop. Ellis has always had his detractors but one item he can rarely be criticised on is a blasé attitude towards the balance sheet; on the contrary. The return of Ellis into Villa was synonymous of a strict schoolteacher who had briefly left the classroom only to return to find pupils throwing paper airplanes, having conker fights, talking at excessive volume, sitting on desks and generally getting up to mischief.

Ellis was now revelling in a much-changed landscape at Villa Park to the one he had departed in 1979. Then, he was humiliated and metaphorically run out of town by his fellow board members, with the spectre of his long-term adversary Ron Saunders calling the shots in the background. Now, though, the Bendalls were gone, Saunders was gone and his old opponents on the board like Bill Dugdale, Alan Smith and Harry Cresswell were also long since departed. While Kartz was still there, his tone towards Ellis had mellowed. Kartz and the board of late 1982 welcomed Ellis with a respect and warmth that was bordering on sickly; for despite the club's precarious financial position, which Ellis spoke openly about when interviewed for this book, the board proposed that Ellis became the first paid director in the club's history; he was recompensed by £50,000 a year and received £10,000 expenses. Ellis 'magnanimously' agreed to accept only £30,000 a year with the £10,000 expenses. He even 'kindly' instructed that the new word processor that was required for the admin staff was to be purchased from his own property services company, Ellmanton.

Ellis admits he was glad of the extra power and control when he returned, unlike during his previous involvement when his influence was usually challenged by fellow directors. Now all-powerful, after gobbling up all of Bendall's shares, not one director ever disagreed with him and this new dictatorial regime was just how Ellis liked it. 'My previous spell at Aston Villa made me realise that you have to have a proper chain of command and that you could not have a situation where the manager and/or players "picked off" individual board members when they had a particular grievance and wanted someone to fight their case. If a player has a playing issue he must resolve it with the manager. It was only when there was a contractual matter or personal matter – like financial or property advice – that I would get involved and that was always together with or with the knowledge of the manager.'

Ellis made his mark instantly – on and off the pitch.

The late Tony Barton's son, Chris, said his dad 'was not happy' by the news Ellis was coming back to Villa because he knew what to expect. Barton's widow, Rose, said she will always remember the time Ellis returned because they were going away to Arsenal on a Tuesday night 7 December and if they won they would have leapfrogged Manchester United to go second in the league following six wins in seven games. 'Tony said he detected the atmosphere around the club change – and not for the better.' Certainly, the mood in the dressing room was also affected and there was a feeling of apprehension. Players like Dennis Mortimer, Jimmy Rimmer and Ken McNaught all knew what Ellis had been like at Villa in his first spell but, to look at this in a balanced way, they were all very close to the then manager Ron Saunders and it is to be expected they would view Ellis with suspicion.

Tony Morley said the atmosphere in the dressing room changed within a couple of weeks from a tight-knit group to a bunch of players insecure about whether they were staying or not. He remembers Jimmy Rimmer saying, 'That's it now, lads, now Doug's back, I'm off and this club will never be the same again.'

In a season that Villa had secured their first shirt sponsorship agreement ever, with Davenports Brewery worth £25,000, Ellis struck another deal with a local car maker for all the players to drive sponsored MG Maestros. Villa were to be paid £168,000 for receiving 22 fully taxed and serviced cars if the players committed to the sponsorship. However, Ken McNaught, Peter Withe and Dennis Mortimer, three of the most senior players remaining, all refused to accept them. McNaught was sold to West Bromwich Albion at the end of the season, while Mortimer and Withe were subsequently offered new contracts on the basis that they drove the sponsored car. Boardroom minutes state: 'Withe took delivery of his Maestro shortly after.'

McNaught found the situation comical but it was not entirely surprising to him, he said. 'Our contracts stated we could have a car of our choice to a certain value. I had a Volvo estate because I had two Old English Sheepdogs and two kids yet he wanted me to hand it back and take a Maestro!

'When we found out that Doug was buying the club back off Bendall, we knew what to expect. He called a meeting very early on at Bodymoor Heath where the players and staff, including the canteen girls, were present. He requested a private meeting with the first-team squad so we went into the changing room where he advised us that we need[ed] to take a pay cut because the club couldn't afford to keep paying our bonuses. We pointed out our pay was built around bonuses and that our basic salaries were generally inferior to players at Birmingham City and West Bromwich Albion. When I subsequently went to West Brom, the win bonus was just £25 because their basic was so high.' Players and staff were also invoiced to the tune of around £200 for small glass replicas of the European Cup, despite initially believing them to be gifts from the club. The general feeling around the club, though, was that because Ellis was not at Villa when the European Cup was won, any reminders of it were unwelcome.

'It's an open secret that Doug has always been a bit miffed that he wasn't there when those two big trophies were won,' Chris Barton said. 'He wasn't there at the club's finest hour and that has always stuck in his [craw]. My mum even had a memorial plaque dedicated to Dad handed to her as Doug wouldn't agree to have it on the wall anywhere at the club. You would expect for the boardroom to have a photo of the European Cup winners on the wall, wouldn't you?'

Austerity was not a promising environment for players asking for a pay rise but that is exactly what Allan Evans did. Fresh from a European Cup final win followed by his summer at the World Cup with Scotland, Evans met with the Villa hierarchy over his pay and demanded £800 a week and an annual loyalty bonus of £10,000 – this would have been double what most of his teammates were on at the time. Evans had been one of only two Villa players at the World Cup and, clearly, he was trying to exploit his elevated status, understandably, and bring his wages into line with his international teammates. The only problem was, if he was hearing in the Scotland dressing room what the likes of Kenny Dalglish, Graeme Souness and Alan Hansen were earning at Liverpool it was never going to be a relevant yardstick for life at Villa, which had never traditionally been a club that paid as attractively as other supposedly big clubs. Villa offered him an extra £100 a week.

Soon into his new reign, Ellis emphasised to manager Tony Barton 'the desperate need' to reduce the playing staff. But the deals on the table were not ones that were likely to generate much money to reduce the debt, and his targets were not ones that would lift the crowd. Norwich City manager Ken Brown bid £70,000 for Brendan Ormsby but the Villa board did not accept this valuation. And in October 1982, Barton attempted to swap David Geddis for Brighton's Andy Ritchie, but that never materialised. The manager then tried to bring in another striker, Dave Swindlehurst from Derby County, for £75,000 plus Terry Donovan; that, too, never worked out. The Rams asked for £150,000 for Swindlehurst plus Pat Heard and Eamonn Deacy. Villa, though, were only prepared to increase their offer to £100,000 plus Deacy. West Ham eventually paid £160,000 for the burly striker later that year.

Tony Morley voiced his surprise that, having just won the European Cup, Villa were not looking to recruit the likes of England-quality players, rather than targeting journeymen or selling their best players.

'Buy them with what? There was no money at the club,' Ellis hit back. 'Tony is right – *if* there was the money to bring in the best players. You have to remember at that time there was no Sky media rights deal in place or huge shirt sponsorship deals. The club's income was derived mainly through the turnstiles and the relatively small shirt and sponsorship deals. That is why one of my priorities was to increase the commercial revenue of the club. I had to personally negotiate deals with the television companies for the right to broadcast our subsequent European games at home and abroad. I was often criticised by supporters for only caring about money but if you want the best players you have to be able to pay the transfer fee. Salaries were not a problem then as they are today – it was the fee that prevented you from signing the player you wanted.'

When Ken McNaught was stalling on a new contract offer, Barton made enquiries for Brighton's Steve Foster, who was a member of England's 1982 World Cup squad, and Sunderland's Shaun Elliott, who played three times for England B. Neither were signed then but Foster did eventually join during the following season.

McNaught remembers some of the senior players suggesting to Ellis that he look at the Far East to capitalise on Villa's commercial potential, having just won the European Cup. But Ellis chose to ignore those opportunities, according to McNaught.

The Far East certainly was a growing marketplace for football. Villa's clash against Uruguayan club Penarol in Tokyo's Olympic Stadium for the World Club Championship or Toyota Intercontinental Cup as it was known at the time was played in front of 63,000 spectators. Penarol, the South American club champions who qualified by winning the Copa Libertadores, overcoming the likes of River Plate from Argentina and Flamengo of Brazil, won 2–0 on 12 December 1982. With no Swain and Colin Gibson out, there was a rare appearance for right-back Mark Jones. Man of the match Jair Gonçalves Prates, who made one appearance for Brazil, scored in the 27th minute with a free-kick dinked over the wall; though Jimmy Rimmer scrambled across to deflect it against the woodwork, the backspin took the ball over the line.

Uruguayan Walkir Silva scored a second in the second half.

While Allan Evans considered the game 'a bit of a nuisance' because league matches had to be rearranged to accommodate it, Jimmy Rimmer thought Villa played very well but the South Americans had good technique and profited from a counter-attacking game.

'We watched them train and didn't think they were very good,' recalled Gordon Cowans. 'They beat us with a couple of sucker punches. I hit the bar with a free-kick early on. Jimmy made a mistake with one of the goals and they scored with a breakaway for their second – two soft goals.'

The build-up to that match, which was Ellis's first overseas trip since returning to Villa, was a colourful one for Cowans and team-mate Tony Morley. The team arrived in Japan three days before the match so there was plenty of time to relax. 'Me and Tony went out on the first night for a few drinks to this place that had about six floors with a different bar on each one, so we made sure we had a drink on every level … We had a good night and as we were walking down the street back to the hotel, a police car pulled over and this officer starts shouting at us, "Aliens, aliens." This was at a time when there weren't many Westerners in Tokyo and it would have been before most of our supporters turned up. We couldn't understand him and he couldn't understand us so they hauled us into the car, arrested us and took us to the police station where, thankfully, an interpreter helped us reach our hotel with a phone call. Tony Barton had to come and get us out of the cell and take us back to the hotel. He didn't make much of it. But if it had been Saunders, he'd have given us a serious bollocking.'

The travelling for the showpiece match was draining on the players, who had flown from London Heathrow to Anchorage in Alaska and then onward for another ten-hour flight to Tokyo. They had been warned officially beforehand by Barton that they could not drink beer on the trip but they could drink wine, which confused them, as wine dehydrates the body even more than beer. On the eve of the game, the players struggled to sleep because of the jetlag. So, in the early hours of the morning they were hitting golf balls on a multi-storey driving range. Then, after the game, their flight back into Birmingham was routed via Paris, where they faced a ten-hour delay at Charles de Gaulle Airport because of fog. By the time they reached England, they only had the Friday to prepare for a crucial home match against Liverpool on the Saturday. 'Everybody was spaced out and didn't know what day it was so you can imagine what happened in the game,' Ken McNaught recalled. 'We were all over the place and were three down in no time. We were so underprepared.'

The jetlag clearly influenced Villa's next two results as they slipped from third in the league to seventh after a 4–2 loss to Liverpool and then an embarrassing 3–0 defeat to Birmingham City, the first competitive meeting between the teams since Ron Saunders crossed to the blue side of the city. The most significant aspect of that local derby setback, though, was it spelled the end of goalkeeper Jimmy Rimmer's Aston Villa career. He never played again for the club where he had been so successful since his switch from Arsenal in 1977, seemingly paying the price for four straight defeats and shipping eleven goals in four games – that's if football reasons were the excuse for dropping him. However, it would seem harsh given Rimmer had let in just one goal in the previous five games prior to that losing streak. The player is adamant it was Doug Ellis's decision to freeze him out and promote Nigel Spink as Villa's number-one goalkeeper, but handling his demotion in that way made little sense because Rimmer was contracted until the end of the season and would still have had to have been paid his basic salary.

Ellis insists he has never told a manager which player to sell or to pick or leave out of the team, which might well be true; however, the extreme pressure he was putting Barton under to cut costs almost certainly had an impact. Either way, it was a disrespectful manner to treat a player who had been arguably the best goalkeeper in Villa's history. He joined relegated Swansea City at the end of the campaign, where he played for three years.

'I stayed until the end of the season but I never played a game,' Rimmer said. 'Tony never told me I was dropped. He named the team for the next match against Ipswich and I wasn't in – I had to accept it, but he never did tell me I was getting dropped or why. But I knew what it was all about. I was the highest-paid player at the club and therefore I was Doug Ellis's number-one target to offload.'

Harry Kartz admitted there were 'quite a few arguments' about the sales or planned sales of members of the European Cup-winning team but because Doug owned the club by then he could do as he wanted.

Ellis never could accept not being present at Villa during the league and European Cup wins. Many club sources of that time felt those triumphs were an embarrassment to him, as he knew he had no attachment to Villa then. Ellis was at least able to be a part of the two-legged glamour tie with Barcelona in January 1983 for the Super Cup, which pitted the European Cup winners against the Cup Winners' Cup champions. Argentina's legendary Diego Maradona was at Barça then but missed both the home and away legs through illness.

It was a particularly aggressive contest in which seven Barcelona players were yellow-carded and two sent off at Villa Park, while three Villa players were booked with Allan Evans sent off late on for a lunging tackle, trying to win the ball back after he had played an under-hit pass to Gordon Cowans. Villa trailed 1–0 from the first leg at the Camp Nou and were struggling to level the score on aggregate until stand-in captain McNaught advised striker Peter Withe they needed to 'mix it up a bit' in an effort to unsettle Barcelona. The tactic worked, as a vicious elbow by Withe on Barcelona's tigerish central defender Migueli was missed by the referee and led to Gary Shaw's goal that brought about extra time. Cowans missed a penalty in extra time but scored from the rebound to make it 2–0 and McNaught's diving header sealed the win.

'That win was fantastic, the atmosphere was great,' Evans recalled. 'They were nasty. Once Withey sorted their centre-half out the game changed. We had to get physical because they were unbelievable. When Sid scored after missing his penalty kick, he went to pick the ball out of the net and their keeper wellied him so hard that he did a somersault. It was one of the most physical games I have ever been involved in – but I loved it.'

The fringe members of Villa's team were by now gradually heading out of the door as the starting XI rarely altered, although Mark Walters, who earned a Super Cup medal, did manage to break through and was the first major success story from Villa's 1980 FA Youth Cup final team. Gary Shelton had already left for Sheffield Wednesday and he then called up Pat Heard to say the Owls manager Jack Charlton was interested in him. Once Heard met the charismatic Charlton, he signed on at Hillsborough. He said Barton indicated he was in his plans but he was realistic enough to see that Mortimer, Cowans and Bremner was still the first-choice midfield and even Andy Blair was ahead of him in the pecking order, with Paul Birch coming through from the reserves, too. In fact, Blair started against Barcelona at Villa Park and that was his finest moment in a Villa shirt. 'Rotterdam was much bigger for the club but the Super Cup meant a lot more to me, as I played,' said Blair. 'I was disappointed not to get more games at Villa after Rotterdam, but for whatever reason it didn't work out.'

Terry Donovan also departed Villa in 1983 having served the club well as a reliable back-up striker and was perhaps unlucky not to have played more after eleven goals in 24 games, but Peter Withe and Gary Shaw were a permanent pairing up front, with David Geddis always the preferred replacement. 'The writing was on the wall that Villa wanted to get rid of me so I went on loan to Oxford and eventually signed for Burnley [for £20,000],' Donovan said. 'I had a bad knee injury not long after and had to pack it in. I have no complaints as I wasn't good enough consistently at that level.'

The Barcelona double-header, as an occasion, was invaluable preparation for Villa's European Cup quarter-final against Juventus a month later. However, whereas Barça were a huge club, they had a team that played like butchers and blacksmiths with the emphasis on aggression and stopping the opposition from playing. Juve, though, were an altogether different prospect, as they started the first leg at Villa Park with six players who had appeared in the 1982 World Cup final when Italy overcame West Germany 3–1. This challenge was seemingly on a par with Bayern Munich, probably even another step up. Outside of that Italian

ASTON VILLA: THE RISE AND FALL OF A EUROPEAN CHAMPION

group of World Cup winners there were also French star midfielder Michel Platini and Polish striker Zbigniew Boniek.

Villa lost the first leg 2–1 in front of a febrile crowd of 45,531, but it might have been much worse once they were a goal down after just forty seconds. Italy goal-poacher Paolo Rossi headed in Antonio Cabrini's left-wing cross, after makeshift centre-half Des Bremner had left Rossi in space. In fairness to Bremner, he was never a central defender, yet here he was, given the task of marking one of the best strikers in the world. It exposed Villa's lack of depth in their squad once more that when experienced centre-back Allan Evans was unavailable they replaced him with their established right-midfielder. It made no sense. Gordon Cowans' diving header from Colin Gibson's cross levelled the scores just after half-time, but Villa were unable to hang on for a draw as Platini's classy defence-splitting pass with the outside of his right foot played in Boniek to score the winner. Juventus eased to a 3–1 win in the second leg in Turin.

Gary Shaw realised after those matches just why Italy were world champions and why Juventus would go on to the European Cup final, only to lose to Hamburg. 'I played with and against some great players in my career, like Platini, Rummenigge and teammates like Tony Morley and Gordon Cowans. But the best of them from a personal viewpoint has to be Claudio Gentile, who marked me out of the game for 180 minutes. They man-marked a lot more in Europe and I never minded that as it was a challenge to get the better of your man and lose them. But Gentile was tough, quick, good on the ball and literally followed me all over the pitch. He brought me down for a penalty, which we didn't get, but that was as close as I came to getting the best of him. We swapped shirts after the two games and I could still smell the aftershave on it ...'

So that was it as far as Aston Villa and the European Cup would go. It had been a truly magical two seasons. A Villa team once considered no more than a group of journeymen had written their names into European football lore. Sadly, their dismal away form in the league meant they finished in sixth when the runners-up position behind Liverpool was within their grasp. They would actually have finished second had they taken at least a win and a draw from just two of their later away matches, which they lost against relatively mediocre opposition in Luton Town, West Ham United and Swansea City. Curiously, they drew their final away match of the campaign at Liverpool, who won the league by eleven points. Therein told the story, of how inconsistency cost them dearly.

A Great Team Broken... Too Soon?

'How can you be regarded the best player in Europe one year and the year after you can't even get into Villa's reserves? I went and saw Tony Barton and he told me he wanted me there for life but he wasn't in charge of what was going on with sales by then. He struggled to look me in the eye. I felt sorry for Tony because he was a nice man and he was put in a terrible position.' – **Tony Morley**

THE OPEN-AIR CHARITY CONCERT AT VILLA PARK ON 23 JULY 1983, by global chart-topping pop group Duran Duran, who formed at a Birmingham nightclub five years earlier, was an example of the way Doug Ellis was thinking. In 1968, when he first became chairman of Villa, he announced how he would like for the ground to become a 365-day-a-year venue for all manner of events that extended outside of football. Fifteen years later, Villa had now also agreed new shirt and kit sponsors, with Japanese electronics company Mita Copiers and French sportswear group Le Coq Sportif signing deals. The Le Coq contract was worth £40,000 a year, which just about covered Ellis's salary and expenses as the club's first paid director in its history. Ellis's new drive towards commercialising the club came in a summer in which he announced that 'total income decreased by £362,669' and went on to say, 'with the decline in match-day attendances throughout Britain your board are constantly looking for ways and means of increasing the income and decreasing the expenditure', which was a not so thinly veiled hint that player sales would be forthcoming.

What would astound many neutrals and business analysts is that he was at the helm of a club that were the champions of Europe only a year earlier, yet the effort to commercially exploit that historic and monumental achievement seemed casual at best. At this time Liverpool and Manchester United were backed by household Japanese brands like Hitachi and Sharp Electronics. With Villa playing in Tokyo in the Toyota Intercontinental Cup, a clear opportunity to negotiate more significant brand partnerships appeared to have been missed. Allan Evans remembers there being an overwhelming atmosphere of austerity once Ellis returned to Villa, which might have been different had he been able to resolve his inner demons over not being around for the major triumphs won in his enforced absence. 'Doug didn't appreciate the European Cup,' Evans said. 'He didn't use it like the club would use it now, to generate commercial interest. It was always hidden away but as players there was nothing we could do about it.'

In the absence of major commercial contracts, Villa had to do business the old-fashioned way. For Ellis that meant selling players and lowering expenditure; offloading the higher earners and nurturing youth.

Notable incoming transfers saw midfield general Steve McMahon arrive from Everton, right-midfielder Alan Curbishley from Birmingham City, 1975 FA Cup-winning goalkeeper Mervyn Day from Orient, and rookie striker Paul Rideout from Swindon Town, while Brighton & Hove Albion stopper Steve Foster joined later in the season for £210,000, with the £50,000-rated Mark Jones going to the Goldstone Ground as part of the package. The naturally kind-natured Tony Barton did not help himself by agreeing for the club to pay Steve McMahon's £2,400 legal fees and stamp duty fees after his move even though a frustrated Ellis pointed out there was no clause in the player's contract for this; because Barton had agreed, he made the payment through gritted teeth. It was gestures like that which made Barton so popular among the players but did little to endear himself with the board. Inevitably, when Barton requested a contract extension midway through that 1983/84 season he was swiftly advised that his position would be reviewed at the end of the season, when his contract was to expire.

McMahon viewed the move to Villa as a significant upward curve in his career and was only too happy to leave Everton, the club he supported as a boy. He even turned Liverpool down to sign for Villa.

'I was really pleased to be signing for the European champions,' McMahon said. 'We had Gary Shaw, Gordon Cowans, Gary Williams, Colin Gibson, Nigel

Spink and many other top players. They signed Paul Rideout and myself – we had the nucleus of a fantastic team with senior guys like Peter Withe and Allan Evans. I had the opportunity to sign for Liverpool but I chose Villa instead.'

Jimmy Rimmer completed his £20,000 transfer to Swansea City, while two more key members of Villa's league championship and European Cup-winning side also departed. Tony Morley was surprisingly allowed to leave after the season had started, but first central defender Ken McNaught was sold to West Bromwich Albion for £125,000. He was half-expecting to become either David O'Leary's new central defensive partner at Arsenal or become the latest recruit from Villa by Ron Saunders at Birmingham City. McNaught had little interest in going to Birmingham other than the opportunity to play under his old manager again. Saunders attempted to fund the transfer through a brewery sponsorship deal but it never worked out.

McNaught's potential switch to Arsenal was advanced enough for him to discuss areas to live in London with O'Leary after a chance meeting at the National Exhibition Centre on the outskirts of Birmingham. And when he was on Villa's pre-season tour in Spain, manager Tony Barton advised him to return to his room because Gunners boss Terry Neill would be calling. They spoke about the move and Neill hung up after telling McNaught he had a board meeting on Monday and he hoped the transfer would be completed by the Tuesday. In the event, that move never materialised and Arsenal instead put faith in Chris Whyte and teenager Colin Hill, who played most of that season as O'Leary's central defensive partner, while a young Tony Adams also made his debut. Neill was sacked later in the year but would first sign England Under-21 international defender Tommy Caton from Manchester City. 'When the Arsenal move didn't happen I agreed terms with Tony Barton to stay at Villa for less money but for three years – I was looking for four but Tony agreed three,' McNaught recalled. Boardroom minutes show the Villa directors did agree he would be offered a two-year contract at £600 per week with end-of-season loyalty payments of £7,000 and then £8,000. 'I hoped if I could get another four years at Villa I would be on for a testimonial. I was struggling with my leg but was getting through games. That deal was never signed though and Doug accepted a bid from West Brom.'

McNaught's presence as a leader on the field, in the dressing room and on the training ground left a significant void and he was one of the most popular members of that Villa team. Before he left he did have a scrape, though, with new arrival

Steve McMahon. They clashed when socialising on a pre-season training camp in Devon. Those who knew the six-foot-two Scottish defender might have advised McMahon to steer clear of the player who 'sorted out' a fair few centre-forwards in his time. When Gordon Cowans was belted up the backside by the right boot of the Barcelona goalkeeper during the 1983 Super Cup final, it was the stand-in captain McNaught who squared up to Urruti, jokingly shadow boxing with him and then turning on eight of the overly aggressive Barça players. The duo left a disagreement in the bar one night and, according to Gordon Cowans, McNaught then paid a visit to McMahon's hotel room later on in an effort to end the bad blood. Cowans was McMahon's room-mate at the St Mellion Hotel and he remembers what happened next.

'Steve had had a few cross words with Ken while we were playing pool and having a few drinks,' Cowans recalled. 'Later that night Ken knocked our door, presumably to sort things out, and Steve opened our door and punched Ken. But Ken just stood there and said, "I'll see you in the morning," and he went back to his room. Steve shut the door and went to bed. Ken's a big mate of mine and I knew Steve was going to get it in the morning but I didn't say anything and just went to sleep, but I did think to myself, "Fucking hell, Macca, you've done the wrong thing there." And he knew he was going to get it in the morning.'

Allan Evans, McNaught's long-time central defensive partner and fellow Scot, remembers vividly what occurred the next morning. 'We were setting up for a five-a-side, a proper training session on an area of the golf course, after there had been a problem the night before in the bar. Steve wound up Ken on the night but Ken mostly ignored it. But the next morning, Ken came into training and went straight up to Steve and bang! There was no wind-up to it, he just came out and went, whack! There was a lot of that in those days. Not punch-ups but aggressive jostling after tackles had gone in that players thought were a bit out of order. Me and Peter Withe used to have a few ding-dongs. I love Peter as a bloke but he wound me up sometimes. It happens. I thought it was healthy.'

McMahon said the incident was 'a storm in a teacup' and, as Evans suggested, those types of occurrences did happen at football clubs in those days.

'It was nothing,' McMahon said, playing down the incident. 'There was nothing to it. If it happened now there would be a hoo-ha. Me and Ken got on well and I never had a problem with him.' McNaught also played down the incident: 'He was a new arrival at the club and I hadn't got anything against him – I thought he would be a great boost to the team. But at that time I had a few concerns about his attitude. But that's water under the bridge and I wouldn't want to go into any details.'

The midfielder certainly became appreciated and admired by Villa's supporters for his committed, consistent performances, but he was unpopular in Birmingham City's dressing room after the derby clash on 15 October 1983. The typically ill-tempered match, in which Colin Gibson was sent off, was won 1–0 by Villa after Peter Withe followed up a Pat van den Hauwe back-pass that stuck in a puddle and poked the ball past goalkeeper Tony Coton. The game was so aggressive the *Sunday Mercury's* headline was 'The Horror Show'. McMahon was involved in a controversy after the final whistle with ex-Villa defender Noel Blake, who head-butted the Villa midfielder. Blake said he had been upset by a taunt from McMahon.

'Derbies were always fierce,' Blake said. 'Villa–Blues is one of the biggest rivalries you can get. There was a lot of excitement and I was copping the "Villa reject" taunts and fans were throwing coins at me. There were a few things going on in the game. Spinksy saved a penalty off me, it was a really wet day, and I was disgusted with a few tackles that were flying in. 'After the game Macca said something derogatory towards me, nothing racist, he questioned my parentage and I reacted. The referee didn't take any action but subsequently the video was given to the FA by local media and I had to go down to Lancaster Gate and was suspended. It's not something I'm proud of when I look back but we were fighters and we fought our corner. If someone gets in your face you get in their face. Over the years Steve and myself have always got on well. He was a damned good player. On the same evening, both sets of players ended up in the same bar as we all got on, though I never saw Steve.'

Another absence for one of Villa's European stars was forced through injury rather than transfer as Cowans broke his leg on the pre-season tour of Zaragoza and was forced to miss the whole season. Villa were up against Mexican club America when Cowans snapped his leg just above his ankle, breaking his tibia and fibula. 'Gary Shaw played a ball to me that was a bit short and their guy came in with his studs over the ball – so I blame Shawry,' Cowans said in jest. 'My foot was facing the wrong way and was only attached by my skin. The pain was ridiculous, I was in agony. They took me to hospital, gave me a painkilling injection in my backside and put me in a pod to straighten my leg. I had to stay at the team hotel until I flew home for the surgery. It wasn't ideal, especially when the lads came back from being on the piss and were bouncing around on my bed and walking on my bad leg and all kinds.'

His loss was felt significantly and, although McMahon proved himself an exceptional signing with his combative presence in the midfield, the creative flair of Cowans was sorely missed. Skipper Dennis Mortimer, Alan Curbishley, rookie Paul Birch and Andy Blair less so took on more responsibility in Cowans' absence while Des Bremner started just fourteen league games. Ironically, before his leg-break, Cowans was given a second opportunity in three years by Brian Clough to join him at Nottingham Forest. But, again, he turned Clough down. His decision this time, though, was not based on loyalty to Villa, for he was under the impression he would be signing for Napoli.

'I went to see Cloughie with my wife at his house this time, while young Nigel was there,' Cowans remembered. 'Mrs Clough said, "Do you want a glass of wine?" Go on then, thank you. Brian turned up after he had been shopping. He cooked us steaks and then got down to business. "I want to offer you a three-year contract and I'll give you ten grand now, which I've got in the loft, and ten grand when you sign." In those days that was a lot of money. My wage was about five hundred pounds a week then. He said, "Here's a bottle of champagne, go and have a walk round the garden with your Mrs and come back and tell me what you want to do." I was there over an hour and gave it some thought as I knew then I wanted to leave Villa with what was going on with all my mates being sold, but I was also under offer to Napoli at the time. After I made sure we drank all the champagne, I returned to the house and told him I'd decided to try my luck with Napoli. He shook my hand and said, "All the best," which really was a polite "fuck off now then" because he wasn't one to mess around with small talk.'

Just when Tony Barton believed things could not get any worse, he lost striker Gary Shaw four games into the new season to a knee injury that would effectively end his promising career that looked destined for international glory. Despite sporadic comebacks in the 1983/84 season he would miss the entire 1984/85 campaign and subsequently make only another fourteen starts for Villa over the next four seasons, which ultimately led to his release in 1988. The injury was sustained freakishly, when he felt a clicking in his knee after Nottingham Forest midfielder Ian Bowyer lifted him to his feet following a crunching challenge. 'I had a few tweaks in the knee beforehand, which were probably the warning signs that something major was going to happen,' Shaw revealed. 'While trying to get back

I had four knee ops and was still feeling pain every time I tried to come back. Over that twelve-month period from September '83 it was one thing after another and I couldn't get back. Four operations on one knee in twelve months took its toll, they wasted all my muscle and I lost a yard of pace. I was inactive for eighteen months – it was a hard time for me.'

Shaw achieved more in his brief career than most do in a full one, but those who knew of his talents would say it was a tragic case of what might have been. 'Had Gary not have had his injury you would be talking about him in the same breath as the likes of [Marco] van Basten and [Dennis] Bergkamp – his first touch was magnificent,' lauded Colin Gibson.

Shaw, on the back of his most successful campaign in which he had scored 24 times, had started the new season well, with two goals, and even returned temporarily in the New Year to score a further four goals in an eight-game spell. Yet he could not escape the treatment room. Even prior to this injury, Shaw had been unlucky: while on England's tour of Australia in the 1983 summer, he looked set to make his international debut only to tear his thigh muscle in his first training session.

'Even after that first setback I still felt I had time on my side to come back and get into the England team,' Shaw said. 'That season of 1983/84 was going to be my big year. I still had household names in front of me like [Trevor] Francis, [Paul] Mariner and [Tony] Woodcock – Peter Withe was also in there, but once Peter broke in I thought I might have had a chance to get in there alongside him, but it wasn't to be. Injury cost me a lot. I'd love to have played abroad like my good mate Gordon Cowans did with Bari. I would have enjoyed playing in Europe, as much to have secured my future and learning another language as trying a different style of football. But once my injury came all that ended.'

Minutes from Villa board meetings indicate the club maintained faith in Shaw, one of their homegrown favourites. Despite his ongoing knee issues, the documents state he was made several contract offers over the next three years as the club sought to retain his services in the hope he would once again return to full fitness. Manager Tony Barton had no choice but to focus on his forwards who *were* fit, namely Peter Withe, Paul Rideout and Mark Walters. It could be debated that Villa performed well to finish as high as tenth in that season after the sales of Ken McNaught and Tony Morley, and the long-term injuries to Cowans and Shaw.

Morley's sale was undoubtedly the most controversial of all the departures from the European Cup-winning team. He was 29 but still at his peak, an England international who had been a dominant force in Villa's European triumph eighteen months earlier. It was clear that he had not declined enough as a player to merit the Villa exit. That left-winger Mark Walters was coming through may have eased Morley's departure but there could have been room for both of them, as they were comfortable on either foot.

Supporters have listened to the arguments of the European Cup winners over the years that Doug Ellis returned to Villa only to destroy a winning legacy that might otherwise have extended long into the 1980s. 'If everyone hadn't started leaving I think we would have won the league again, and a couple of cups,' remarked Jimmy Rimmer. 'I am not so sure we could have won in Europe again, but we would certainly have remained a top-four team in the league.'

Villa were eleventh the year after they won the European Cup and sixth the year after that when the nucleus of the league championship and European Cup-winning side was still at the club, despite the squad being stretched far too thinly.

'Maybe the team needed breaking up at some point, but it happened too quickly,' Allan Evans insisted.

'It would have been nice if the team had not have been broken up and perhaps we could have achieved more for a while longer,' Colin Gibson said. 'Nobody will ever know because it was not allowed to happen, by one man [Doug Ellis].'

Des Bremner added: 'It was disappointing it was broken up as soon as it was, as most of the lads would have loved to have played their days out at Villa.'

That final comment smacks a little of over-sentimentality, as much as Bremner and his teammates deserved great respect for their feats. The likes of Bob Paisley, Sir Alex Ferguson, and none more so than Ron Saunders all displayed great ruthlessness when it came to freshening up their squads.

These claims – of ripping apart Villa's golden generation too soon – need to be looked at in detail and with a balanced view. Let's start with Rimmer. He was certainly treated poorly with the way he was dropped midway through a season and never to play again, but he was the club's highest earner amid a time of financial review. He was 35 when Villa sold him to Swansea, with Nigel Spink having already shown in Rotterdam that he was ready to step up.

Right-back Kenny Swain, meanwhile, admitted he was desperate to go, keen to play for maverick boss Brian Clough at Nottingham Forest. Little blame can be apportioned there. Tony Barton could have shown more faith in him, as he identified a younger successor and made Swain his first casualty of the post-Rotterdam changes. Swain was sold just after Ellis returned to Villa but his initial loan move occurred pre-Ellis.

Then there was Ken McNaught: still as committed as any player Villa had in their ranks when he left for West Bromwich Albion, but even the player himself has admitted he was not the same force after his blood-clotting issues, which left him with what felt to him like a wooden leg.

Des Bremner was eventually sold in 1984, when almost 32. Many would argue Villa reaped the best five years of his career. It is unlikely his sale would have upset too many at that stage, with the younger, equally tireless Paul Birch breaking through in his position.

Captain Dennis Mortimer was not sold until three years after Rotterdam and, while he was certainly treated poorly in his latter days at Villa having fallen out with the new management, he was 33 when he left and his best days were behind him. Villa's failing in that regard was not replacing him and Steve McMahon after he moved to Liverpool, leaving a clear void in the centre of the midfield.

Gary Shaw was never sold while he was fit and still an asset, with injury wrecking his career, and while Gordon Cowans was sold to Bari in Italy in 1985, he also wanted to go at that stage. Villa were guilty though in allowing him, and Paul Rideout, to be sold for just £475,000. Cowans was an England international and Rideout an England under-21 player. The then manager, Graham Turner, held the view, subsequently proven wrong, that Cowans would not be the same classy player as he was before his leg break.

Peter Withe, like Mortimer, also did not leave until 1985 and was even offered a new contract to stay, despite approaching his 34th birthday. Once he did leave for Sheffield United he never played in the top flight again.

Colin Gibson also stayed on for over three years and hardly had a downwards career move in signing for Manchester United. Reliable left-back Tony Dorigo had also broken into the first team by then and his ability was such that he had to play. Gibson was pushed further forward into midfield, but was such a versatile and experienced player his absence did hurt Villa once he left.

So, the one clear and shocking sale of them all was Morley's. That item of business demonstrated a reckless tendency, on Ellis's part, to cash in on a player long before his 'use by' date. 'The trouble with Doug,' suggested Steve Stride, 'was that he could never resist an offer on a player and he never wanted to pay top dollar in wages to players.'

One fact that cannot be denied is that Ellis's revolution meant that the special kinship that had been developed in the Villa dressing room under Ron Saunders and then Tony Barton was lost.

'How can you be regarded as the best player in Europe one year and then the year after, you can't even get into the reserves?' a still puzzled Morley asked. 'I went to see Tony Barton and he told me he wanted me there for the rest of my career but he wasn't in charge of what was going on with sales by then. He struggled to look me in the eye. I felt sorry for Tony because he was a nice man and he was put in a terrible position.

'Ron Wylie signed me for West Brom. I didn't want to leave and I was also owed loyalty money by Villa for four years' service. Ron said I would get the same wage at West Brom as I was on at Villa and Doug told me "whatever you're owed, you will get". But I never did.

'I scored on my debut for West Brom against QPR and the fans still booed me. I thought, "This ain't right, I don't deserve this." It didn't change much after that. I fell out of love with football after all that business and never played at my best again, consistently.'

The exodus could have been worse as Manchester United sent a scout to watch Allan Evans, but he reported back to Ron Atkinson that he had lost his pace. Further, Peter Withe submitted a written transfer request in summer 1983 but withdrew this after meeting with Ellis. However, director Harry Kartz tried to engineer the sale of Withe at a board meeting on 29 February 1984, which saw a lengthy and general discussion about the playing squad and transfers required – both incoming and outgoing – as well as the budget available to facilitate them.

This was at a time when Tony Barton was close to securing the signing of Steve Foster from Brighton. It is interesting to note that board directors were advising the manager on the requirements of the team, yet the man most reviled in some quarters for interfering in team matters too often, Doug Ellis, actually stayed out of the finer points of the transfer talk and merely pointed out to Barton that there was a £500,000 deficit between outgoing player transfers and incoming, and that further purchases would have to be taken from the summer fund. This seems like sensible logic that a chairman should interject with during a board meeting. It was actually former chairman Harry Kartz who suggested to Barton that 'the club should consider selling players such as Peter Withe whilst they were saleable assets'.

Maybe, then, Ellis is harshly judged by former players and supporters for his actual influence into those who came and went at Villa Park. It is quite likely he deserves the criticism he receives in terms of his failing to honour certain agreements with so many players unhappy at leaving under a cloud financially, like Colin Gibson and Tony Morley to name just two. He certainly had a keen eye on the balance sheet, as all prudent businessmen do. But the evidence does not point as strongly to him engineering the exits of as many players as is commonly attributed him.

The late Tony Barton might have disagreed. According to his widow, Ellis advised him to sell Mortimer and Morley. However, his successor Graham Turner stated that Ellis never once told him who to buy or sell.

What is certain, though, is that Ellis did put Barton under great pressure to improve the financial health of the club. In November 1983 he again reminded Barton of the need to sell players, without naming names. West Brom initially showed interest in a loan move for Morley, while AEK Athens also made contact about his availability. Brighton and Sunderland enquired after Des Bremner but nothing materialised then. Morley ultimately paid the price for a wretched streak of results that saw a 6–2 defeat at home to Arsenal as Tony Woodcock scored five. And Villa were eliminated from the UEFA Cup after a 2–1 loss at home to Spartak Moscow. There was also a 5–2 defeat to Notts County away from home, although Morley did not feature at Meadow Lane.

The one shining light that season was the League Cup – that is, until Villa crashed out to Everton in a two-legged semi-final. Kevin Richardson's undetected handball on the goal-line cost Villa dearly as they lost 2–1 on aggregate. 'The only person who didn't see Richardson handball Dennis Mortimer's shot on the line was the referee!' Chris Barton reflected with a lingering frustration. 'In between the first and second legs he hurt his wrist and when Mum saw him at Villa wearing this plaster-cast she said, "Is that the arm you knocked the bloody ball off the line with?" The players knew they had been robbed. Had they got through to that cup final Doug's hands would have been tied as you can't sack someone for getting into a cup final, can you?'

Barton paid the price for many things. A league position of tenth seems respectable enough given he was deprived of two of his leading players, with

Gordon Cowans' and Gary Shaw's injuries. But Ellis saw it as a failure, which was a harsh judgement considering the underinvestment in new players. Not only that, Ellis did not like Barton's extreme loyalty to his players at the expense of loyalty to the board. Barton was an old-school football man and was never likely to change. 'Doug Ellis misread my dad,' Chris Barton said. 'I think he sensed there was an opportunity to take more control of things, as dad had a reputation as one of the nicest men in football, but he also knew his own mind and could be quite stubborn. If Ellis ever came to him saying, "We are going to have to get rid of these players," Dad would have no problem in saying, "No, we're not."' The last straw for Ellis, according to Rose Barton and various players, was when Barton refused to sack his assistant Roy McLaren on the chairman's orders.

Ellis sacked Barton five days before his son Gary was due to be married – and the reception was booked at the McGregor Suite, Villa Park. The one dissenting voice on the board was that of Harry Kartz. The Barton family believe Ellis's timing was no accident as he was upset at not receiving an invitation to the wedding. When the mild-mannered and sensitive Barton returned to his home after being sacked, or at least learning that his contract would not be renewed, he sat at the bottom of his beloved garden for hours, collecting his thoughts. There was an offer from an alternate venue to host the reception, to spare the Barton family what could have been an uncomfortable day, but Barton decided it would go ahead as planned, at Villa Park.

The ousted manager faced up to a stream of news reporters camped on the doorstep of his family home and answered all their questions. 'He felt he hadn't done anything wrong and certainly it came out of the blue because he had a long-term vision for Villa,' Rose Barton explained. 'Apart from Dennis Mortimer, Des Bremner, Jimmy Rimmer and Withey, he felt the core of the team were still young enough and good enough to take them forward.

'Just after the news had got out, we had Steve McMahon and Alan Curbishley at our house for most of the day. I was panicking because I had the wedding to organise, but these lads didn't want to go. They were gutted. It showed how the players felt about Tony.'

McMahon explained why he felt so dejected by the sacking.

'It was Tony Barton who convinced me to sign for Villa and not Liverpool,' explained McMahon. 'I was very sad how it turned out. He was too nice and certainly one of the most decent men in football.'

Mervyn Day said he cannot remember Barton ever 'giving a player a rollicking', which was quite unusual in that era. 'I have seen Howard Wilkinson at Leeds throw a medicine ball across a room and kick a table and break his toe. Tony, though, was what Villa needed at that time because they had a strong set of players and they just needed to be guided. That group of players all respected him.'

Perhaps the saddest part of Barton's story is of the ill-health he suffered after leaving Villa. He became Northampton Town's manager only a month later, dropping down three levels to the Fourth Division. He spent nine months in that job before suffering a heart attack that subsequently led to a quadruple bypass. Rose Barton is not surprised in hindsight when she thinks back to how hard he always worked and the stress he was under at Villa. She lost count of the times he would return home at one in the morning after watching a game. And then he would not retire to his bed but would pick up a list of messages he usually had waiting for him.

When in hospital, another setback jolted the Barton family when tests revealed that he had suffered more than one heart attack while he was manager of Aston Villa.

'When Tony went into Good Hope Hospital [after] his first heart attack, the big one, they gave him an ECG and told him that it wasn't actually his first heart attack,' Rose revealed. 'It was his first major heart attack but there were at least a couple of bleeps on the graph that showed he had a couple before when he would have been at Villa.

'We can't be sure when they were but we wouldn't be surprised if they came when he was manager. We know he faced his share of challenges and problems and Tony was not one to share them with us and would keep them to himself, as he would not want to worry his family. Maybe that was to his cost.' Tony Barton died in 1993 of another heart attack. He was 56. All the Villa players and their wives attended his funeral in Southampton.

Giants of Europe Hire Shrewsbury Boss

'There were always likely to be issues with some players when a young manager
goes in with new ideas, which can upset one or two of the established players.
I had to change a few things. Dennis Mortimer was a strong character and had had
a very good career and he was one who wasn't particularly happy with my
appointment or the events of my early months at Aston Villa.' – **Graham Turner**

WHEN ASTON VILLA APPOINTED GRAHAM TURNER, THE 36-YEAR-OLD Shrewsbury Town player-manager, in the summer of 1984, it raised eyebrows. A lot of eyebrows. Especially within the Villa dressing room.

It appeared to be a fairytale move for Turner, who had impressed with his ability to succeed on a shoestring budget at Gay Meadow, but as good as a first-season promotion was in 1979 from the third tier of English football and, latterly, two top-ten finishes with the Shrews in the Second Division, expectations were much, much higher at Villa, where the league title win and European Cup final victory were still fresh in the memory.

Doug Ellis placed a significant amount of faith in Turner – some observers viewed the appointment as a huge gamble, but few are aware that the rookie manager was far from Ellis's first choice. Though Turner was always a potential candidate, Ellis favoured a safer, more experienced pair of hands for the job, but was rebuffed by as many as six manager targets. He offered the job to Ron Atkinson, Keith Burkinshaw, David Pleat, interviewed Gordon Lee and also sounded out John Toshack and Lawrie McMenemy. Despite Villa's success around that period, it was the job nobody really wanted.

'Doug wanted me to leave Manchester United for Villa in 1984 but I didn't,' Atkinson revealed. 'I did actually go down to Doug's house and he asked me there and then to come to Villa. I weighed it all up and thought, "I can't." How could I leave Man U then? We'd just won the FA Cup and were building for bigger things.

'It wasn't an easy decision because Villa is a club that has always been close to my heart. I know more about Villa than most people as I was a kid there and I often argue with people about how big a club Villa is. It's a massive club, just below the very biggest. I'm thankful I had another opportunity to manage them. And that was after I had to turn them down a second time when Graham Taylor came to see me the year he left for England to say he was going to recommend me as his replacement. But we had just been relegated at Sheffield Wednesday and there was no way I could walk out on them then.'

Burkinshaw was also approached, before and after he won the UEFA Cup in his final game as Tottenham Hotspur manager. The first occasion came before Tony Barton had even been sacked. The second time was before Ellis made Billy McNeill his manager in the ill-fated 1986/87 season.

'Tony Barton had not long won the European Cup and was still manager and I told the chairman that while there was a manager in his job at the club I could not even consider his offer,' Burkinshaw recalled. 'It wasn't a great advert for the job, knowing the chairman was recruiting a manager while he still had one, who was clearly unaware of what was going on behind his back. If it wasn't for the manner of how I was approached I might have fancied the Villa job because I knew by then I was leaving White Hart Lane at the end of the season.'

Luton manager Pleat was exceeding expectation with the Hatters. Consequently, he claims he was approached by a clutch of high-profile clubs to be their new manager, including Sunderland, QPR, Southampton and Villa. When Ellis came calling, Pleat's choice between turning his back on an improving Luton team for a rapidly declining Villa, even with their history, was a simple one for him. It said much of how people's impression of Villa was quickly changing, and not for the better.

'I was building something at Luton so was happy to remain there until the time felt right,' Pleat explained. 'I wanted to go to a really big club and Tottenham were hard to resist in 1986.

'Doug was in hospital with a neck brace on when my wife and I went to see him in Solihull about the Villa job. It was behind Tony's back while he was on the rocks in the job, but I rang Tony anyway. I understand Doug also spoke to John Toshack and Graham Turner around the same time. I remember coming away and thinking the job wasn't for me, as Doug had certain ideas of his own that were different to mine about how to take the club forward. But I believe the job was mine if I wanted it.'

After the initial rejections came in, and following casual conversations with other candidates that came to nothing, secretary Steve Stride remembers how former Newcastle and Everton manager Gordon Lee, from the West Midlands and who won the League Cup with Villa in 1961, became favourite for the job. Lee, a Wolverhampton Wanderers supporter as a boy until that changed through spending eleven years at Villa as a player, had such an affection for the club he said if he was given a choice where to play his last football match it would have been at Villa Park.

'I was extremely disappointed not to get the job as I felt with my experience I could have built on their success around that time,' Lee said. 'I was confident I could help to consolidate their position along with the big clubs. I never understood then why they went with a less experienced manager and to this day I still don't know why I never got the job.'

In fact, Lee was interviewed for the post by Stride, director Tony Alderson and Doug Ellis at the chairman's home in Four Oaks. Maybe Lee wanted the job too much as, out of either desperation or nervousness, he talked his way out of the position.

'The job was his but he went on and on and on,' Stride recalled. His inquisitors considered that if he'd lost their interest so quickly in a one-hour interview, what effect would he have on the players in a dressing-room environment? Therefore, they passed on him.

Ellis finally insisted to the board that they had tried to appoint the more experienced managers but none of them had shown sufficient interest, so they really had no choice but to turn to the younger, hungrier candidate, who was Turner. Seventh time lucky they had their manager, but even Turner – a top-flight rookie – almost rejected them too. His status as an up-and-coming manager then was growing and he said Villa were not the only team chasing him, having spoken to two other clubs.

'I've got to be honest,' Turner recalled, 'when they offered me the job, I wasn't all that happy with the contract. I'm not referring to the financial aspect but more the terms and what the manager would and would not control there. Details surrounding things like pre-season tours bothered me as much as anything to do with the hiring and firing of players. I suppose times were changing, yet I wasn't happy that the commercial department would have a bigger say on where we went to prepare for the season than I did. But we talked one or two things through – and how I might have a bit more control of the playing side – and it was an amicable agreement in the end. There were still elements I wasn't totally happy with, but how can someone who was managing Shrewsbury turn down the opportunity of managing a club like Aston Villa? So, whatever was in there that didn't suit me, I had to compromise on to take the job.'

Turner signed a two-year contract worth £30,000 a year to him, rising to £33,000 by his second year, according to boardroom accounts. The most frequent accusation that Turner faced then and even now, more than thirty years after his reign, was that Ellis employed an inexperienced manager so he could gain more control of the club, especially the incoming and outgoing player transfers. This would let him oust the remnants of the European Cup-winning team and further his aggressive cost-cutting in the presence of a rookie manager unlikely to put up too much of a protest. 'Ellis's puppet' was a frequently used term by the media and supporters to describe Turner. Some of this is true, for the evidence during Tony Barton's regime proved that the chairman forced Barton's hand on Tony Morley's sale at the very least. The aspect that is most accurate is how Ellis operated a frugal transfer policy, despite some rather ambitious transfer targets that Turner proposed to Ellis and the board. It may well be that a more experienced boss such as Ron Atkinson or Keith Burkinshaw would have tried to force the chairman's hand more on extra funds for transfer fees. Turner, though, insists that, while he was not totally comfortable with his contract with regards to the hiring and firing of players, Ellis never once overruled him on a player he wanted or on an existing player he wished to sell.

'Any manager that stood up too much to Doug wouldn't have been there long,' Steve Stride commented, 'which is why Ron Saunders didn't take him on directly and used allies in the boardroom.'

Turner bought into Ellis's vision to buy good-value players where possible, to blood the younger players more quickly in an attempt to develop future stars and to keep expenditure at a minimum. Whereas Tony Barton was infamously reluctant to carry out Ellis's orders when he wished for the playing or coaching staff to be trimmed as when refusing to sack his assistant Roy McLaren, Turner went along with Ellis's cost-cutting plan with greater enthusiasm. According to boardroom minutes, Turner announced in one meeting that he would be prepared to trim the coaching staff down from to six to four by offloading Malcolm Beard and Bill Shorthouse.

'I had a good relationship with Doug Ellis and anyone who knew us at the club would not doubt that – I worked well with him,' Turner confirmed. 'I wouldn't have too much wrong said about Doug Ellis.

'I made all the football decisions and would refute any suggestions that Doug made decisions on the playing side. I'm sure he would verify that. And I don't think there would be a manager out there who would put up with it anyway.'

Turner's toughest challenge was not to prove himself to Ellis, the board or even supporters who are generally swayed by results and player signings. His biggest test was to walk onto the training ground at Bodymoor Heath and command instant respect from a tight-knit, experienced group after they had been so successful and in spite of his own shortcomings in terms of his pedigree. Turner was a reliable centre-back for Wrexham, Chester City and Shrewsbury but the fact he had never played above the old Second Division, nor managed above it, was a problem for him. It probably should not have been, for modern-day managers like José Mourinho and Arsène Wenger have shown they did not have to be superstars as players to be successful in coaching. Nonetheless, this was a hurdle for Turner.

'Graham had come from Shrewsbury Town – nothing wrong with Shrewsbury, a great little club – but to go from there in the lower leagues to managing the recent champions of Europe is quite a big step,' Colin Gibson suggested. 'If Graham is honest I think he would admit at that stage he was not equipped to take Villa to the next level, even though he was a good young manager then'

Goalkeeper Mervyn Day will never forget a significant faux pas Turner committed early in his tenure, and the fallout never really left him until he was able to offload senior players who opposed him and his methods.

'I remember Graham coming in and one of his first sessions was set-plays,' Day said. 'You have a squad full of European Cup winners and he said, "This is what we used to do at Shrewsbury." Whichever manager you are and whatever club you have been at, that's one thing you don't do, go on about your previous club, because none of the players care – especially if you are at Villa and you are banging on about Shrewsbury.

'It must have been very difficult for him going into that environment because they were very strong characters, players like Peter Withe, Dennis Mortimer, Allan Evans, Des Bremner – they didn't have big egos as individuals, they were just such a tight-knit group that it would have been quite intimidating for Graham at that stage in his career.'

Gibson said he enjoyed playing for Turner, while Allan Evans also did not mind playing for him, but felt he lacked conviction in his methods, which compounded the doubts that his critics already had of him. Evans added of himself that he was always able to walk onto a training pitch, as a coach at Leicester City and Villa, and feel completely comfortable around the players and never insecure because he knew he had won the league, the European Cup and played at the 1982 World Cup. Turner could not say the same.

'I liked Graham but I didn't think he was big enough for Villa,' Evans admitted. 'I don't think the fans or the players accepted him as the manager enough. He wasn't commanding and players pick up on that. It happens in any industry; if a manager isn't strong enough they don't get the respect they probably should have.'

Indeed, Turner clearly detected the resistance to his appointment from a group of players, but mostly the captain, Dennis Mortimer. There was little surprise, then, when Turner offloaded Mortimer at the end of the season. That was 100 per cent Turner's decision, like with Des Bremner's transfer to Birmingham City after he started just four games for him. Gordon Cowans reasoned that Mortimer was usually a quietly spoken, composed man but because he had the instinct to see what was going on with different players leaving the club and with youth overtaking experience, he felt it was his job to stand up as captain and say something. Mortimer, remember, was Ron Saunders' most loyal lieutenant who was central to a successful culture that was now being destroyed in his eyes.

'I found some of the senior players like Allan Evans and Peter Withe decent fellas and there were no problems with the likes of them,' Turner recalled, 'but there were always likely to be issues with some players when a young manager goes in with new ideas, which can upset one or two of the established players. I had to change a few things. Dennis Mortimer was a strong character and had had a very good career and he was one who wasn't particularly happy with my appointment or the events of my early months at Aston Villa.'

It could be justifiably debated that Turner's appointment was a poisoned chalice for him and would have been for any other manager going in at that time; after Ron Saunders' golden generation and then Tony Barton's stint that included a European Cup final triumph. Not only that, but having to contend with a time of austerity, too, when wages and transfers were being scrutinised vigorously by Ellis; any good player signing generally meant one existing player had to leave to balance the books, so there was rarely a time when the squad's strength in depth seemed to be improving.

'I was never likely to say no to the Villa job but it was a difficult time to go in as there were a number of players who had been in the European Cup side who had left like Ken McNaught, Tony Morley, Kenny Swain and Jimmy Rimmer,' Turner reflected. 'There were also a couple of serious injuries to deal with as Sid Cowans had broken his leg quite badly and Gary Shaw was having a difficult time with a knee injury and was never the same player again.

'It was a transitional time for the club. With hindsight, it was a massive jump for me to go from a club the size of Shrewsbury to a club the size of Villa while still only thirty-six and not much older than some of the senior players. Looking back, now I'm more mature, I would say if I had gone to a club in between Shrewsbury and Villa in terms of size, it would have helped my career more, as this was too big a jump to make. But I never felt that at the time and was confident in my ability.'

Doug Ellis soon became aware that his young manager was having problems on the training ground and knew some of the players had no respect for him and were not happy about playing under his management. But by this stage, with a new era well and truly upon the club, he was more enthusiastic about changing the players than the new manager. Ellis, then, was only too happy when Turner advised him he wanted to offload some of the established players and invest in youngsters who would not oppose him. But Turner admits in retrospect this policy cost the club dearly as although most of his signings were good, the influx of youth from outside and from within was too much too soon.

'I probably didn't have the respect of the senior players,' Turner conceded. 'It was difficult in those first few months. They probably looked at me and thought, "What's his background, put your medals on the table!" So those are the things I had to put up with. When I assessed the situation, I felt I needed to buy young players with the money that was available. I bought young players with a lot of potential like Paul Elliott, Martin Keown and Steve Hodge, while the likes of Tony Dorigo and Mark Walters were already there but just establishing themselves and I gave them a chance. Tony Daley was given an opportunity. So, the bulk of the side became quite young but with a lot of potential. Mistakes were made because of that inexperience and we paid the penalty. I put too much money into too many young players, while looking to the future for the club. Unfortunately, in football you don't always get the time to see these plans come to fruition.'

Des Bremner's final game was a 5–0 defeat at home to Nottingham Forest, when journeyman striker Trevor Christie scored a hat-trick in the last thirty minutes. Turner's men were smashed 5–0 at Leicester City the following month, too. Villa legend Kenny Swain was playing for Forest that night and he took a moment to reflect on Villa's situation after the final whistle. 'I thought, "Bloody hell, how things have changed around here."' Seven of the league championship-winning regulars were still in the team on that Wednesday evening and Turner then decided changes were needed. Bremner never played for Villa again and, like former teammates, his bowing out came after a heavy defeat as if he had been made the scapegoat for an appalling result. Kenny Swain's final match had been a 5–0 loss to Everton, Jimmy Rimmer's was a 3–0 defeat to Birmingham City, while Tony Morley's two-penultimate games were a 6–2 defeat at home to Arsenal and a 2–1 home reverse to Spartak Moscow as Villa exited the UEFA Cup.

Dennis Mortimer would play only two more games for Villa spread over the next six weeks, before taking a loan move to Second Division Sheffield United. His last match for Villa's first team was a substitute appearance for Steve McMahon. Not exactly a fitting farewell for one of the club's greatest servants and the man who had held aloft the European Cup two and a half years before. But he paid the price for his opposition to the new manager. He was club Player of the Year in 1983/84 yet a year later he was making his final appearance in a Villa shirt, somewhat ignominiously, in the Birmingham Senior Cup final as Villa's reserves overcame non-league Wednesfield Social. Captain Dean Glover sportingly allowed Mortimer to lift the trophy, bringing an end to a Villa career in which he scored 36 goals in 405 first-team appearances.

As for Bremner, he knew his position was vulnerable after a pre-season meeting with his new manager when, he claims, he was told he would be on trial for the first few matches of the campaign along with Mortimer. Bremner still thinks to this day that Ellis orchestrated his exit but Turner, with no reason to conceal the truth more than thirty years on, insists he made the decision.

'They [Bremner and Mortimer] were under contract, but I felt I had to put my stamp on the team, on the squad, so there were always going to be difficult decisions that had to be made and players who would be upset by the change,' Turner explained. 'Ultimately I felt there was a need for change and that's the way I felt best to go about it. With any appointment of a new manager at any club, there are always players who will be upset.'

Bremner had recently turned 32 when he left Villa to sign for Birmingham City after he telephoned his former boss Ron Saunders to enquire if he might be in the market for an industrious right-sided midfielder. Saunders told him there and then he would be delighted to sign him, as he always knew what he would get from the player – total commitment to the cause and an engine in his midfield that rarely faltered. This was at a time when a core of Birmingham players were attracting negative headlines for bar brawls and general misdemeanours, so Bremner's professionalism was identified as a way of cleaning their act up. He also met with Luton manager David Pleat and spoke with Manchester City boss Billy McNeill, but the cross-city switch enabled Bremner to remain in the West Midlands where his family was settled. He would spend four years at St Andrew's, outlasting Saunders' tenure.

'I enjoyed my best days at Villa for the five years I was there and I wanted to see my career out there, but Graham Turner told me I was not part of his plans and I didn't want to play reserve-team football at that stage of my career,' said Bremner.

'The writing was on the wall before the season began when me and Morty were the first two brought into Turner's office. He told us, "You're all on trial, I will judge you after six or seven games. So, let's see how you go." It was his way of seeing who he wanted to keep and who he wanted to let go. We started the season well but one morning he pulled me and Morty in and said, "You're not a part of my future plans. You can go and search yourself out a new team." It was clear if we stayed we'd have been making up the numbers. Morty chose to wait until the end of the season.'

Andy Blair had already left for Sheffield Wednesday in the summer of 1984 for £80,000 and he left with an ex gratia payment of £16,000, boardroom minutes state. Steve Foster and Alan Curbishley followed him out of Villa before the year was out. Gary Williams could also have left after he submitted a written transfer request in November 1984 but no clubs made an offer after being alerted to his availability. He resolved his differences with Turner and stayed for another three years.

The board were making financial decisions that could only be described as 'inconsistent', maybe even 'strange' for Curbishley was paid an ex gratia sum of £30,000 before he signed for Charlton Athletic. Yet board room minuted documents state a league championship and European Cup winner like Bremner received £17,500, after Ken McNaught had been paid £25,000 a year earlier. 'I like to think that five finals or showpiece games would merit such an ex gratia payment,' McNaught said. 'In those days there were no agents so we got what we were given pretty much.' There seemed no logic to the 'loyalty' pay-outs. Steve Foster did not manage to complete a year at Villa before his £85,000 sale to Luton yet he was paid an ex gratia amount of £12,500 'in recognition of the player's loyal service', according to club records.

Veteran striker Peter Withe, one of the senior players who made Turner's life at Villa more bearable, attracted a bid of £200,000 from Coventry City in September 1984. This was rejected after Turner advised the board that although Withe would be 33 at the end of the season, and despite the club's precarious financial situation, they would have to pay considerably more to replace a player of Withe's ability. Turner admired the work ethic and attitude that Withe gave the Villa team and he actually quashed a possible move by Withe to Southampton that had been agreed prior to Turner's appointment. Everton manager Howard Kendall had also enquired about Withe but Villa frightened them off with a request of £400,000.

The board supported Turner's view on the Coventry bid, though the player refused to sign the new one-year contract offer that the board hoped he would sign to retain ownership over his services. Coventry subsequently bought Cyrille Regis for £250,000 from West Bromwich Albion. This episode, though, does give further weight to Turner's viewpoint that he – and not Ellis – had control of the comings and goings of the players. If Ellis really did have the power and was totally motivated to sell the European Cup winners, as some of that team believe, Withe might well have been on his way to Highfield Road then. But instead boardroom minutes, which were routinely signed off by the Villa directors at the start of the next board meeting documenting the previous meeting, reveal there was a real intention to retain his services and they document that Withe was offered a five-year contract that would have seen him play on for another two years and then take up a coaching job. Further boardroom minutes from another meeting state that manager Turner made a final offer to Withe of a two-year contract with the option of a third if he played in 20 league games in the second year. A further document minuted the board agreeing to give Turner clearance to make the latter offer. But Withe signed for Sheffield United and, according to the minutes, left with an ex gratia payment of £25,000 for his services. Withe, however, denied ever receiving those contract offers or the payment. "Doug would only offer me one year," Withe said. "If they offered me two years I would have stayed but they didn't so I signed for Ian Porterfield at Sheffield United."

Ellis and the club continued to be supportive to the luckless, injury-plagued Gary Shaw, although the player felt Turner was not too happy to have him around. Turner did advise a board meeting in late 1984 that Shaw 'was ten pounds overweight, a poor trainer' and he was 'not convinced the player would ever reach full fitness again'. History shows Turner was not far off the truth in terms of Shaw's fitness, but Ellis's decision to retain Shaw demonstrated a human side that many would not credit him for. While Ellis could be ruthless and certainly was in some cases, he was not all of the time. This revolution, like a twister of player exchanges, that was taking place at Aston Villa should be attributed as part-Ellis but mostly Turner's work, with Tony Barton having already started the weeding out of Villa's golden generation.

Youth coach and club legend Brian Little observed Turner's new era with interest from his vantage point inside the corridors of power and he did not like what was happening. Little resigned in protest at the player sales that were taking place – the likes of Mortimer and Bremner were his former teammates. 'I didn't get on great with Graham,' Little said in an understated manner. 'I left before some of the other guys like Withey and Morty but the writing was on the wall. I had a great job as youth-team coach; I could have been there still now. But I didn't agree with what the manager was doing. But, playing devil's advocate having been a manager, I understand why Graham did what he did.

'No disrespect to any of those players who were sold, but most of those guys have never been a football manager and do not appreciate that tough decisions have to be made when changing a team. There must be people who look back in anger about players I've sold. I got rid of Kevin Richardson, Ray Houghton and most of Ron Atkinson's team, so I know that tough decisions need to be made at times, whether they were right or wrong.'

One item of positive news that season came with the arrival of France winger Didier Six, who was signed on a season-long loan from Mulhouse. He earned £600 a week with a signing-on fee of £50,000 that was paid in three instalments. Turner had been searching all over Europe for quality players when the opportunity to sign Six presented itself, at a time when few players from the continent played in England. They initially trialled him in a behind-closed-doors game against Tranmere Rovers and he impressed immediately with his touch. The Frenchman struggled with the physicality of the English game and actually suffered a flaked ankle bone while playing against West Bromwich Albion. Six failed to embrace the English language and played just thirteen games, so an extended deal was not pursued, probably to the player's favour according to Tony Dorigo.

'Poor Didier – he couldn't speak a word of English though you could see he had ability,' Dorigo recalled. 'He was trying and nothing went right for him. One night we played QPR away on the Astroturf and he went for this sliding tackle and ripped the side of his leg open, it got infected and he was out for weeks. He was just trying so hard to impress that he went over the top.'

Villa finished tenth in Turner's first season. Ellis was encouraged enough for him to continue his reorganisation of the squad. But at what cost?

In the 1985 summer, Holte End hero Andy Gray returned to Villa and, although he did not realise it at that time, he eventually concluded that Turner had taken on a position that was far above his capabilities. 'I felt the job was too big for Graham,' Gray insisted. 'I liked him as a man, I thought he was a lovely lad, but irrespective of how good a manager he was at Shrewsbury, expectation is so much different at a club like Villa in comparison. I don't think he was ever comfortable there. No doubt he felt it was a job he thought he could do but in hindsight the club was far too big for him.'

'The Right Club at the Wrong Time'

'I don't mean any disrespect to some of the players who were there then but they should never have been put in that situation and the club should have been more ambitious. It was like we were on a train that was out of control and there was only one place we were going to go and it was down.' – **Gary Williams**

WHEN QUESTIONED FOR THIS BOOK IN THE REAR DINING ROOM OF his house in leafy Four Oaks, Birmingham, as to who was the best signing made by Aston Villa during his time in the boardroom, Doug Ellis thought for about five seconds and nominated Gordon Cowans, who came for free as a youth player. He went on to sell him three times yet bought him back twice. Cowans is certainly royalty as far as Villa's history goes. His long-time colleague in the midfield Dennis Mortimer would be regarded in a similarly elevated place. Yet, in one summer of 1985, both departed amid Graham Turner's resolution to develop a more youthful, fresher-looking team and Ellis's desire to please the balance sheet. Both followed Des Bremner out of Villa Park in 1984/85 so, in just one season, the entirety of what was probably Villa's best midfield of all time disappeared.

In fairness to Turner, Cowans was only one season back after a horrific leg-break and the manager took the decision – rightly or wrongly – that the injury had had an impact on his game. Turner made a brave call and opted to cash in on the classy playmaker, selling him to Italian side Bari.

'Gordon was another one missing from the European Cup side who you desperately needed in your team, like Gary Shaw,' Turner said. 'But I never had the benefit of that with their injury troubles. I never wrote Gordon off, he worked tremendously hard to get fit and he did play a lot of games again. But I don't think he was ever the same player as he once was. It took him a long time to fully recover from his injury and though I acknowledge he came back to the England team some years later, I never saw anywhere near the best of Gordon Cowans while I was there. That money helped me to build for the future with guys like Steve Hodge and Paul Elliott.'

Villa's England Under-21 international striker Paul Rideout left for Italy as part of the same deal. Rideout was not even 21, yet had netted fifteen goals to finish as Villa's top scorer in 1984/85. If Turner's regime was all about youth and Ellis's focus was on smaller salaries and transfer fees, it was puzzling that Rideout was also allowed to leave when Gary Shaw was still struggling with injury and Peter Withe was nearing the end of his Villa career. But as Steve Stride always maintained, Ellis could never resist an offer, especially if the club were going to make money. The fee that was recorded in the minutes of the boardroom meeting then was a one-off payment of £475,000 after Ellis accepted £25,000 less than Bari's original offer just to receive the money in one transaction. The money did not seem enough for those players but in Ellis's haste to cash in, and Turner's eagerness to introduce his own men, the deal was finalised.

Cowans was disappointed to be leaving a club he had been at for over a decade but there was also a side of him that was exasperated by the ongoing sales of his trophy-winning teammates. Quite simply, things did not feel the same any more for him and he was quite amenable to a change of scenery. A proposed move to Napoli did not materialise in 1983 – because they opted to sign Diego Maradona instead, after Cowans broke his leg – but when the scout who spotted Cowans moved to Bari he then made sure they signed him on this occasion. So Cowans was finally able to go and sample the Italian life and join the likes of Trevor Francis, Ray Wilkins, Liam Brady and Graeme Souness in Serie A.

'Graham Turner was a nice enough fella,' Cowans reflected, 'but I'd had enough with the way they were breaking that team up and the way things were going at the club. He did tell me he didn't think I was the same player after the injury. My thought was, "If my manager thinks that, I need to go." All he needed to do was give me time but he had written me off quickly and I don't know if Doug had anything to do with it.' Yet more evidence of suspicion of Ellis's involvement, but again this sale was purely the decision of Turner.

'Doug had a say in the finances,' Turner explained, 'as leading the club with a tight rein was always the way Doug did it and everybody knew that. But when we talk of firing people, no, he was quite happy with what I'd done. It would be easy for me to blame Doug Ellis but I wouldn't want to hide behind anyone else.'

If one was to play devil's advocate, removing sentiment from the argument, consider that Bremner was 32 when he left, Mortimer was 33 and, though Cowans was younger, approaching 27, the question mark about whether he would rediscover his form of the glory years was understandable. Where Turner and especially Ellis failed Aston Villa and their supporters was not having a succession plan in place. Steve McMahon was a ready-made, proven replacement for Mortimer as a dynamic midfield presence, but Villa sold him to Liverpool for £375,000 – though this move appeared to be unavoidable such was the player's desperation to return to Merseyside and especially Anfield.

'I was really happy at Villa when Liverpool came calling for a second time,' McMahon revealed. 'You can't turn down the opportunity to play with Kenny Dalglish, Ian Rush and the other greats that were there.'

He added, on the debate of Villa's decline at that time: 'I wouldn't blame the chairman for that because there is no way he could have known Gordon Cowans was going to break his leg so badly or that Gary Shaw would suffer a career-ending knee injury at Nottingham Forest. They were terribly unlucky, freakish events, as Gordon was going to be a top, top England player, and Gary Shaw the same. Yes, there were six or seven players who were not going in the right direction age-wise, but I believe we still had the nucleus of a fantastic young team. The injuries to Cowans and Shaw, though, were significant blows. If there is one area where Doug Ellis might be culpable it's the transfer fees he was accepting, as Liverpool paid less than £400,000 for me, which was nothing.' McMahon went on to earn seventeen England caps and Villa were paid an extra £50,000 by Liverpool once McMahon played in two full internationals.

Frustratingly for Turner, he was only able to recruit the future England midfielder Steve Hodge from Nottingham Forest for £425,000 just one week before McMahon left, when it seemed as though those two would complement one another perfectly in the centre of midfield. 'I was a bit taken aback by that sale as I had no idea it was happening when I signed,' Hodge revealed. 'I presumed it was going to be me and him in midfield. He was a top player, a class act, but Doug and the board had their ideas and it was one in and one out.'

Turner never replaced McMahon and tried to nurture young reserve players into becoming first-team regulars, which left too many players exposed too often, especially a midfield light on quality with Hodge and Paul Birch overburdened. Rookies David Norton 20 league starts, Dean Glover 15, Darren Bradley 15, Ray Walker 5 and Paul Kerr 5 all struggled to adapt to that level. Left-back Tony Dorigo and winger Tony Daley were also rookies then aged twenty and eighteen respectively but they fared better with the step up in quality.

'I don't mean any disrespect to some of the players who were there then but they should never have been put in that situation and the club should have been more ambitious,' Gary Williams commented. 'It was like we were on a train that was out of control and there was only one place we were going to go and it was down.'

Turner was actually very ambitious in his transfer plans. But, sadly for him, the supporters and the players, Ellis was not prepared to speculate to accumulate or, as he saw it, jeopardise the financial well-being of the club. Most of the quality players that Turner made enquiries on would have made a significant difference to a Villa team that was haemorrhaging quality. This was where Ellis let down his club, who would soon pay the ultimate price – with relegation.

Throughout the 1985/86 campaign, Turner was frantically trying to reshape the Villa team with an emphasis on more quality, but he just could not push the deals through for Ellis's unwillingness to pay out more money than what the club was generating.

The players that Turner wanted to bring into Villa were:

Neil Webb: Turner was in regular touch with the Portsmouth midfielder and his parents. Ellis sanctioned a £250,000 bid, plus associated levies. But Nottingham Forest eventually snapped him up in 1985, the year he became an England Under-21 international and two years before he was a full international. It was felt that Villa would not pay the wages Forest were prepared to pay.

Richard Gough: Villa offered Dundee United £550,000 but hastily gave the player an ultimatum that he had to sign before the 1986 World Cup. Gough chose to remain at Tannadice before signing for Tottenham later that year, for £750,000. Even before Gough had been signed, Villa board member Tony Alderson recommended that Turner should sell a player to offset the investment.

Gary Lineker: Turner told the Villa board that he had made enquiries with Leicester City about Lineker but he expected him to remain with the Foxes. Wrong! He signed for Everton for just £800,000 that same year, despite already having made his England debut. Everton sold him to Barcelona a year later for £2.8 million.

Alan Smith: Turner identified Smith as a perfect replacement for Peter Withe and Ellis subsequently lodged an offer to Leicester City of £600,000 for the striker, but it was not enough and he ended up at Arsenal where he spent eight years and played for England.

Terry Butcher: Turner attempted to reverse the sudden influx of youth in the team by adding some experience, but after making enquiries for Butcher he realised he would never be able to compete with the £725,000 transfer fee that Rangers were offering Ipswich for him. Butcher was at his peak then in 1986, aged 28.

John Gidman: Turner tried to re-sign ex-Villa favourite Gidman on a free transfer and offered him £600 a week and £10,000 at the end of a two-year contract. Gidman reportedly wanted £700 a week, a signing-on fee of £25,000, plus all first-team bonuses whether he was in the team or not and a two-year contract. Ellis, who had a great warmth for the player, would still never place sentiment over financial logic and refused his demands. Gidman went to Manchester City.

Villa also looked at West Bromwich Albion centre-half Martyn Bennett, but even though they considered paying a likely fee of £200,000 for him at a tribunal, injuries were a problem with him. They considered taking Everton forward Adrian Heath for £300,000 at a tribunal after his contract expired, but he signed a new one and remained at Goodison Park. Turner checked on Southampton's David Armstrong, too, who had been a transfer target of Ron Saunders six years earlier when he was with Middlesbrough. They also looked at Garry Thompson when he was still at West Bromwich Albion, but he ended up at Sheffield Wednesday instead.

'There were a number of players we pursued, in particular Richard Gough when he was at Dundee United and Alan Smith before he went to Arsenal,' Turner admitted. 'But in the end, the amount of money that was being mentioned was way over the top for us.'

Another Villa favourite was sold before the end of 1985, as left-sided utility player Colin Gibson headed to Manchester United. Turner, with the board's support, initially rejected a bid of £225,000. Although Tony Dorigo was now the regular left-back and Mark Walters could play wide left as a midfielder or winger, Turner tried to fit Gibson into the team but he ultimately annoyed the player by swapping him around into various positions. So, when United increased their offer to £275,000 according to their manager Ron Atkinson, the bid was accepted. Gibson left with an ex gratia payment of £37,500 before tax deductions according to boardroom minutes, though there was a suggestion United helped facilitate the move by contributing to that payment. Most players would view a switch from Villa to United as a terrific career move but Gibson was so upset by the way Ellis handled his transfer, financially, that it has remained a bitter memory for him ever since.

'I had a contract in 1985 and I let it I run out,' Gibson explained. 'I was then handed a brilliant new contract, double what I was getting paid almost, yet within three months I was gone. Doug Ellis had no intention of me fulfilling that contract; it was negotiated purely so that he could receive a healthier transfer fee. He might not admit that but I know it for a fact. He was wise enough not to offer me a signing-on fee up front because he would have had to pay that so instead he offered me a great big loyalty bonus payable at the end of the contract, but knowing all along that he would never have to pay it as he always intended on selling me.

'Apparently, Man United enquired about me in March [1985] though the transfer didn't go through until November. By then I had been well and truly played by Villa, or more accurately Mr Ellis. Even on the field I was being messed around – left-back, right-back, left wing, right wing, all over the place. And all I wanted then was to play left-back, which was my best position. I was as left-footed as they come so why I was playing on the right I don't know. I had enough in the end.

'Ellis never told me about the move. I was on £30,000 a year and £30,000 loyalty. I was loyal but he wasn't. He chopped my legs off. I had nine years at Villa and Doug made sure I didn't get a testimonial as well so I was gone very quickly as my testimonial was in the contract as well. I was stitched up by a ruthless man.'

When Ellis was questioned on Gibson's claims, he rejected his allegations and stated: 'When Colin was given the new contract, it was entirely in good faith.

Remember, you cannot sell a player to another club unless that player wants to go! If he had stayed we would have honoured his contract to the letter.'

Gibson concluded that, while he didn't want to leave Villa because he had been happy there, because he was being played in so many different positions he felt it was time to consider other options. He believes Ellis was advising Turner to make his life uncomfortable so that he would want to leave. United manager Ron Atkinson was delighted to sign Gibson and he felt he was unlucky not to go to the 1986 World Cup in place of Steve Hodge, who did exceptionally well to earn that call-up while playing in a struggling team.

Hodge had also been a target of Atkinson's but Forest manager Brian Clough would not sell him to the Old Trafford club because he did not want to strengthen a club he viewed as a rival for honours. Interesting, then, that Clough was happy to send Hodge to Villa, just three years after they had won the European Cup. Even Clough could see what was happening at Villa Park; their reputation was clearly not what it once was. Hodge himself regretted making the move almost straight away.

'It was the right club at the wrong time,' surmised Hodge, who rejected Queens Park Rangers and Sheffield Wednesday to go to Villa. 'I was unveiled on the pitch before the QPR game. Villa lost 2–1 and I remember thinking, "This team looks a bit young." It made me feel like I hadn't done my homework. Even just a week into my transfer to Villa, just after Steve McMahon had left, I thought to myself, "I'm not sure about this, I think I've made a massive mistake," but I had a four-year contract so I had to get on with it.

'We had a team of rookies, mixed with some experience like Allan Evans, Spinksy, Andy Gray and Gary Williams. I knew it was going to be a long old season.'

Brendan Ormsby, who had become the replacement for Ken McNaught in 1983 without being able to really fully establish himself, was sold to Leeds United for £75,000, as Turner's rebuilding continued. Gary Williams might have followed him if Villa had not rejected Southampton's £100,000 bid. They also refused to allow Mark Walters to speak with Arsenal when their manager Don Howe made an enquiry. Had the Gunners made a firm offer, though, it is difficult to have seen Ellis turning it down with the way he was operating at that time when an offer meant more to him than an established player who was performing well.

Turner was swayed by Ellis into re-signing striker Andy Gray in the 1985 summer, as he returned to play for the club where he had made his name before leaving six years earlier. Glasgow Rangers and his first league club, Dundee United, were also interested. Turner recognised he was losing experience and that Gray would certainly bring that in abundance as Peter Withe departed for Sheffield United. Much had changed for both parties; Gray had won a league championship, an FA Cup and a Cup Winners' Cup at Everton after his goal gave Wolves a League Cup win in 1980. Seemingly, all he had to look forward to at Villa now was a relegation battle, though he did not see that when signing. However, they fared well in the League Cup until they were stunned by eventual winners Oxford United in the two-legged semi-final. Villa had managed to avoid Liverpool as they took on QPR in the other semi-final, and few would have predicted an Oxford versus QPR final. Ellis called an emergency board meeting after this defeat to Oxford. The merits of sacking Turner were debated but they decided to give him to the end of the season. Turner asked for Ron Wylie to be promoted from youth coach to first-team coach, which the board approved.

Villa's cup run had been powered by another new signing, Simon Stainrod from Sheffield Wednesday in September. He notched four goals on his debut in the League Cup tie at Exeter City and finished with 21 for the season after his £220,000 transfer. Stainrod, languid with a neat touch and an eye for goal, proved himself a good signing for Turner and his goals were key to Villa's survival and cup progress that season.

Central defender Paul Elliott arrived from Luton, too, for £490,000 according to club records, and his arrival added some steel to the defence. 'When I was playing for Luton I viewed Villa as the royalty of the Midlands,' said Elliott. 'It always had that prestige because of its history and its stadium. I really loved my time there. They just tried to change too much too quickly. Graham Turner had a really good vision, though I wasn't aware then of the politics he had faced with the great players who had been moved on. They were in transition.'

The two players who made the most significant impact that season, though, were transfer deadline-day signings in March 1986. They undoubtedly prevented Villa from being relegated. Turner re-signed Andy Blair from Sheffield Wednesday for £120,000 – twice what he was sold for – and his fellow midfielder Steve Hunt from West Brom for £140,000 plus Darren Bradley. Blair and Hunt played together at Coventry City so understood one another's game.

'I played OK but Hunty was marvellous and pulled all the strings in the midfield,' Blair recalled modestly. 'The two of us going in as a fresh injection did the trick and we survived.'

Hunt was sold by new Baggies manager Ron Saunders, who had released him at Villa in 1976. As soon as he knew Saunders had been appointed at The Hawthorns, he was aware he would be leaving, but at least he was going back to the club his entire family supported.

'The first time he [Saunders] spoke to me when he came to Albion was on the team coach,' Hunt recalled. 'He shouted out, "Hey, baldy, I want a word." The fact he was bald too didn't seem to occur to him. He was trying to belittle me in front of the team and I thought it was disrespectful. He said to me another time, "I can't have you playing centre midfield because I don't like talented little baldies messing around in the middle of the park." The likes of Des Bremner who ran their socks off were his type. So, it was clear I would be on my way.'

While Turner did good business in bringing both players back to Villa to have such a telling impact on their relegation battle, he attributed much credit to his new first-team coach, Ron Wylie, who knew the players at Coventry when he was assistant manager to Gordon Milne. Further, it was a demonstration of Turner's lack of experience in failing to identify the gaping hole in Villa's midfield after Steve McMahon, Dennis Mortimer, Gordon Cowans and Des Bremner had all left. It was simply naive to think the likes of Paul Kerr and Ray Walker would fill the void.

'We'd got all these young players at Villa but I felt we needed some experience so we brought in Andy and Steve, players who Ron knew well,' Turner admitted. 'There's no doubt we were lacking in midfield, which is why we brought these lads in. We needed their experience and know-how, both had good character references and they did well for us.'

So that was one fire doused for another season. Players celebrated in the dressing room at the end of the campaign on avoiding relegation, remembered Steve Hodge. To him, it was like celebrating failure. In fact it was more a statement of just how far the club had fallen in four years, from champions of Europe to relegation candidates. But more troubles were to come, and they would be far more damaging than had been seen for a long time.

Relegation and 'a Disaster' Called McNeill

'He was a massive disappointment. He had been at Manchester City and came in with a big reputation. We were all expecting things to change but nothing did change. Things just got worse. He was a disaster. He didn't do anything, he never changed anything, he didn't buy a player who improved us, he was a big letdown, even though he had a big reputation at the time.' – **Gary Williams**

BILLY MCNEILL WAS NICKNAMED 'CESAR' AFTER THE ACTOR CESAR Romero and not the Roman military general Julius Caesar despite the obvious association to the iconic leader during his eighteen years as a player at Celtic, where he was idolised for his leadership as an inspirational captain and dominance as a central defender. A one-club man, his loyalty was unimpeachable and his durability equally remarkable throughout his 790 appearances for the Bhoys between 1957 and 1975. His legacy at Parkhead was eternally secured when he lifted the European Cup in 1967 after Celtic triumphed over Inter Milan in Lisbon to become the first British team to claim that prestigious title. He later went into management and won four league titles with Celtic over two spells and, after venturing south of the border, steered Manchester City to promotion to the top flight in 1984/85.

Once Aston Villa dispensed with the services of Graham Turner on 14 September 1986 after five losses from their first six games, they needed a strong leader to take control and to quell the turbulence. After Keith Burkinshaw turned the job down and after Doug Ellis sought Andy Blair's opinion on Howard

Wilkinson, at Villa Park it was a case of 'Hail, Cesar'. No doubt Celtic supporters would have felt Villa had landed the perfect man to galvanise a team that had totally lost their way. Villa fans, though, were less enthusiastic about celebrating his successes of two decades before. This was not a time to pay any tributes to past endeavours but to roll the sleeves up, instil confidence and belief and breathe fresh life into an ailing team; an ailing club. McNeill joined from Manchester City, where he had not been having the best of fortunes, and this struggle at Maine Road was sufficient evidence to offer Villa fans an excuse for apprehension. They would, though, have appreciated his belief in the club, in his apparent identification that Villa were a more ambitious, altogether bigger club that represented an upward curve in his managerial career. City chairman Peter Swales disagreed. He tried to talk McNeill out of the switch and argued that he would support his aspirations once a better job opportunity presented itself. But McNeill already felt it had arrived, not realising just what a difficult challenge he had taken on, in so many ways.

Six weeks into the campaign Villa were rock bottom. It might have encouraged them to see Manchester United only a place above having lost six of their first eight league games. That run would eventually cost Ron Atkinson his job. While United improved under their new manager, another Scot, Alex Ferguson, Villa's form remained dismal and was inspired somewhat less by the arrival of McNeill.

McNeill's first league game in charge was a trip to Liverpool to face the reigning champions. A heartening 3–3 draw and then successive wins against Coventry (1–0 away) and Southampton (3–1 at home) gave McNeill a bright beginning. Despite a 4–2 reverse to Watford at Vicarage Road, Villa added wins against Newcastle and Leicester – both 2–0 at home – before a defeat at McNeill's old club City on 8 November sparked a downward spiral he simply could not stop. Villa's early burst of form during McNeill's honeymoon period proved quite misleading and the team suffered not only for their desperate start to the campaign but also for a run-in from the Christmas period through to the end of the season where they won just two games in their last twenty-one. It was no surprise when they finished in 22nd and last position, three points adrift of Manchester City, also relegated.

Tony Dorigo revealed that McNeill became something of a joke figure to the players pretty quickly. 'We called him Billy McBungle or Billy McBingo. He kept saying "bingo" in his team talks. We would even have a bet to see how many times he would say "bingo". I think forty-seven was the winning number at one time. He'd say, "Right, we need to get it wide, get it in the box, cross it and then, BINGO!" We would all be looking at each other trying not to laugh.'

The manager was honest enough to acknowledge, though, in his 2004 autobiography *Hail Cesar*, that his switch to Villa was the worst mistake of his career and therefore was his unhappiest time in football. The fact he never moved his family to the West Midlands from Greater Manchester and commuted every day was a tell-tale signal to the management of the club and the players that this man's heart was just not in the job. He was feeling low professionally before shifting to Villa Park as he had hoped to be Jock Stein's permanent successor as the manager of the Scotland national team, but instead Andy Roxburgh was appointed. Further, Freddie Pye had become a director at Manchester City and was to be in charge of team affairs, which McNeill interpreted as undermining his authority. So although his instincts told him Villa was not the right move, circumstances and Doug Ellis's charm offensive with promises of backing in the transfer market persuaded him otherwise.

'Villa were in a sorry state but still seemed to offer more in the long term,' McNeill said. 'In the end, I fell for his [Ellis's] sweet talk. It turned out to be the worst eight months of my managerial career. I was barely five minutes in the job when I received the first of many memos from the chairman, informing me that the club had no option but to accept an offer of £650,000 from Spurs for Steve Hodge. So much for strengthening the squad! ... Within a fortnight of becoming Aston Villa manager I realised that I had made a huge mistake.'

Turner had been busy pre-season, further shaping his squad, and he was especially pleased to sign defender Martin Keown who had watched Villa games live in their title-winning season when the club were chasing him as a schoolboy recruit from Arsenal and Garry Thompson from Sheffield Wednesday having missed out on him previously when he was at West Brom. Neale Cooper arrived from Aberdeen but struggled with injury throughout his time at Villa. The trio was supposed to give a more robust 'spine' to the team, according to Doug Ellis.

For the Birmingham-born Thompson it was a dream move, especially as it offered him a way out at Hillsborough where he was not enjoying the football or his relationship with manager Howard Wilkinson. 'I remember the day Villa came in for me, Argentina had just won the World Cup and I got a call from Howard. He said, "Well, I wouldn't say it's worked out, big man, but we have had an offer for you from Aston Villa. Go and have a chat with them." Me and Wilko didn't really like one another so I thought I'd wind him up first and said: "I'm not sure if I want to do that, gaffer, as I am just getting my feet under the table here and I might have another year." His reply was along the lines of: "Go and fucking talk to them!" And with that he put the phone down.'

Villa supporter Thompson was euphoric to sign for the club but had barely been there a day or two when his bubble was burst after a casual chat with new team-mate Gary Shaw, who he had known since their teenage days. 'You're a couple of years too late, big man,' Shaw advised him. 'The good days are gone!' Thompson recalled: 'I was stunned and thought because Shawsy had been injured he was just down on everything. But soon enough I knew what he meant.'

Keown was signed for £200,000 with a weekly wage of £600 and a signing-on fee of £15,000, according to boardroom minutes. He was employed either in the centre of defence with Allan Evans or at right-back. He would go on to win 43 England caps but at the time of his Villa career he was simply a good, fast defender with lots of potential. Unfortunately for the player, he was not the most popular member of the squad and his teammates detected an air of arrogance about him, which did little to endear him to them. Andy Gray wrote in his autobiography *Gray Matters* that Keown was one of the few players he couldn't get along with in his career.

'I was captain when Martin came,' recalled Allan Evans. 'He thought he was the big macho main guy and everything was all about him. He would wind people up and people hated him – really hated him. He was a great player but he struggled to get on with a few of the lads. I regularly had to sit him down on the training ground after everyone else had gone in [to the dressing rooms] and say, "Martin, you're rubbing people up the wrong way and they don't like you because of the way you act and the things you say. You don't have to like them but stop being so big-time." Personally, I got on well with Martin but I was in the minority.'

Another senior player who had a problem with Keown's attitude around the club was Gordon Cowans, after he re-signed for Villa in 1988.

'He was always asking questions like, "Sid, how much are you on?" I would say, "What the hell's it got to do with you, Martin, that's none of your business."'

Midfielder Steve Hunt, who by then was an experienced pro and had won two England caps, considered Keown a misunderstood individual who was simply 'different' to the majority but was essentially a decent guy.

Keown, who went on to win both the Premier League and the FA Cup three times in a second spell with Arsenal, was just twenty years old on arriving at Villa and learned a great deal from his experiences there. One thing none of the players would have doubted of Keown was his worthiness to be in the team, which was not the case with many of the rookies around the squad then. Keown was justifiably a regular pick despite his rawness.

'I found it very difficult in my early days at Villa because we were losing most weeks and I am a very bad loser,' Keown admitted. 'There were a few people who would come into training on a Monday morning and seem more bothered about going off to golf at The Belfry than putting things right on the training ground. I demanded more from certain players and wasn't shy about letting them know. In hindsight I was overly aggressive, but the place was a disaster at that stage. I sensed the disillusionment amongst the fans not long after joining and it became very difficult to play at home. I still saw Villa as recent European Cup winners when I joined and couldn't understand all the negativity. I soon realised, though, things had changed a lot.

'Maybe I would have been better off keeping my head down and getting on with my football but, call it naivety, I didn't do that and was quite vocal. That team, which ended up getting relegated, was in disarray. There was no togetherness and it felt like a dog-eat-dog situation. I learned a lot from that which served me well for the rest of my career. It doesn't matter how good you are as individuals; if there's no team ethic, you will win nothing.'

Steve Hodge returned from the 1986 World Cup with England and was heartened by the signings of Keown and Thompson but he felt 'the nucleus of the team was still too young' and knew after the first six games relegation was probable. Conversely, Doug Ellis wrote to shareholders in his annual summer report that he could not think of a summer when he had felt as positive about the oncoming season as he did at that time. He qualified his optimism with the fact there 'is no doubt that Graham Turner's positive manipulation of the transfer market has become a major talking point within professional football'. That manipulation might have been even better had Ellis supported his more ambitious transfer targets.

The season started badly. Clive Allen scored a hat-trick to give Tottenham a 3–0 win at Villa Park on the opening day of the season. Player confidence drained and further losses followed to Wimbledon (3–2 away), QPR (1–0 away), Oxford

(2–1 at home), and then a crushing 6–0 defeat at Nottingham Forest.

Graham Turner did not forsee such turmoil and was content with the pre-season. He did not remember feeling worried about the upcoming campaign, though he did acknowledge 'the shape of the side wasn't quite right'. Paul Elliott reflected that the transfer strategy from the days of the European Cup was ultimately to blame.

'In hindsight, there was too much change too quickly, but they could not see that at the time,' Elliott said. 'Ultimately, no matter what your vision is, you're judged on results. We should have built more sensibly rather than do it overnight. There was a need to stabilise after the success. Instead, it was all change, straight away. Maybe economics had a say. There was a need for more experience to help the youngsters who were coming through.'

Liverpool and England defender Phil Thompson, a three-time European Cup winner, observed that in those mid-80s days there were many teams who had good players and although Liverpool had a lot of success they well and truly had to earn it. He pointed out how the likes of Villa, Everton, Arsenal, Tottenham and Manchester United were 'always up there', while Ipswich had good players and even Southampton and Watford were runners-up in consecutive seasons, so he understands why Villa fell away.

'We all had small squads in those days so it only needed a loss of form, a few injuries, the sale of a couple of key players and it could cripple a team,' Thompson said.

'Doug Ellis coming back and selling their big players who had been so critical towards Villa's success would have had a huge impact. There was such a good camaraderie and closeness at Villa that it only took a few changes and you can't get back what you had. Even at Liverpool we never made huge changes. We would maybe make two signings every summer just to freshen the squad up and keep people on their toes.'

Following the result at Forest, Turner would ultimately pay the price for his failure to reverse Villa's worrying slide. Morale at the club was non-existent and their star player Steve Hodge was not playing, despite being fit. He was ordered to sit and watch in the stands by Turner because he had submitted a written transfer request the week before after the home defeat to Oxford. Hodge said it was a peculiar game watching his former club thrash his current team – or at least the team he was still registered to.

'That is the most embarrassed I have ever felt on a pitch,' Allan Evans said ruefully. 'I don't know what happened that day. I don't know how many goals I gave away but I can remember after the game I couldn't speak. I was that gutted with it. There is nothing worse than being on the pitch and whenever they attack you're thinking "this could be a goal", which is what that game was like.'

Paul Elliott said although the score was 6–0 it could easily have been ten. Steve Hunt believed that the manager had been terribly let down by his players.

'I felt a bit sorry for Graham because with the players we had we should never have struggled like that,' Hunt admitted. 'Too many players were not putting in 100 per cent every game and looked like they had given up [on survival] or were just biding their time before a move. Graham had a right go at everyone after the Forest game and accused us of not caring, but I thought that had been the case for a long time beforehand. Not me, as I have Villa in my blood, but there were some I felt who were coasting.'

Turner thought it was inevitable after such a result he would receive a phone call from the chairman asking, 'Would you like to come around my house in the morning for a chat?' It was only after the Forest result, though, that he felt his job was on the line.

'Before that game I believed I could pull it round,' Turner said.

Indeed, the next day Ellis made the former Shrewsbury Town manager his fourth sacking victim at Villa following Tommy Docherty, Vic Crowe and Tony Barton, but maintains it was not a decision he made with any relish or satisfaction. Turner was at least, board room minutes state, paid £25,000 ex gratia for his efforts over more than two years. That was more money than several of the European Cup winners received when they departed.

'Graham Turner was a lovely, honest man and I remember walking around my garden with him when I had to sack him,' Ellis said. 'Both of us had tears in our eyes.'

First-team coach Ron Wylie was caretaker manager for one game before McNeill came in, when Villa were pummelled once again in front of their own supporters, this time 4–1 to Norwich City.

Steve Hodge's transfer request had been leaked to the media prior to that match, which helped make the England midfielder an unfortunate scapegoat for all that was rotten about Villa. The Villa fans chanted 'let him die' when Hodge received treatment at one moment in the game.

'That Norwich game was a personal nightmare,' said Hodge, 'though I expected a hostile reception. Who can blame the fans on hearing one of their players wants to leave? But I gave a goal away in the first ten minutes and that made things even worse. It was a tough afternoon to get through.'

Enter Billy McNeill.

The Celtic legend told the Villa board in one of his first meetings with directors the squad was desperate for a major clear-out, though he received little encouragement from Ellis in that regard and eventually he said he 'hated going to work'. Another early contribution from McNeill was to recommend that the specialist goalkeeping coaching from 1966 World Cup winner Gordon Banks was 'no longer necessary and could be dispensed with'.

Like the players, the board was rarely in sync with McNeill but he never helped himself by making no attempt to relocate from his Greater Manchester home to the West Midlands, citing it was because he could not source the right school for his son. He commuted from Hale Barnes, spending two nights a week living in hotels.

While McNeill got on well enough with some players like Paul Elliott and Andy Blair, the general view in the dressing room was that he was using Villa as a stepping stone to return to Celtic, which he did in fact do the same year he was axed by Villa.

'Billy McNeill was a massive disappointment,' Andy Gray summed up. 'He was a giant of a footballer to me as I was growing up and I played against him when I was a kid at Dundee United. He was an absolute giant of Scottish football who had won so much as a player and when I heard he was coming down to Villa I thought, "Brilliant". But I don't think Villa meant enough to Billy and it was a token gesture by him to come down from Man City.

'There were enough good players at Villa then and there is not a doubt in my mind that with a better, more committed manager that team would not have been relegated.'

Steve Hunt claimed McNeill 'lost the dressing room very quickly'. He never helped himself and for some reason showed none of the leadership skills he was known for at Celtic. In one training session early in his tenure he called an unofficial meeting with senior players Allan Evans, Andy Gray and Hunt and asked them, "What do you think we should we do? What formation should we go with?" This at a time when the players were desperate to see some strong leadership and direction from their new manager; instead, they had only someone who appeared to not have a clue about the best way forward. 'It's OK managers getting the opinion of players but ultimately they need to know what they will be doing and having some plan on how to play,' Hunt said. 'That smacked of desperation to me.'

McNeill clashed with captain Allan Evans very early into his tenure to the extent that they never spoke again for the rest of his time at Villa – not in a civil manner anyway. Evans explains, 'We went out for training one day and it was sunny but I seldom wore shorts in training and always wore tracksuit bottoms. Not even with shorts underneath, just a jock-strap. That's how I felt comfortable and had always done that. He brought us all together for a chat and he pointed at me, the club captain, and said, "Get your bottoms off." I told him this is how I trained, he kept on and I said, "I am not going to take them off." I hardly spoke to him after that – and I'm not the kind to fall out with people. It was a shame because when Billy came to us I can remember thinking, "This guy is a legend, a Lisbon Lion, he will sort us out, I'm going to get on with this bloke." It never happened.'

Most of the players were disappointed in McNeill's lack of man-management skills, his lack of tactical awareness and his one-dimensional training, which was mostly five-a-sides, while the players also noticed McNeill was very quick to leave the training ground for home.

'He was a massive disappointment,' Gary Williams reflected, echoing Andy Gray's words. 'He had been at Manchester City and came in with a big reputation. We were all expecting things to change but nothing did change. Things just got worse. He was a disaster. He didn't do anything, he never changed anything, he didn't buy a player who improved us, he was a big letdown, even though he had a big reputation at the time.

'All he kept talking about was Celtic. He would keep referring back to how things were dealt with at Celtic. It was Celtic, Celtic, Celtic, and I became bored with it. To be fair to him, when I had to travel down to London after I was sent off, he came with me, but all he talked about was Celtic.'

Oh yes, those two red cards for Williams. The defender had never been sent off in the previous ten years of his career but now in this nightmare of all nightmare seasons, he was sent off not once but twice. The first was against Wimbledon in the second match of the campaign and the second was at Southampton in an ill-tempered League Cup match when Mark Dennis and Martin Keown were also dismissed. Williams' uncharacteristic lack of discipline typified the state of the club then. 'It was chaos, everything seemed to be going wrong. I showed my frustration a couple of times, with those red cards being the obvious results of the way I felt at the time. It was no excuse but the discipline in the team then was non-existent and I retaliated in a way I shouldn't have. The wheels were falling off.

'You had a sense all through that season something wasn't right. We had good individuals, but we played like individuals. We weren't a team. There was no shape, no plan, nothing.'

Even the long-serving secretary, Steve Stride, had had enough and started working a trial period with Sheffield Wednesday, a role he did not really want but he was just so disillusioned by events at Villa he was looking for a way out. He was, though, persuaded to return by Ellis.

'It was doom and gloom at Villa,' Stride recalled. 'We were in utopia one minute and battling relegation the next. I remember a match against Southampton in the 1985/86 season where we had a crowd of just over 8,000 – for a First Division league match! It was a depressing time.'

There was no excuse for some of Villa's defeats. Quite simply, it was often inadequate management from McNeill, whose heart was never in the job. His team selection for the League Cup match at Southampton that Williams referred to, for instance, is puzzling at best. He selected just one recognised midfield player, Steve Hunt, who was single-handedly up against a competitive Saints midfield of Jimmy Case, Glenn Cockerill and George Lawrence. He played two strikers, Garry Thompson and Simon Stainrod, with nineteen-year-old winger Tony Daley ahead of Hunt and six defenders – two natural right-backs, Williams and David Norton who sometimes played out of position in midfield, a left-back Tony Dorigo and three centre-backs, Allan Evans, Paul Elliott and Martin Keown.

Events were even worse when Villa returned to the Dell to play Southampton in the league on 21 March. They lost 5–0 and McNeill later pointed the finger at his chief dressing-room adversary, Allan Evans, for a performance he felt cost his teammates.

'I have never been a violent person off the pitch, although I played hard on it,' Evans said. 'But Billy McNeill was the one person I nearly clobbered, a few weeks before he was sacked. We were hammered at Southampton and came in after and Billy went for me, blamed me for every goal. I can take it and I said, "I'm not talking to you now, I'll talk to you on Monday," and I walked away. I went into his office on Monday and he accused me of not caring for the club. I had been there ten years and he had been there for a few months. I said, "I'm going to get out of this office right now or I'm going to do something I will regret." I walked out and he followed me and was abusing me in my ear. The assistant coach Ron Wylie must have heard the commotion and came out of the coaches' room and I said, "Ron, get him away from me now or I will hit him." He was soon gone but was a nightmare for the club. He didn't care about Aston Villa, or at least he gave that impression.'

McNeill told the Villa players, in an effort to raise morale, that he was going to buy a striker who would keep them up. Subsequently, his one and only signing as Aston Villa manager was nineteen-year-old striker Warren Aspinall from Everton. Villa paid £215,000 and £400-per-week wages, plus £200 per appearance on a player who had never started a game in the top flight and had made just seven substitute appearances without a single goal.

Aspinall's success to that point had been with Wigan Athletic in the old Third Division. This was not the guaranteed match-winning goalscorer McNeill had committed to sign but a rookie striker from Everton's reserve team – it was a huge gamble. Aspinall said he had been scoring freely in Everton's reserves but was just biding his time waiting for Graeme Sharp or Adrian Heath to allow him an opening through injury. Instead, Villa came calling.

"It came out the blue and as Villa were a massive club the move was a no-brainer," recalled Aspinall. "I never felt like I was put under any pressure because they had been struggling to score with experienced strikers long before I arrived and they were leaking goals as well. So I just felt excitement going in.

"I noticed pretty soon though that the manager had lost the dressing room by the time I came in. His tactics were strange, though. He would bring a Subbuteo board into the dressing room and say, "Right, that man passes to that man, then he crosses for him and Bingo! Goal." It was weird and the lads weren't very impressed. There was no leadership or direction from the management."

On Aspinall's arrival, Gary Williams said: 'I felt sorry for Warren because there was an unfair expectation put on him, as though he was going to make all the difference. It didn't happen for him and he received quite a bit of stick. He was only a young lad and was like a rabbit in the headlights who couldn't cope, but it wasn't his fault. He should never have been put in the position where he was seen as some sort of saviour. He was never going to be that.'

Doug Ellis was generally avoided by the players as none wished to be known as a 'chairman's snitch', but given the nature of the divide between McNeill and his players, some players who were comfortable speaking with the chairman fed him dressing-room opinion, which McNeill suspected. In a board meeting on 22 April 1987, Ellis informed his fellow directors that various members of the team had aired their negative views on McNeill's management ability. The chairman opted to defer judgement until Villa's relegation was certain. McNeill knew Ellis had players in his ear but he never could find out who they were. All he did know was that he had several enemies in the dressing room.

Ellis sacked McNeill and first-team coach Ron Wylie before the final game of that horrendous season. Boardroom documents reveal that McNeill was paid £15,000 compensation and Wylie £17,500, given his service as a player and as a coach. Ellis described McNeill's attitude in a meeting a day before the sacking as 'aggressive and provocative', as he refused to accept any blame for the team's dismal performances.

'I felt Ellis took great pleasure telling me that I was sacked,' said McNeill. 'He called me into his office and delivered the unsurprising news as coldly and clinically as he possibly could … I found Doug Ellis a despicable character. I can't help but admire the way he managed to survive in the face of so much opposition from a cross-section of the Villa fans.'

Coach Frank Upton took charge of the team for the final game of the season, against Manchester United at Old Trafford – a fixture cruelly timed to kick Villa while they were down if ever there was one. They lost 3–1 after selecting a team that might not have looked out of place in a youth-team league, such was the number of rookies among them, like Warren Aspinall aged nineteen and Phil Robinson, Bernie Gallacher and Martin Keown all twenty. There was no Allan Evans, no Gary Shaw, no Gary Williams, no Andy Blair. The average age of the team, once the eighteen-year-old Stuart Ritchie was introduced for Andy Gray, was just 22, even though Nigel Spink 28, Simon Stainrod 28 and Steve Hunt 30 were all playing. It had been a familiar story for two or three seasons as Graham Turner's investment in youth, Doug Ellis's penchant for low wages and Billy McNeill's lack of commitment to the club all came to a head. Namely, with relegation. For someone like Andy Gray, who had built his reputation at Villa after he signed first time round in 1975, finishing bottom of the league and being relegated was extremely painful. Unlike many participants in this stage of Villa's history, though, he does not hold Ellis responsible.

'It was awful, just dreadful,' Gray reflected, even though Villa had been officially relegated the game prior after losing 2-1 at home to Sheffield Wednesday. 'I can remember after that hammering up at Old Trafford, I was coming back to Birmingham on the team bus and was absolutely gutted. I said to myself, "There will be a guy sitting in his house now feeling as bad as I do." So, I went around to Doug Ellis's house that night, knocked on his door and he was in, as I thought he would be. He was sat on his own having a drink. I tried to console him on an awful day and spent a couple of hours with him, shared a couple of bottles of wine, while talking about Villa and the things he had to do to resurrect this great club and get them back to where they belong. Then I left him.

'I maintain Doug had Villa in his heart one hundred per cent,' Gray added. 'You only have to look around that stadium, walk around the training ground, see where that club was when Randy Lerner bought it. Everything was in place. He did a brilliant job, not everyone says that, I know, but I liked him.'

Ellis is aware of the criticism. He knows of the common perception that he manipulated Tony Barton and Graham Turner's transfer activity, but he ultimately maintains the manager always made his own decisions on hiring and firing, while he interfered only on the financial side of business. When the relegation came, many would say Ellis deserved it. Steve Stride worked alongside Ellis over four decades and he knows better than anyone his attitude towards money. He was never a chairman that spent loosely on box-office names to raise his football club if he thought a younger talent or an untapped one could be signed for a quarter of the price. That approach cost him, ultimately, in 1987.

'The best way I could describe Doug is like this ...' Stride explained. 'If we needed twelve new running machines at the gym at Bodymoor Heath, Doug would more than likely do a deal somewhere on eight reconditioned ones. Whereas his successor, Randy Lerner, in his first few years as chairman, would buy sixteen of the best running machines on the market. That was the difference.'

Whatever one's viewpoint, there was certainly nobody more upset than Doug Ellis when Villa's relegation was confirmed.

'They were very painful times and I was never the kind of chairman who could come home at night and switch off from Aston Villa,' Ellis revealed. 'It wasn't a nine-to-five job. I always lived and breathed Aston Villa through the good times and the bad. And any time a club you are in charge of is relegated, you feel it more than anyone.'

Everything that could have gone wrong in that season, went wrong. The overreliance on youth was one obvious error – and not just youth but inadequate youth, utilising players who were unable to cut it at the highest level. Players used over the three seasons leading up to this capitulation like Warren Aspinall, Dean Glover, Paul Kerr, David Norton, Ray Walker, Kevin Poole, Darren Bradley and Phil Robinson went on to enjoy substantial careers in professional football, but predominantly in the lower tiers. Even the likes of Tony Dorigo, Martin Keown, Mark Walters, Tony Daley and Paul Elliott – all quality players who went on to have excellent careers in the top flight – were surrounded by too many other youthful players too soon when they would have benefitted from being surrounded by more experience.

Graham Turner insisted, though, the squad that McNeill inherited should never have been involved in a relegation, despite the horrendous early results under his stewardship.

'There was plenty of time and ability to recover from the bad start we had,' said Turner. 'I was quite surprised that the poor run continued throughout the season. There was enough ability in that changing room to get away from any danger.'

Aston Villa had degenerated so badly and so quickly as a team and a club by this time that even quality experienced players coming in struggled, almost certainly due to the environment that had been created in the dressing room and the boardroom. Steve Hunt would be an exception, but Andy Gray is a prime example. He failed to score a single goal in 21 appearances in the league and FA Cup in the relegation season, managing two in a League Cup game against Reading. He believes the rotting state of Villa then had an infectious effect on players, himself included.

'I had a shocker,' Gray admitted. 'People might say it was Old Father Time catching up with me but I like to think I still had more to offer than what we saw that season. You don't decline that quickly after the season we had had at Everton. It was just very difficult for all of us, we didn't create chances, maybe I was trying to do too much as a senior player for everyone else because of the decline. You can't have the season I had at Everton, winning things and competing at the top as we were, to suddenly become a bad player overnight while Villa were struggling so badly. I came back full of optimism. But it was a shocking season that I consign to the back of my memory, never to be brought out.'

Another verdict on the relegation goes to a Birmingham-born Villa fan who enjoyed the best days of his career at fellow West Midlands clubs Coventry City and West Bromwich Albion. Garry Thompson, a Villa supporter from his childhood, felt the pain of the relegation as much as any fan or player.

'That relegation was the saddest experience of my life,' he admitted. 'The whole club needed sorting out. I could blame Billy McNeill for the relegation because he wasn't a good manager but basically we, the players, fucked up. I didn't score enough goals, we didn't defend properly, we didn't create enough. The players didn't do their jobs, that's the bottom line. We weren't Aston Villa.'

Another Birmingham-born Villa supporter who also enjoyed his best days away from Villa before returning for this sad time was Steve Hunt.

He said: 'I wasn't right for ages. Villa was unfinished business for me after I didn't stick around long early on, so to come back and get relegated was the lowest point in my career. I had never been relegated before so to suffer that at Villa – my club – it was hard to take.'

Allan Evans never supported Villa as a boy like Thompson and Hunt, but after a decade at Villa Park and the medals he won he became as much a converted Villa fan as there had ever been; the league position of last in the First Division was something that did not sit too well with him. More so, because he had savoured the club's greatest highs not long before.

'When we won the league and then the European Cup, I thought it was always going to be like that, but it wasn't,' Evans said. 'When we were eventually relegated that hit me so hard I was actually depressed for ages. That relegation hurt me more than anything.'

Andy Blair, who had first-hand experience of Villa's greatest high from his vantage point of the substitutes bench in Rotterdam when the European Cup was won, said the relegation was 'absolute agony' and the whole club 'needed cleansing'. Similarly, Tony Dorigo felt he had 'hit the jackpot' when he came to the club as a fifteen-year-old in 1981 after arriving from Australia. He wrote to the top twelve clubs in the First Division and the only club that bothered to write back was Villa. He did enough to earn an apprenticeship after a four-day trial. But as he worked his way through the ranks, he observed a disintegration of most things that were positive about the club.

'We would sell quality, experienced players and replace them with young gambles, like Warren Aspinall and guys like that,' Dorigo said. 'It was tough as the great players like Gordon Cowans moved away. Relegation was inevitable.'

The last word on the horror season goes to Martin Keown, who puts the carnage into perspective when he said: 'If Chelsea had been relegated five years after beating Bayern Munich in the Champions League in 2012, it would have been viewed as a massive catastrophe. Well, that is exactly what happened to Aston Villa. It was a massive fall from grace for us.'

Epilogue:
Graham Taylor's
Reconstruction

'Graham Taylor was what Villa needed at that time. I was depressed by the relegation but got over it within two days of Graham Taylor coming in. As soon as I saw Graham at work I thought, "This club is going to get sorted."' – **Allan Evans**

IF EVER THERE WAS A MONUMENTAL JOB IN FOOTBALL THAT A GREAT DEAL of respectable managers would have happily avoided, it was taking on the wreckage that was Aston Villa in the summer of 1987. Watford manager Graham Taylor, though, was up for the challenge and Villa would not look back for a long time thereafter.

Keith Burkinshaw is one manager who admits to rejecting the Villa job then, for a second time in his case, but Taylor chose to see the positives in the challenge of resurrecting a once great club. He was hired on 18 May 1987 on a four-year contract after chairman Doug Ellis paid Watford £25,000 compensation to buy him out of his contract. Taylor instantly became Villa's highest-paid manager of all time with a £60,000-a-year salary plus double the bonuses of the players. His track record, though, certainly justified every penny Villa invested in him. He started in management with five seasons at Lincoln City, with whom he won promotion to the third tier in his penultimate season there. But it was at Vicarage Road where he built his reputation as one of the best managers in the country. Consecutive promotions in his first two seasons with the Hornets lifted them from the old Fourth Division to the Second, until he won another promotion to the elite of English football. One year later, in 1982/83, he demonstrated remarkable talent as a team-builder in raising Watford to the runner-up position behind champions Liverpool in Watford's maiden campaign in the top tier. Players such as John Barnes, Luther Blissett, Pat Rice and Kenny Jackett inspired their dream campaign that witnessed an 8-0 win over Sunderland when Blissett scored four. They also reached the 1984 FA Cup final, losing to Everton.

The cynics pointed to Taylor's direct, long-ball style as a way of undermining his achievements but what he did have was a solid game-plan that he stuck to wherever he went, and his players knew what was expected of them. Taylor's teams were generally made up of solid, reliable defenders, like Steve Terry and John McClelland at Watford, midfielders who could keep the ball like Les Taylor and Jackett, and wide men like Barnes and Nigel Callaghan to deliver accurate crosses for dominant strikers who were good in the air like Blissett and George Reilly. Taylor repeated the same formula at Villa and his players appreciated they were working with a manager who at least had 100 per cent conviction in his methods, probably for the first time since Ron Saunders left more than five years earlier.

'I didn't really agree with his direct style of long-ball football but, whatever anyone says about Graham, one thing he had was strong leadership and total conviction in what he was trying to do,' Steve Hunt said. 'He was also the most organised manager I ever played under. In pre-season before we started our promotion bid he sat us down in the centre circle at a ground in Sweden and told us exactly how he planned for us to play and what everyone's jobs were. His attention to detail was outstanding.'

That attention to detail extended way beyond the football field. He brought with him a professionalism that had long been missing from the club and also highly professional staff who improved players in all kinds of ways. Striker Garry Thompson, for instance, had been troubled by a mystery injury throughout the previous season and kept trying to play through it despite obvious discomfort. The medics through the Turner and McNeill eras could not identify what was wrong with him and were even considering taking bone from his hip and fusing it somewhere else.

'They were clueless,' remembered Thompson, who the Villa supporters affectionately nicknamed 'Bruno' after the heavyweight boxer Frank. 'I was taking dog's abuse because I was struggling but I was still trying to play on. I would roll out of bed of a morning, crawl to the bog, and bit by bit I'd stand up. But every time I played I kept ripping my stomach. Andy Gray said to me in one game against

Man City, 'Get up, big man, what's the matter with you?' And I just couldn't get up. The medical expertise was so bad they didn't know what was happening. I endured that for eleven months until Graham Taylor came in with physio Jim Walker. He kept getting me fit, I'd break down, would get me fit, I'd break down. He said it wasn't right and asked me if I'd ever been examined. I hadn't. It took this specialist who Jim took me to see about ten seconds to diagnose that I had a hernia. That was Villa for you at that time.'

Taylor introduced discipline off the field, which he believed would translate on it. He made the players train at Villa Park as a way of encouraging them to see their home ground as a familiar environment to be defended with pride and to savour the experience rather than fear it in front of supporters who had become understandably impatient and critical of their team's performances. Taylor made the squad wash their own kit and he ensured all the players 'worked their arses off' until they had attained optimum fitness levels.

'I thought me and him weren't going to get on but I loved what he was trying to do,' Thompson added. 'Graham made us a club again.'

Taylor's professionalism impressed all the players and Gary Williams regretted leaving for Leeds United, admitting he acted on impulse because of frustrations with the previous regime. Disillusioned and disaffected, Williams made a dash for the exit at the first decent opportunity. Had he taken more time to consider that the future might just be rosier under Taylor, he almost certainly would not have left. Taylor tried hard to keep him and even offered to arrange a testimonial. He had taken the time to research his squad and he seemingly knew everything about Williams, including the names of his wife and children.

'With that man in charge I could tell straight away Villa would be close to getting promotion, or at least challenging,' Williams remembered. 'There was no question he was going to change Aston Villa.

'The only reason I left was because it was the right time for me to go, as all my mates had gone and it wasn't the same any more. Graham didn't want me to go, my contract was up and he said if my decision was about money he would sort it out. But I was adamant I wanted to leave. In hindsight, I wish I had stayed. Leaving Villa was the worst decision I ever made in my career. If I had just hung on for another month I am sure the new manager would have rejuvenated me and my desire to stay at the club.'

Another veteran from the league championship and European Cup wins who was still there to meet Taylor was Allan Evans. The Scottish stopper insists he learned more about defending from Taylor's deputy, Steve Harrison, in the first six months of Taylor's reign than he had learned in his entire career. Evans incorporated elements of Harrison's approach when he became a coach in later years.

'Graham Taylor was what Villa needed at that time,' said Evans. 'I was depressed by the relegation but got over it within two days of Graham coming in. As soon as I saw Graham at work I thought, "This club is going to get sorted." He was so authoritative in the dressing room and did not leave any stone unturned in his organisation. You couldn't catch him out on anything, with his training, team selection, anything.'

Taylor also stood firm when Doug Ellis attempted to interfere in team matters or other areas where the manager felt his interest was not welcome. Taylor owned *his* space and Ellis had not felt so out of the loop as far as the football side of things were concerned since Ron Saunders' days. The key difference between Taylor and Saunders though was that Taylor was firm and had total conviction in his own methods, but he was also a diplomat and could 'play' Ellis in such a way that he denied the chairman any control he might have been seeking but at the same time did it in a way that still made Ellis feel part of things. Saunders was not interested in these kinds of games or politics. 'My dad was told many times by friends, "If you can get on with Doug better you'd get a lot more money out of him [for players],"' Ron Saunders Jr revealed. The facts support this view too, as club accounts show that expenditure for player and staff wages increased from 1987 to 1988 by more than £470,000.

Ellis's reputation for spending money was not a positive one and his over-prudent nature in this regard certainly contributed to Villa's barren spell in the mid-80s – if not being totally his fault. Taylor and, later, Ron Atkinson would attest to Ellis's free spending once cajoled in the right way by his manager. Atkinson managed Villa between 1991 and 1994.

'He had certain personality quirks,' said Atkinson, 'but what money he had got you could get. Quite often the type of money he made available would not get us anything better than what we had already so I'd tell him, "Keep your money and at the end of the season when you haven't got to spend any more money on the ground, we'll go for a couple of biggies like Les Ferdinand," who was my big target.'

At various stages of his chairmanship, over both spells, Ellis genuinely wanted to sign star quality but his old habits of frugality always cost him. He enquired about George Best in the 70s before he went to Fulham; he met with Paul Gascoigne during Italia '90 but no move was forthcoming, while Les Ferdinand met him at Villa Park when leaving QPR but Newcastle offered him £20,000-a-week wages when Ellis was willing to offer only £15,000. And, of course, we have already heard of how Graham Turner enquired about the likes of Gary Lineker, Terry Butcher and Alan Smith only to be rebuffed on budgetary grounds. Ellis always stopped short of going that extra mile to take Villa from being a good club into a huge, great club on the level of Liverpool and Manchester United.

Graham Taylor, though, had a way of sweet-talking Ellis. Therefore, he was able to persuade Ellis to release so much more money for his imperative squad-rebuilding programme that he set about immediately. He knew when to be matey with Ellis but also when to be firm on boundaries that were agreed when he joined. Taylor had never had such problems previously with pop singer Elton John as his chairman at Watford. There, he had a free rein. But now the landscape was very different.

'Tony Barton did magnificent with Roy McLaren in keeping the wheels turning after Ron Saunders left, but Graham Turner and Billy McNeill were not strong enough to stop Doug Ellis in his tracks when he tried to overstep his role,' commented Nigel Spink. 'That is what Graham Taylor did. Graham said, "Yes, I will come and manage your club, but I am in charge. I am recruiting players and you are not going to tell me which players I bring in." He understood the financial aspects, he wanted to oversee the youth, the reserves and the first team, too. He was in charge of the football at Aston Villa. Whether Doug really knew what he was taking on with Graham I am not too sure. Graham was such a stern man and very forceful in his beliefs. But he was exactly what we needed then.'

Ellis, though, has no regrets about his appointment of Taylor and revels in stories that involve the two of them operating almost as a double act. Like when he sat on the substitutes' bench at a friendly match in Tobago on 5 March 1989 during Villa's mid-season tour. He supposedly tapped Taylor on the shoulder and suggested he took a closer look at a boy out there called Dwight Yorke, who would eventually sign for Villa before winning the Champions League with Manchester United. Taylor's version of that event would almost certainly have been different. However, he was happy for the famously egotistical Ellis to boast in such a way if it meant he stayed on the right side of him when it came to requesting more funds for player wages or transfer fees.

Taylor was shrewd and knew perfectly how to conduct himself with Ellis. Appeal to his better nature and you would see a charming, football-loving, intelligent gentleman. Players, though, sometimes saw the other side of Ellis: the painfully tight businessman who would dig his heels in over payments that players believed were owed to them. Colin Gibson, Garry Thompson and Tony Morley are just three players who still consider themselves denied loyalty payments they felt were owed to them. Steve Stride revealed the anti-Ellis feeling from the European Cup-winning squad remains very strong.

'I didn't know it at the time but I know now that a number of players from that team hate him,' said Stride.

'I don't like to use the word "hate",' said Colin Gibson, 'but let's just say this man is not on my Christmas card list and never will be. He decimated our team. People say he had success but it depends how you measure that. They won a couple of League Cups, but never won an FA Cup, never won the league again or threatened in Europe. All he did was get Villa relegated and take the club back into the Dark Ages.'

Garry Thompson believed he was owed £25,000 on his Villa exit yet received £15,000, and he only pocketed that much because of Taylor's intervention with Ellis. There was no diplomatic figure like Taylor around to approach Ellis on these matters when Morley and Gibson left Villa. Ellis always admired Taylor's work, which is why he employed him again in 2002. 'Graham Taylor did a tremendous job in his first stint as Aston Villa manager,' Ellis confirmed, 'and brought discipline and structure to the playing side of the club, which was essential when we needed to fight our way back.'

Martin Keown played for two seasons under Taylor, one in the old Second Division when Villa battled their way to the runners-up spot to regain promotion at the first attempt; and then his final season was spent helping to maintain Villa's position in the top flight in 1989.

Whereas Keown survived Taylor's sweeping changes near enough a dozen players left and a dozen came in with Taylor when he revamped the whole squad, many did not. The new manager preferred to introduce many of his own signings to complement other players still at Villa who he wished to retain. Taylor used twenty-six players in league action in that 1987/88 promotion-seeking campaign. He was finding out about players as he went along.

Tony Dorigo did not play one game in the second tier for Villa and was one of the first to depart, in somewhat harsh circumstances. Chelsea had attempted to sign Dorigo during the previous campaign and their interest was always in the media spotlight. But the player had not asked to leave nor had he declared he wanted to leave. However, Taylor interpreted the speculation as unnecessary distraction to his hard-line promotion plans and subsequently he viewed Dorigo as someone who did not want to stick around for the fight in the Second Division. He joined Chelsea for £475,000, six years after arriving from Australia for a trial while still a schoolboy.

'In my last team meeting at Villa and Graham's first one he came in with this big speech about us playing for the shirt, saying all the right stuff, and then goes, "And you, Dorigo, if you want to bugger off to Chelsea, then go on, off you go." But he was pointing to Gary Williams and everyone starts laughing. Someone told him, "Boss, Tony's over there." I start laughing, he starts laughing and it was a case of "OK, thanks, I'm off." And that was it. I didn't ask for the move. We had some good young players and if we could have kept them together, the likes of Mark Walters, myself, Paul Elliott, Martin Keown et cetera, who knows what might have been.

'I guess after Chelsea's interest before a move was always possible. But I was absolutely shocked that Villa were preparing to sell me. I had no idea what was going on. I got a call from Doug before the old March transfer window shut. I'm twenty-one, I was player of the year, I'm absolutely flying, loving my time at the club and Doug tells me, "I'm picking you up in an hour and taking you down to Chelsea. We are going to swap you for David Speedie as we can't score goals and the only way they will let him go is if we sacrifice you." So, there we are in this corridor of the Posthouse Hotel, with me, Deadly Doug and my agent on one side and Ken Bates, David Speedie and John Hollins on the other side. And they swapped players. As we walked past each other it felt like both parties were giving a hostage back. It was funny because we ended up in adjoining rooms, me with Ken Bates and John Hollins and Speedie in the next room with Deadly Doug and all we could hear early on was Speedie letting out this huge, great laugh and Ken Bates said, "That will be Villa's first offer…" It didn't actually go through in the end because, apparently, Speedie didn't want to move to Villa and was holding out for Liverpool. Although he was sold to Coventry it was only a stop-gap before he ended up at Anfield. Chelsea kept coming back in for me, though, and eventually I decided I wanted to go because it was clear Villa were not bothered about keeping me.'

Another key departure was that of Paul Elliott, who left for Pisa before reuniting with Billy McNeill at Celtic, while Mark Walters signed for Rangers for £575,000 after rejecting three contract offers to remain at Villa. One of those offers was worth £600 a week and a signing-on fee of £25,000, club documents reveal. Villa graduate Walters, though, who won the Super Cup in 1983 and had been a loyal, talented player over the years, was paid £25,000 ex gratia, according to boardroom minutes. Walters went on to join Graeme Souness's revolution at Ibrox and withstood some of the most sickening racial abuse in British football only to win over his ignorant detractors and become one of the most successful English exports north of the border. Villa legend Andy Gray moved to West Bromwich Albion for £32,000; Dean Glover £55,000, Mark Burke £40,000 and Kevin Poole £28,000 all joined their former team-mate Paul Kerr at Middlesbrough; Simon Stainrod shifted to Stoke City for £100,000.

Incoming transfers saw Taylor return to his former club to buy central defender Steve Sims for £57,000 plus a £10,000 bonus for achieving promotion; midfielder David Hunt arrived on a free transfer from Notts County with a £10,000 signing-on fee; Kevin Gage, a right-back who Taylor played mostly in central midfield, came from Wimbledon for £140,000; combative midfielder Andy Gray joined from Crystal Palace for £150,000 with an £18,000 signing-on fee and an £8,000 promotion bonus; his namesake Stuart Gray, with a 'sweet' left foot who was able to play at left-back or left midfield, arrived from Barnsley for £175,000; midfielder Mark Lillis signed from Derby County for £175,000 with a £10,000 promotion bonus; Alan McInally arrived from Celtic for £250,000 and although the Scotsman was not the highest earner he did well from the move after agreeing a £22,500 signing-on fee and a £10,000 promotion bonus all above figures stated in board room minutes. Villa more than reaped the rewards from this signing, though, when McInally joined Bayern Munich for £1.2 million in 1990. Meanwhile, long-serving club legend Gary Shaw signed a one-year extension as Taylor hoped he could see the player return to fitness to help Villa's promotion bid.

It was clearly a busy summer's transfer activity for Taylor but was worth it when Villa held on to the second automatic promotion place on the final day of the season courtesy of a goalless draw at Lou Macari's Swindon Town.

'Graham Taylor saved Aston Villa and without him the club could easily have gone down all the divisions, such was the level of disarray before he arrived,' Keown said. 'In his first meeting with the players, at the training ground, he was introduced to us by the chairman and once that was over he told the chairman to be on his way. That made an instant statement to us straight away. He said, "Who wants to come with me on this journey? Those who don't fancy it can leave now." He knew exactly what he wanted and how we were going to achieve it.

'That promotion-winning campaign in 1987/88 remains one of the most satisfying achivements of my career. We were like a band of brothers, a real tight-knit group that was in it together. I could have left after we were relegated but I didn't want to leave with the club in a worse state than when I joined and I am so pleased I did stay because I loved that season. When I was leaving Villa in 1989, Graham tried to keep me and said he was signing a big-name defender he wanted to play me alongside but he wouldn't tell me who it was. I chose to go, but if I had known then it was Paul McGrath I might just have stayed on.'

Certainly for Warren Aspinall this campaign was much happier as he finished top goalscorer for Villa with thirteen goals. It at least allowed him to show the Villa supporters he was not as inferior a signing as they might have initially thought when he was unfairly touted as the club's supposed saviour from relegation the season before. Taylor was happy to have the striker in his ranks after he had tried to sign him for Watford when he left Wigan but opted for Goodison Park instead.

"That season was hard work because Graham really put us through it with double training sessions and such like," Aspinall said. "Graham got rid of the dead wood who were causing issues in the dressing room. I don't want to mention any names but certain players were out drinking too often and didn't seem to care about results as long as they got paid. All that changed when Graham came in.

"His attention to detail was amazing; he knew everything about every player. He had spies with bouncers at certain nightclubs and was aware when we were in the Bel Air nightclub at The Belfry on a Monday night. I had a house move that was days from going through when he came to me and said, "I hear you're moving to the Stafford area?" His intel was spot on. He said, "You're going to have to change your plans because that's 33 miles from Villa Park. The rule is you have to be within 25 miles of Villa Park!" I ended up moving to Walmley five miles from the ground.'

Taylor's revolution was well under way and Aston Villa were back among the elite. The overall recovery was not sudden, though, for their first season back in the top flight saw Villa avoid relegation by one place, as they finished a point above relegated Middlesbrough in seventeenth position. Ellis might have sacked a manager a few years before for such a close escape but he had totally bought into Taylor's methods and supported him, seemingly for the long term.

The first genuine evidence of real progress came the season after in the 1989/90 campaign when Taylor led the team to the runners-up position behind Liverpool. They never threatened the title, trailing the Reds by nine points, but that they finished seven points ahead of third-placed Tottenham did exhibit a significant improvement from where they had been the season before.

Taylor utilised a three-man central defence to good effect with his inspirational signing Paul McGrath, Danish international Kent Nielsen and ex-Everton league title winner Derek Mountfield ahead of the veteran goalkeeper Nigel Spink. Another Taylor signing, David Platt, registered nineteen league goals to earn a place in England's Italia '90 squad, while other players like Tony Daley, Kevin Gage and Gordon Cowans, who Taylor brought back to Villa Park from Italy, functioned fluently in a well-organised, enterprising team that was attractive to watch, contrary to Taylor's reputation for producing teams that played the long ball and bypassed midfield.

Cowans recalled how his return to Villa Park revealed a ruthless streak that Taylor had, which he was not always given credit for because of his placid nature in media interviews.

'On my last night in Italy I went out with the lads, had too much to drink, then got on the plane and was met by Graham Taylor at the other end,' Cowans said. 'I thought he was going to take me to Bodymoor Heath to chat or train. But instead he took me to Lilleshall for a fitness test, not a medical. I had to do these uphill treadmill drills for about half an hour with a mask on, suffocating myself with alcohol fumes. I told Graham on the way that I'd had a big night the evening before but he said, "I don't care, you're going!"

'Somehow I did OK and the local physio said no footballer had ever recorded such good stats, so I am not sure how I managed that.'

Taylor left Villa to succeed Bobby Robson and take up the England manager's job after the 1990 World Cup. It was a jolt to the club's progress.

There would be further sporadic triumphs over the next three decades, such as another runners-up finish under Ron Atkinson's management in 1992/93, and League Cup victories the following season and again in 1996 during Brian

Little's tenure. But never again would they experience the extreme highs of the early 1980s.

Another relegation to the second tier in 2016 was the latest reminder of how sorely missed the glory days are. Especially as clubs such as Manchester City and Chelsea, deemed inferior to Aston Villa not so long ago, seemingly grow forever stronger.

The seasons of 1980/81 and 1981/82 remain a source of pride to Villa supporters, who will always have something to be proud of no matter how painful the club's situation becomes. Yet as each decade goes by with further underachievement, frustration grows and some would be forgiven for wondering, 'How the hell did we get here, from where we once were?'

Aston Villa:
Seasons 1974 – 88

Season 1974/75

Aug 17	Division 2	A	York City	1-1	Graydon
Aug 20	Division 2	A	Hull City	1-1	Robson
Aug 24	Division 2	H	NORWICH CITY	1-1	Graydon
Aug 28	Division 2	H	HULL CITY	6-0	Morgan (3), Little, Hamilton, Graydon
Aug 31	Division 2	A	Bolton Wanderers	0-1	
Sep 04	Division 2	H	ORIENT	3-1	Graydon (2), Morgan
Sep 11	League Cup R2	H	EVERTON	1-1	Nicholl
Sep 14	Division 2	A	Bristol Rovers	0-2	
Sep 18	League Cup R2r	A	Everton	3-0	Morgan, Graydon, Carrodus
Sep 21	Division 2	H	MILLWALL	3-0	Graydon (3)
Sep 28	Division 2	A	Southampton	0-0	
Oct 02	Division 2	H	NOTTINGHAM FOREST	3-0	Leonard, Graydon, Hamilton
Oct 05	Division 2	A	Oldham Athletic	2-1	Hicks (og), Graydon
Oct 09	League Cup R3	A	Crewe	2-2	Morgan, Leonard
Oct 12	Division 2	H	BLACKPOOL	1-0	Graydon
Oct 16	League Cup R3r	H	CREWE	1-0	Hamilton
Oct 19	Division 2	A	Sunderland	0-0	
Oct 26	Division 2	H	SHEFFIELD WEDNESDAY	3-1	Graydon (pen), Nicholl, Phillips
Nov 02	Division 2	A	Fulham	1-3	Little
Nov 09	Division 2	H	NOTTS COUNTY	0-1	
Nov 12	League Cup R4	A	Hartlepool	1-1	Aitken
Nov 16	Division 2	A	Manchester Utd	1-2	Hamilton
Nov 23	Division 2	H	PORTSMOUTH	2-0	Hamilton, Little
Nov 25	League Cup R4r	H	HARTLEPOOL	6-1	Little (2), Graydon (2, 1pen), Hamilton (2, 1pen)
Nov 29	Division 2	H	OXFORD UNITED	0-0	
Dec 03	League Cup R5	A	Colchester United	2-1	Graydon, Little (Alan)
Dec 07	Division 2	A	Bristol City	0-1	
Dec 14	Division 2	H	YORK CITY	4-0	Graydon, Nicholl, Little, Hamilton
Dec 21	Division 2	A	West Bromwich Albion	0-2	
Dec 26	Division 2	H	BRISTOL ROVERS	1-0	Graydon
Dec 28	Division 2	A	Cardiff City	1-3	Hamilton
Jan 04	FA Cup R3	A	Oldham Athletic	3-0	Graydon, Nicholl, Little
Jan 11	Division 2	H	BRISTOL CITY	2-0	Little, Hamilton

Season 1974/75 Continued

Jan 15	League Cup SF	A	Chester	2-2	Graydon, McDonald
Jan 18	Division 2	A	Oxford United	2-1	Little, Nicholl
Jan 22	League Cup SF	H	CHESTER	3-2	Leonard (2), Little
Jan 25	FA Cup R4	H	SHEFFIELD UNITED	4-1	Leonard (2), Graydon, Nicholl
Feb 01	Division 2	A	Notts County	3-1	Little (2), Carrodus
Feb 08	Division 2	H	FULHAM	1-1	Nicholl
Feb 15	FA Cup R5	A	Ipswich Town	2-3	McDonald, (Alun Evans
Feb 18	Division 2	A	Portsmouth	3-2	Graydon, Little, Carrodus
Feb 22	Division 2	H	MANCHESTER UTD	2-0	Graydon, Aitken
Mar 01	League Cup F		Norwich City	1-0	Graydon
Mar 05	Division 2	H	BOLTON WANDERERS	0-0	
Mar 08	Division 2	A	Nottingham Forest	3-2	Little, Graydon (2)
Mar 15	Division 2	H	SOUTHAMPTON	3-0	Holmes (og), Graydon, Leonard
Mar 22	Division 2	A	Orient	0-1	
Mar 29	Division 2	H	WEST BROMWICH ALBION	3-1	Leonard (2), Hamilton
Apr 01	Division 2	A	Millwall	3-1	Leonard, Hamilton (pen), Little
Apr 09	Division 2	H	CARDIFF CITY	2-0	Little (2)
Apr 12	Division 2	H	OLDHAM	5-0	Little (3), Hicks (og), Hamilton
Apr 19	Division 2	A	Blackpool	3-0	Phillips, Little, Hatton (og)
Apr 23	Division 2	A	Sheffield Wednesday	4-0	Leonard, Ross (pen, Little (2)
Apr 26	Division 2	H	SUNDERLAND	2-0	Ross (pen), Little
Apr 30	Division 2	A	Norwich City	4-1	McDonald, Leonard, Gidman, Carrodus

Top Scorers League and Cup

Ray Graydon 27
Brian Little 24
Ian 'Chico' Hamilton 13
Keith Leonard 12

Season 1975/76

Aug 16	Division 1	H	LEEDS UNITED	1-2	Phillips
Aug 19	Division 1	A	QPR	1-1	Leonard
Aug 23	Division 1	A	Norwich City	3-5	Aitken, Graydon (2)
Aug 27	Division 1	H	MAN CITY	1-0	Leonard
Aug 30	Division 1	H	COVENTRY CITY	1-0	Graydon
Sep 06	Division 1	A	Newcastle United	0-3	
Sept 10	League Cup R2	H	OLDHAM	2-0	Nicholl, Leonard
Sept 13	Division 1	H	ARSENAL	2-0	Phillips, Leonard
Sept 17	UEFA R1	A	Royal Antwerp	1-4	Graydon
Sept 20	Division 1	A	Liverpool	0-3	
Sept 23	Division 1	A	Wolves	0-0	
Sept 27	Division 1	H	BIRMINGHAM CITY	2-1	Hamilton, Little
Oct 01	UEFA R1	H	ROYAL ANTWERP	0-1	
Oct 04	Division 1	A	Middlesbrough	0-0	
Oct 08	League Cup R3	H	MANCHESTER UTD	1-2	Gray
Oct 11	Division 1	H	TOTTENHAM HOTSPUR	1-1	Gray
Oct 18	Division 1	A	Everton	1-2	Nicholl
Oct 25	Division 1	H	BURNLEY	1-1	Noble (og)
Nov 01	Division 1	A	Ipswich Town	0-3	
Nov 08	Division 1	H	SHEFFIELD UNITED	5-1	Hamilton (2), Deehan, Gray Graydon
Nov 15	Division 1	A	Manchester Utd	0-2	
Nov 22	Division 1	H	EVERTON	3-1	Gray (2), McNaught (og)
Nov 29	Division 1	H	LEICESTER CITY	1-1	Graydon
Dec 06	Division 1	A	Stoke City	1-1	Graydon
Dec 13	Division 1	H	NORWICH CITY	3-2	Graydon, Deehan (2)
Dec 20	Division 1	A	Leeds United	0-1	
Dec 26	Division 1	H	WEST HAM UNITED	4-1	Deehan (2), Hamilton, Gray
Dec 27	Division 1	A	Derby County	0-2	
Jan 03	FA Cup R3	A	Southampton	1-1	Gray
Jan 07	FA Cup R3r	H	SOUTHAMPTON	1-2	Graydon
Jan 10	Division 1	A	Arsenal	0-0	
Jan 17	Division 1	H	NEWCASTLE UNITED	1-1	Mahoney (og)
Jan 31	Division 1	H	QPR	0-2	

Season 1975/76 Continued

Feb 07	Division 1	A	Manchester City	1-2	Gray
Feb 14	Division 1	A	Sheffield United	1-2	Graydon
Feb 21	Division 1	H	MANCHESTER UTD	2-1	Gray, McDonald
Feb 24	Division 1	H	WOLVES	1-1	Graydon (pen)
Feb 28	Division 1	A	Burnley	2-2	Gray, Graydon
Mar 06	Division 1	H	IPSWICH TOWN	0-0	
Mar 13	Division 1	A	Tottenham Hotspur	2-5	Graydon, Gray
Mar 20	Division 1	A	Leicester City	2-2	Nicholl (2), (Nicholl also scored 2 og's)
Mar 27	Division 1	H	STOKE CITY	0-0	
Apr 03	Division 1	A	Birmingham City	2-3	Graydon (pen), Gray
Apr 10	Division 1	H	LIVERPOOL	0-0	
Apr 13	Division 1	A	Coventry City	1-1	Nicholl
Apr 17	Division 1	A	West Ham United	2-2	Deehan, Hunt
Apr 19	Division 1	H	DERBY COUNTY	1-0	McDonald
Apr 24	Division 1	H	MIDDLESBROUGH	2-1	Deehan, Carrodus

Top Scorers League and Cup

| Ray Graydon 14 |
| Andy Gray 12 |
| John Deehan 7 |
| Chris Nicholl 5 |

Season 1976/77

Aug 21	Division 1	H	WEST HAM UNITED	4-0	Graydon (2, 1 pen), Gray (2)
Aug 25	Division 1	A	Manchester City	0-2	
Aug 28	Division 1	A	Everton	2-0	Lyons (og), Little
Sep 01	League Cup R2	H	MANCHESTER CITY	3-0	
Sep 04	Division 1	H	IPSWICH TOWN	5-2	Graydon, Gray (3), Little
Sep 11	Division 1	A	QPR	1-2	Gray
Sep 18	Division 1	H	BIRMINGHAM CITY	1-2	Gray
Sep 21	League Cup R3	H	NORWICH CITY	2-1	Gray (2)
Sep 25	Division 1	H	LEICESTER CITY	2-0	Graydon (pen), Gray
Oct 02	Division 1	A	Stoke City	0-1	
Oct 16	Division 1	A	Sunderland	1-0	Cropley
Oct 20	Division 1	H	ARSENAL	5-1	Mortimer, Gray (2), Little, Graydon
Oct 23	Division 1	H	BRISTOL CITY	3-1	Gidman, Graydon, Nicholl
Oct 27	League Cup R4	H	WREXHAM	5-1	Little (2), Carrodus, Nicholl, Gray
Oct 30	Division 1	A	Liverpool	0-3	
Nov 06	Division 1	H	MANCHESTER UTD	3-2	Gray (2), Mortimer
Nov 10	Division 1	A	West Bromwich Albion	1-1	Mortimer
Nov 20	Division 1	H	COVENTRY CITY	2-2	Gidman, Gray
Nov 27	Division 1	A	Norwich City	1-1	Little
Dec 01	League Cup R5	H	MILLWALL	2-0	Little, Nicholl
Dec 11	Division 1	A	Leeds United	3-1	Gray (2), Cropley
Dec 15	Division 1	H	LIVERPOOL	5-1	Gray (2), Deehan (2), Little
Dec 18	Division 1	H	NEWCASTLE UNITED	2-1	Deehan (2)
Dec 27	Division 1	A	Middlesbrough	2-3	Gray, Hughes
Jan 01	Division 1	A	Manchester Utd	0-2	
Jan 08	FA Cup R3	A	Leicester City	1-0	Gray
Jan 22	Division 1	A	West Ham United	1-0	Gray
Jan 29	FA Cup R4	H	WEST HAM UNITED	3-0	Mortimer, Deehan (2)
Feb 01	League Cup SF	A	QPR	0-0	
Feb 05	Division 1	H	EVERTON	2-0	Gray, Little
Feb 12	Division 1	A	Ipswich Town	0-1	
Feb 16	League Cup SF	H	QPR	2-2	Deehan (2)
Feb 22	League Cup SFr		QPR	3-0	Little (3)

Season 1976/77 Continued

Feb 26	FA Cup R5	H	PORT VALE	3-0	Little, Nicholl, Deehan
Mar 02	Division 1	H	DERBY COUNTY	4-0	Mortimer, Little, Gidman, Cowans
Mar 05	Division 1	A	Leicester City	1-1	Deehan
Mar 12	League Cup F		Everton	0-0	
Mar 16	League Cup Fr1		Everton	1-1	Kenyon (og)
Mar 19	FA Cup R6	A	Manchester Utd	1-2	Little
Mar 23	Division 1	H	SUNDERLAND	4-1	Gray, Gidman, Deehan (2)
Apr 02	Division 1	A	Bristol City	0-0	
Apr 05	Division 1	H	MIDDLESBROUGH	1-0	Deehan
Apr 09	Division 1	A	Derby County	1-2	Little
Apr 13	League Cup Fr2		Everton	3-2	Little (2), Nicholl
Apr 16	Division 1	A	Coventry City	3-2	Cowans, Deehan, Little
Apr 20	Division 1	H	TOTTENHAM HOTSPUR	2-1	Little, Deehan
Apr 23	Division 1	H	NORWICH CITY	1-0	Little
Apr 25	Division 1	A	Arsenal	0-3	
Apr 30	Division 1	A	Tottenham Hotspur	1-3	Deehan
May 04	Division 1	H	MANCHESTER CITY	1-1	Little
May 07	Division 1	H	LEEDS UNITED	2-1	Deehan, Cropley
May 10	Division 1	A	Birmingham City	1-2	Deehan
May 14	Division 1	A	Newcastle United	2-3	Little (2)
May 16	Division 1	H	STOKE CITY	1-0	Gray (pen)
May 20	Division 1	H	QPR	1-1	Cowans
May 23	Division 1	H	WEST BROMWICH ALBION	4-0	Gray (3), Nicholl

Top Scorers League and Cup

Andy Gray 29
Brian Little 24
John Deehan 18
Chris Nicholl / Ray Graydon 6

Season 1977/78

Aug 20	Division 1	A	QPR	2-1	Webb (og), Carrodus
Aug 24	Division 1	H	MAN CITY	1-4	Deehan
Aug 27	Division 1	H	EVERTON	1-2	Gray
Aug 31	League Cup R2	A	Exeter City	3-1	Gray (3)
Sep 03	Division 1	A	Bristol City	1-1	Little
Sep 10	Division 1	H	ARSENAL	1-0	Cropley
Sep 14	UEFA R1	H	FENERBAHCE	4-0	Little, Gray, Deehan (2)
Sep 17	Division 1	A	Nottingham Forest	0-2	
Sep 23	Division 1	H	WOLVES	2-0	Deehan, Brazier (og)
Sep 28	UEFA R1	A	Fenerbahce	2-0	Little, Deehan
Oct 01	Division 1	H	BIRMINGHAM	0-1	
Oct 05	Division 1	A	Leeds United	1-1	Gray
Oct 08	Division 1	A	Leicester City	2-0	Cowans, Gray
Oct 15	Division 1	H	NORWICH CITY	3-0	Gray, Cowans, Little
Oct 19	UEFA R2	H	GORNIK ZABRZE	2-0	McNaught (2)
Oct 22	Division 1	A	West Ham United	2-2	Gray, McNaught
Oct 26	League Cup R3	H	QPR	1-0	Gray (pen)
Oct 29	Division 1	H	MANCHESTER UTD	2-1	Cropley, Gray
Nov 02	UEFA R2	A	Gornik Zabrze	1-1	Gray
Nov 05	Division 1	A	Liverpool	2-1	Gray (2)
Nov 12	Division 1	H	MIDDLESBROUGH	0-1	
Nov 19	Division 1	A	Chelsea	0-0	
Nov 23	UEFA R3	H	ATHLETIC BILBAO	2-0	Iribar (og), Deehan
Nov 29	League Cup R4	A	Nottingham Forest	2-4	Carrodus, Little
Dec 03	Division 1	A	Ipswich Town	0-2	
Dec 07	UEFA R3	A	Athletic Bilbao	1-1	Mortimer
Dec 10	Division 1	H	WEST BROMWICH ALBION	3-0	Gray, Cowans, Gidman
Dec 17	Division 1	A	Middlesbrough	0-1	
Dec 26	Division 1	H	COVENTRY CITY	1-1	Deehan
Dec 27	Division 1	A	Derby County	3-0	Little, Gray, Deehan
Dec 31	Division 1	A	Manchester City	0-2	
Jan 02	Division 1	H	QPR	1-1	Little
Jan 07	FA Cup R3	A	Everton Division 1	1-4	Gray

Season 1977/78 Continued

Jan 14	Division 1	A	Everton	0-1	
Jan 28	Division 1	H	BRISTOL CITY	1-0	Deehan
Feb 04	Division 1	A	Arsenal	1-0	MacDonald (og)
Feb 25	Division 1	A	Birmingham City	0-1	
Mar 01	UEFA QF	H	BARCELONA	2-2	McNaught, Deehan
Mar 04	Division 1	H	LEICESTER CITY	0-0	
Mar 11	Division 1	A	Norwich City	1-2	Gregory
Mar 15	UEFA QF	A	Barcelona	1-2	Little
Mar 18	Division 1	H	WEST HAM UNITED	4-1	Gregory (2), Deehan, Mortimer
Mar 21	Division 1	A	Coventry City	3-2	McNaught, Little, Gray
Mar 25	Division 1	H	DERBY COUNTY	0-0	
Mar 29	Division 1	A	Manchester Utd	1-1	Deehan
Apr 01	Division 1	H	LIVERPOOL	0-3	
Apr 05	Division 1	H	NOTTINGHAM FOREST	0-1	
Apr 08	Division 1	A	Newcastle United	1-1	Evans
Apr 15	Division 1	H	CHELSEA	2-0	Wicks (og), Cowans
Apr 17	Division 1	H	NEWCASTLE UNITED	2-0	Gray, Cowans
Apr 22	Division 1	A	West Bromwich Albion	3-0	Mortimer, Cowans, Deehan
Apr 26	Division 1	H	LEEDS UNITED	3-1	Deehan, Little, Mortimer
Apr 29	Division 1	H	IPSWICH TOWN	6-1	Deehan (2), Cowans, Carrodus, Little, Gray
May 02	Division 1	A	Wolves	1-3	Carrodus

Top Scorers League and Cup

Andy Gray 20
John Deehan 16
Brian Little 11
Gordon Cowans 7

Season 1978/79

Aug 19	Division 1	H	WOLVES	1-0	Gray
Aug 23	Division 1	A	Tottenham Hotspur	4-1	Shelton, Little, Evans, Gregory
Aug 26	Division 1	A	Bristol City	0-1	
Aug 30	League Cup R2	H	SHEFFIELD WEDNESDAY	1-0	Shelton
Sept 02	Division 1	H	SOUTHAMPTON	1-1	Gray
Sept 09	Division 1	A	Ipswich Town	2-0	Gregory, Gray (pen)
Sept 16	Division 1	H	EVERTON	1-1	Craig
Sept 23	Division 1	A	QPR	0-1	
Sept 30	Division 1	H	NOTTINGHAM FOREST	1-2	Craig (pen)
Oct 04	League Cup R3	H	CRYSTAL PALACE	1-1	Little
Oct 07	Division 1	A	Arsenal	1-1	Gregory
Oct 10	League Cup R3r1	A	Crystal Palace	0-0	
Oct 14	Division 1	H	MANCHESTER UTD	2-2	Gregory (2)
Oct 16	League Cup R3r2	N	Crystal Palace	3-0	Gregory, Gray (2)
Oct 21	Division 1	A	Birmingham City	1-0	Gray
Oct 27	Division 1	H	MIDDLESBROUGH	0-2	
Nov 04	Division 1	H	MANCHESTER CITY	1-1	Deehan
Nov 08	League Cup R4	H	LUTON TOWN	0-2	
Nov 11	Division 1	A	Wolves	4-0	Shelton, McNaught, Deehan, Mortimer
Nov 18	Division 1	H	BRISTOL CITY	2-0	Deehan, Cowans
Nov 21	Division 1	A	Southampton	0-2	
Nov 25	Division 1	A	West Bromwich Albion	1-1	Evans
Dec 09	Division 1	A	Chelsea	1-0	Evans
Dec 16	Division 1	H	NORWICH CITY	1-1	McGuire (og)
Dec 23	Division 1	A	Derby County	0-0	
Dec 26	Division 1	H	LEEDS UNITED	2-2	Gregory (2)
Jan 10	FA Cup R3	A	Nottingham Forest	0-2	
Jan 31	Division 1	A	Everton	1-1	Shelton
Feb 24	Division 1	A	Manchester Utd	1-1	Swain
Mar 03	Division 1	H	BIRMINGHAM CITY	1-0	Cowans
Mar 07	Division 1	H	BOLTON WANDERERS	3-0	Swain, Gray, Jones (og)
Mar 10	Division 1	A	Middlesbrough	0-2	
Mar 20	Division 1	H	QPR	3-1	Gidman (pen), Mortimer, Evans

Season 1978/79 *Continued*

Mar 24	Division 1	H	TOTTENHAM HOTSPUR	2-3	Gidman (pen), Gray
Mar 28	Division 1	H	COVENTRY CITY	1-1	Evans
Apr 04	Division 1	A	Nottingham Forest	0-4	
Apr 07	Division 1	A	Coventry City	1-1	Deehan
Apr 11	Division 1	H	DERBY COUNTY	3-3	Cowans (2), Gidman (pen)
Apr 14	Division 1	A	Leeds United	0-1	
Apr 16	Division 1	H	LIVERPOOL	3-1	Evans, Thompson (og), Deehan
Apr 21	Division 1	A	Norwich City	2-1	Shelton, Cropley
Apr 25	Division 1	H	ARSENAL	5-1	Deehan (2), Shelton (3, 1 pen)
Apr 28	Division 1	H	CHELSEA	2-1	G. Wilkins (og), Swain
May 02	Division 1	H	IPSWICH TOWN	2-2	Swain, Deehan
May 05	Division 1	A	Bolton Wanderers	0-0	
May 08	Division 1	A	Liverpool	0-3	
May 11	Division 1	H	WEST BROMWICH ALBION	0-1	
May 15	Division 1	A	Manchester City	3-2	Cropley, Mortimer, Deehan

Top Scorers League and Cup

John Deehan 9

Andy Gray / John Gregory / Gary Shelton 8

Season 1979/80

Aug 18	Division 1	A	Bolton Wanderers	1-1	Cowans
Aug 22	Division 1	H	BRIGHTON	2-1	Evans (pen), Morley
Aug 25	Division 1	H	BRISTOL CITY	0-2	
Aug 28	League Cup R2		Colchester United	2-0	Shaw (2)
Sept 01	Division 1	A	Everton	1-1	Morley
Sept 05	League Cup R2	H	COLCHESTER UNITED	0-2	(Villa won 9-8 on pens)
Sept 08	Division 1	H	MANCHESTER UTD	0-3	
Sept 15	Division 1	A	Crystal Palace	0-2	
Sept 22	Division 1	H	ARSENAL	0-0	
Sept 25	League Cup R3	H	EVERTON	0-0	
Sept 29	Division 1	A	Middlesbrough	0-0	
Oct 06	Division 1	H	SOUTHAMPTON	3-0	Bremner, Mortimer, Evans (pen)
Oct 09	League Cup R3r	A	Everton	1-4	Swain
Oct 13	Division 1	H	WEST BROMWICH ALBION	0-0	
Oct 20	Division 1	A	Derby County	3-1	Little, Shaw, Mortimer
Oct 27	Division 1	A	Wolves	1-1	Shaw
Nov 03	Division 1	H	BOLTON WANDERERS	3-1	Shaw, Evans, Mortimer
Nov 10	Division 1	A	Ipswich Town	0-0	
Nov 17	Division 1	H	STOKE CITY	2-1	Mortimer, Evans (pen)
Nov 24	Division 1	H	LEEDS UNITED	0-0	
Dec 01	Division 1	A	Norwich City	1-1	Evans
Dec 08	Division 1	H	LIVERPOOL	1-3	Little
Dec 15	Division 1	A	Tottenham Hotspur	2-1	Geddis, Cowans (pen)
Dec 19	Division 1	H	COVENTRY CITY	3-0	Donovan, Little (2)
Dec 26	Division 1	A	Nottingham Forest	1-2	Shaw
Dec 29	Division 1	A	Bristol City	3-1	Shaw (3)
Jan 04	FA Cup R3	A	Bristol Rovers	2-1	Shaw, Cowans
Jan 12	Division 1	H	EVERTON	2-1	Gibson, Donovan
Jan 26	FA Cup R4	A	Cambridge United	1-1	Donovan
Jan 30	FA Cup R4r	H	CAMBRIDGE UNITED	4-1	Donovan (2), Evans, Little
Feb 02	Division 1	H	CRYSTAL PALACE	2-0	Cowans, Mortimer

Season 1979/80 *Continued*

Feb 09	Division 1	A	Arsenal	1-3	Mortimer
Feb 16	FA Cup R5	A	Blackburn Rovers	1-1	Geddis
Feb 20	FA Cup R5r	H	BLACKBURN ROVERS	1-0	Evans
Feb 23	Division 1	A	West Bromwich Albion	2-1	McNaught, Little
Feb 27	Division 1	H	MANCHESTER CITY	2-2	Shaw, Donachie (og)
Mar 01	Division 1	H	DERBY COUNTY	1-0	Evans
Mar 03	Division 1	A	Brighton & Hove Albion	1-1	Evans
Mar 08	FA Cup R6	A	West Ham United	0-1	
Mar 10	Division 1	H	WOLVES	1-3	Shaw
Mar 15	Division 1	A	Southampton	0-2	
Mar 19	Division 1	H	MIDDLESBROUGH	0-2	
Mar 22	Division 1	H	IPSWICH TOWN	1-1	Morley
Mar 26	Division 1	H	NORWICH CITY	2-0	Cowans (pen), Hopkins
Mar 29	Division 1	A	Stoke City	0-2	
Apr 05	Division 1	H	NOTTINGHAM FOREST	3-2	Bremner, Evans, Lloyd (og)
Apr 07	Division 1	A	Manchester City	1-1	Geddis
Apr 19	Division 1	A	Leeds United	0-0	
Apr 23	Division 1	A	Manchester United	1-2	Bremner
Apr 26	Division 1	H	TOTTENHAM HOTSPUR	1-0	Cowans
Apr 29	Division 1	A	Coventry City	2-1	Gibson, Cowans (pen)
May 03	Division 1	A	Liverpool	1-4	Cohen (og)

Top Scorers League and Cup

Gary Shaw 12
Allan Evans 10
Gordon Cowans 7
Brian Little / Dennis Mortimer 6

Season 1980/81

Aug 16	Division 1	A	Leeds United	2-1	Morley, Shaw
Aug 20	Division 1	H	NORWICH CITY	1-0	Shaw
Aug 23	Division 1	A	Manchester City	2-2	Withe (2)
Aug 27	League Cup R2	H	LEEDS UNITED	1-0	Morley
Aug 30	Division 1	H	COVENTRY CITY	1-0	Shaw
Sept 03	League Cup R2	A	Leeds United	3-1	Withe, Shaw (2)
Sept 06	Division 1	A	Ipswich Town	0-1	
Sept 13	Division 1	H	EVERTON	0-2	
Sept 20	Division 1	H	WOLVES	2-1	Hughes (og), Geddis
Sept 23	League Cup R3	A	Cambridge United	1-2	Morley
Sept 27	Division 1	A	Crystal Palace	1-0	Shaw
Oct 04	Division 1	H	SUNDERLAND	4-0	Evans (2), Morley, Shaw
Oct 08	Division 1	A	Manchester United	3-3	Withe, Cowans (pen), Shaw
Oct 11	Division 1	A	Birmingham City	2-1	Cowans (pen), Evans
Oct 18	Division 1	H	TOTTENHAM HOTSPUR	3-0	Morley (2), Withe
Oct 22	Division 1	H	BRIGHTON & HOVE ALBION	4-1	Motimer, Withe, Bremner, Shaw
Oct 25	Division 1	A	Southampton	2-1	Morley, Withe
Nov 01	Division 1	H	LEICESTER CITY	2-0	Shaw, Cowans
Nov 08	Division 1	A	West Bromwich Albion	0-0	
Nov 12	Division 1	A	Norwich City	3-1	Shaw (2), Evans
Nov 15	Division 1	H	LEEDS UNITED	1-1	Shaw
Nov 22	Division 1	A	Liverpool	1-2	Evans
Nov 29	Division 1	H	ARSENAL	1-1	Morley
Dec 06	Division 1	A	Middlesbrough	1-2	Shaw
Dec 13	Division 1	H	BIRMINGHAM CITY	3-0	Geddis (2), Shaw
Dec 20	Division 1	A	Brighton & Hove Albion	0-1	
Dec 26	Division 1	H	STOKE CITY	1-0	Withe
Dec 27	Division 1	A	Nottingham Forest	2-2	Lloyd (og), Shaw
Jan 03	FA Cup R3	A	Ipswich Town	0-1	
Jan 10	Division 1	H	LIVERPOOL	2-0	Withe, Mortimer
Jan 17	Division 1	A	Coventry City	2-1	Morley, Withe
Jan 31	Division 1	H	MANCHESTER CITY	1-0	Shaw
Feb 07	Division 1	A	Everton	3-1	Morley, Mortimer, Cowans (pen)

Season 1980/81 *Continued*

Feb 21	Division 1	H	CRYSTAL PALACE	2-1	Withe 2
Feb 28	Division 1	A	Wolves	1-0	Withe
Mar 07	Division 1	A	Sunderland	2-1	Evans, Mortimer
Mar 14	Division 1	H	MANCHESTER UNITED	3-3	Withe (2), Shaw
Mar 21	Division 1	A	Tottenham Hotspur	0-2	
Mar 28	Division 1	H	SOUTHAMPTON	2-1	Morley, Geddis
Apr 04	Division 1	A	Leicester City	4-2	Withe (2), Bremner, Morley
Apr 08	Division 1	H	WEST BROMWICH ALBION	1-0	Withe
Apr 14	Division 1	H	IPSWICH TOWN	1-2	Shaw
Apr 18	Division 1	H	NOTTINGHAM FOREST	2-0	Cowans (pen), Withe
Apr 20	Division 1	A	Stoke City	1-1	Withe
Apr 25	Division 1	H	MIDDLESBROUGH	3-0	Shaw, Withe, Evans
May 02	Division 1	A	Arsenal	0-2	

Top Scorers League and Cup

| Peter Withe 21 |
| Gary Shaw 20 |
| Tony Morley 12 |
| Allan Evans 7 |

Season 1981/82

Aug 21	Charity Shield	N	Tottenham Hotspur	2-2	Withe (2)
Aug 29	Division 1	H	NOTTS COUNTY	0-1	
Sept 02	Division 1	A	Sunderland	1-2	
Sept 05	Division 1	A	Tottenham Hotspur	3-1	Donovan (2), Mortimer
Sept 12	Division 1	H	MANCHESTER UTD	1-1	Cowans
Sept 16	European Cup R1	H	FC VALUR	5-0	Morley, Withe (2), Donovan (2)
Sept 19	Division 1	A	Liverpool	0-0	
Sept 23	Division 1	H	STOKE CITY	2-2	Withe (2)
Sept 26	Division 1	H	BIRMINGHAM CITY	0-0	
Sept 30	European Cup R1	A	FC Valur	2-0	Shaw (2)
Oct 03	Division 1	A	Leeds United	1-1	Shaw
Oct 07	League Cup R2	H	WOLVES	3-2	Bremner, Morley, Blair
Oct 10	Division 1	A	Coventry City	1-1	Shaw
Oct 17	Division 1	H	WEST HAM UNITED	3-2	Morley, Geddis, Mortimer
Oct 21	European Cup R2	A	Dynamo Berlin	2-1	Morley (2)
Oct 24	Division 1	A	Wolves	3-0	Shaw (2), Palmer (og)
Oct 27	League Cup R2	A	Wolves	2-1	Cowans (2), (1 pen)
Oct 31	Division 1	H	IPSWICH TOWN	0-1	
Nov 04	European Cup R2	H	DYNAMO BERLIN	0-1	
Nov 07	Division 1	H	ARSENAL	0-2	
Nov 11	League Cup R3	A	Leicester City	0-0	
Nov 21	Division 1	A	Middlesbrough	3-3	Withe, Cowans, Shaw
Nov 25	League Cup R3r	H	LEICESTER CITY	2-0	Cowans (pen), Withe
Nov 28	Division 1	H	NOTTINGHAM FOREST	3-1	Bremner (2), Withe
Dec 01	League Cup R4	A	Wigan Athletic	2-1	Cowans (pen), Withe
Dec 05	Division 1	A	Manchester City	0-1	
Dec 15	Division 1	A	Swansea City	1-2	Thompson (og)
Dec 19	Division 1	A	Everton	0-2	
Dec 28	Division 1	A	Brighton & Hove Albion	1-0	Morley
Jan 05	FA Cup R3	A	Notts County	6-0	Richards (og), Shaw, Geddis (3), Cowans (pen)
Jan 16	Division 1	A	Notts County	0-1	
Jan 20	League Cup R5	H	WEST BROMWICH ALBION	0-1	
Jan 23	FA Cup R4	A	Bristol City	1-0	Shaw
Jan 30	Division 1	H	LIVERPOOL	0-3	

Season 1981/82 *Continued*

Feb 02	Division 1	H	SUNDERLAND	1-0	Geddis
Feb 06	Division 1	A	Manchester United	1-4	Geddis

New Manager: Tony Barton

Feb 10	Division 1	H	SOUTHAMPTON	1-1	Withe
Feb 13	FA Cup R5	A	Tottenham Hotspur	0-1	
Feb 17	Division 1	H	TOTTENHAM HOTSPUR	1-1	Withe
Feb 20	Division 1	A	Birmingham City	1-0	Withe
Feb 27	Division 1	H	COVENTRY CITY	2-1	Cowans (pen), Shaw
Mar 03	European Cup QF	A	Dinamo Kiev	0-0	
Mar 06	Division 1	A	West Ham United	2-2	Cowans, Withe
Mar 13	Division 1	H	WOLVES	3-1	Donovan, Morley, Shaw
Mar 17	European Cup QF	H	DINAMO KIEV	2-0	Shaw, McNaught
Mar 20	Division 1	A	Ipswich Town	1-3	McNaught
Mar 27	Division 1	A	Arsenal	3-4	Shaw, Morley, Heard
Mar 30	Division 1	H	WEST BROMWICH ALBION	2-1	Shaw, Withe
Apr 07	European Cup SF	H	ANDERLECHT	1-0	Morley
Apr 10	Division 1	A	Southampton	3-0	Nicholl (og), McNaught, Morley
Apr 12	Division 1	H	BRIGHTON	3-0	Geddis (2), Evans
Apr 17	Division 1	H	MIDDLESBROUGH	1-0	Evans
Apr 21	European Cup SF	A	Anderlecht	0-0	
Apr 24	Division 1	A	Nottingham Forest	1-1	Cowans (pen)
Apr 28	Division 1	H	LEEDS UNITED	1-4	Geddis
May 01	Division 1	H	MANCHESTER CITY	0-0	
May 05	Division 1	A	Stoke City	0-1	
May 08	Division 1	A	West Bromwich Albion	1-0	Heard
May 15	Division 1	H	EVERTON	1-2	Cowans
May 21	Division 1	H	SWANSEA CITY	3-0	Morley, Bremner, Withe
May 26	European Cup F	N	Bayern Munich	1-0	Withe

Top Scorers League and Cup

Peter Withe 17
Gary Shaw 14
Gordon Cowans / Tony Morley 11
David Geddis 7

Season 1982/83

Date	Competition		Opponent	Score	Scorers
Aug 28	Division 1	H	SUNDERLAND	1-3	Cowans
Aug 31	Division 1	A	Everton	0-5	
Sep 04	Division 1	A	Southampton	0-1	
Sep 08	Division 1	H	LUTON TOWN	4-1	Mortimer, Withe, Cowans (2 pens)
Sep 11	Division 1	H	NOTTINGHAM FOREST	4-1	Mortimer, Withe (2), Cowans (pen)
Sep 15	European Cup R1	H	BESIKTAS	3-1	Withe, Morley, Mortimer
Sep 18	Division 1	A	Manchester City	1-0	Shaw
Sep 25	Division 1	H	SWANSEA CITY	2-0	Mortimer, Evans
Sep 29	European Cup R1	A	Besiktas	0-0	
Oct 02	Division 1	A	West Bromwich Albion	0-1	
Oct 06	League Cup R2	H	NOTTS COUNTY	1-2	Withe
Oct 09	Division 1	A	Notts County	1-4	Shaw
Oct 16	Division 1	H	WATFORD	3-0	Withe, Morley (2)
Oct 20	European Cup R2	A	Dinamo Bucharest	2-0	Shaw (2)
Oct 23	Division 1	A	Norwich City	0-1	
Oct 26	League Cup R2	A	Notts County	0-1	
Oct 30	Division 1	H	TOTTENHAM HOTSPUR	4-0	Cowans (2, 1 pen), Morley, Shaw
Nov 03	European Cup R2	H	DINAMO BUCHAREST	4-2	Shaw (3), Walters
Nov 06	Division 1	A	Coventry City	0-0	
Nov 13	Division 1	H	BRIGHTON & HOVE ALBION	1-0	Withe
Nov 20	Division 1	H	MANCHESTER UTD	2-1	Shaw, Withe
Nov 27	Division 1	A	Stoke City	3-0	Parkin (og), Shaw (2)
Dec 04	Division 1	H	WEST HAM UNITED	1-0	Cowans (pen)
Dec 07	Division 1	A	Arsenal	1-2	McNaught
Dec 12	Intercontinental Cup	N	Penarol	0-2	
Dec 18	Division 1	H	LIVERPOOL	2-4	Shaw, Withe
Dec 27	Division 1	A	Birmingham City	0-3	
Dec 29	Division 1	H	IPSWICH TOWN	1-1	Withe
Jan 01	Division 1	A	Manchester United	1-3	Cowans (pen)
Jan 03	Division 1	H	SOUTHAMPTON	2-0	Cowans (pen), Evans
Jan 08	FA Cup R3	A	Northampton Town	1-0	Walters
Jan 15	Division 1	A	Sunderland	0-2	
Jan 19	European Super Cup	A	Barcelona	0-1	

Season 1982/83 *Continued*

Jan 22	Division 1	H	MANCHESTER CITY	1-1	Shaw
Jan 26	European Super Cup	H	BARCELONA	3-0	Shaw, Cowans, McNaught
Jan 29	FA Cup R4	H	WOLVES	1-0	Withe
Feb 05	Division 1	A	Nottingham Forest	2-1	Withe (2)
Feb 12	Division 1	H	EVERTON	2-0	Morley, Withe
Feb 19	FA Cup R5	H	WATFORD	4-1	Shaw, Morley, Gibson, Cowans
Feb 26	Division 1	A	Watford	1-2	Walters
Mar 02	European Cup QF	H	JUVENTUS	1-2	Cowans
Mar 05	Division 1	H	NORWICH CITY	3-2	Withe, Deacy, Shaw
Mar 08	Division 1	H	NOTTS COUNTY	2-0	Withe, Shaw
Mar 12	FA Cup R6	A	Arsenal	0-2	
Mar 16	European Cup QF	A	Juventus	1-3	Withe
Mar 19	Division 1	H	COVENTRY CITY	4-0	Shaw, Withe
Mar 23	Division 1	A	Tottenham Hotspur	0-2	
Mar 26	Division 1	A	Brighton & Hove Albion	0-0	
Apr 02	Division 1	A	Ipswich Town	2-1	Shaw, Withe
Apr 04	Division 1	H	BIRMINGHAM CITY	1-0	Shaw
Apr 09	Division 1	A	Luton Town	1-2	Shaw
Apr 19	Division 1	H	WEST BROMWICH ALBION	1-0	Mortimer
Apr 23	Division 1	A	West Ham United	0-2	
Apr 30	Division 1	H	STOKE CITY	4-0	Cowans, McNaught, Morley, Evans
May 02	Division 1	A	Swansea City	1-2	Shaw
May 07	Division 1	A	Liverpool	1-1	Shaw (pen)
May 14	Division 1	H	ARSENAL	2-1	Shaw, Gibson

Top Scorers League and Cup

Gary Shaw 24
Peter Withe 20
Gordon Cowans 13
Tony Morley 7

Season 1983/84

Aug 27	Division 1	H	WEST BROMWICH ALBION	4-3	Evans, Walters, Shaw, Ormsby
Aug 29	Division 1	H	SUNDERLAND	1-0	Walters
Sep 03	Division 1	A	QPR	1-2	Withe
Sep 07	Division 1	A	Nottingham Forest	2-2	Withe, Shaw
Sep 10	Division 1	H	NORWICH CITY	1-0	Mortimer
Sep 14	UEFA Cup R1	A	Vitoria Guimaraes	0-1	
Sep 17	Division 1	A	Liverpool	1-2	Gibson
Sep 24	Division 1	H	SOUTHAMPTON	1-0	Withe
Sep 28	UEFA Cup R1	H	VITORIA GUIMARAES	5-0	Withe 3, Ormsby, Gibson
Oct 01	Division 1	A	Luton Town	0-1	
Oct 04	League Cup R2	A	Portsmouth	2-2	Gibson, Evans
Oct 15	Division 1	H	BIRMINGHAM CITY	1-0	Withe
Oct 19	UEFA Cup R2	A	Spartak Moscow	2-2	Gibson, Walters
Oct 23	Division 1	A	Wolves	1-1	Withe
Oct 26	League Cup R2	H	PORTSMOUTH	3-2	Evans (pen), Withe, Walters
Oct 29	Division 1	H	ARSENAL	2-6	Morley, Evans (pen)
Nov 02	UEFA Cup R2	H	SPARTAK MOSCOW	1-2	Withe
Nov 05	Division 1	A	Manchester United	2-1	Withe (2)
Nov 09	League Cup R3	H	MANCHESTER CITY	3-0	Gibson, Evans, Mortimer
Nov 12	Division 1	H	STOKE CITY	1-1	Withe
Nov 19	Division 1	H	LEICESTER CITY	3-1	Withe, Rideout, McMahon
Nov 26	Division 1	A	Notts County	2-5	Mortimer, Evans (pen)
Nov 30	League Cup R4	A	West Bromwich Albion	2-1	Walters, Mortimer
Dec 03	Division 1	H	WEST HAM UNITED	1-0	Rideout
Dec 10	Division 1	A	Everton	1-1	Rideout
Dec 17	Division 1	H	IPSWICH TOWN	4-0	Withe, Rideout, McMahon, Evans (pen)
Dec 26	Division 1	A	Watford	2-3	Curbishley, Walters
Dec 27	Division 1	H	TOTTENHAM HOTSPUR	0-0	
Dec 31	Division 1	H	QPR	2-1	Evans (pen), McMahon
Jan 02	Division 1	A	Southampton	2-2	McMahon, Shaw
Jan 07	FA Cup R3	H	NORWICH CITY	1-1	Withe
Jan 11	FA Cup R3r	A	Norwich City	0-3	
Jan 14	Division 1	A	West Bromwich Albion	1-3	Shaw

Season 1983/84 *Continued*

Jan 17	League Cup R5		Norwich City	2-0	Shaw, Rideout
Jan 20	Division 1	H	LIVERPOOL	1-3	Mortimer
Feb 04	Division 1	H	LUTON TOWN	0-0	
Feb 11	Division 1	A	Norwich City	1-3	Shaw
Feb 15	League Cup SF	A	Everton	0-2	
Feb 18	Division 1	A	Arsenal	1-1	Evans (pen)
Feb 22	League Cup SF	H	EVERTON	1-0	Rideout
Feb 25	Division 1	H	WOLVES	4-0	Withe (2), Birch, Walters
Mar 03	Division 1	H	MANCHESTER UNITED	0-3	
Mar 10	Division 1	A	Stoke City	0-1	
Mar 13	Division 1	A	Coventry City	3-3	Evans (pen), Withe, Rideout
Mar 17	Division 1	H	NOTTINGHAM FOREST	1-0	McMahon
Mar 24	Division 1	A	Sunderland	1-0	Walters
Mar 31	Division 1	A	Birmingham City	1-2	Withe
Apr 07	Division 1	H	COVENTRY CITY	2-0	Ormsby, Birch
Apr 14	Division 1	A	Leicester City	0-2	
Apr 18	Division 1	A	Tottenham Hotspur	1-2	Walters
Apr 21	Division 1	H	WATFORD	2-1	Mortimer, Foster
Apr 28	Division 1	H	NOTTS COUNTY	3-1	Walters (2), Withe
May 05	Division 1	A	West Ham United	1-0	Mortimer
May 07	Division 1	H	EVERTON	0-2	
May 12	Division 1	A	Ipswich Town	1-2	Withe

Top Scorers League and Cup

Peter Withe 22
Mark Walters 11
Allan Evans 10
Paul Rideout / Dennis Mortimer 7

Season 1984/85

Aug 25	Division 1	H	COVENTRY CITY	1-0	Bremner
Aug 27	Division 1	A	Stoke City	3-1	Walters (2), Withe
Sep 01	Division 1	A	Newcastle United	0-3	
Sep 05	Division 1	H	NOTTINGHAM FOREST	0-5	
Sep 08	Division 1	H	CHELSEA	4-2	Withe (2), Foster, Rideout
Sep 15	Division 1	A	Watford	3-3	Foster, Withe, McMahon
Sep 22	Division 1	H	TOTTENHAM HOTSPUR	0-1	
Sep 24	League Cup R2	A	Scunthorpe United	3-2	Kerr (2), Gibson
Sep 29	Division 1	A	Ipswich Town	0-3	
Oct 06	Division 1	H	MANCHESTER UNITED	3-0	Withe, Evans, Rideout
Oct 10	League Cup R2	H	SCUNTHORPE UNITED	3-1	Cowans, Gibson, Rideout
Oct 13	Division 1	A	Everton	1-2	Withe
Oct 20	Division 1	H	NORWICH CITY	2-2	Withe (2)
Oct 27	Division 1	A	Leicester City	0-5	
Oct 30	League Cup R3	A	QPR	0-1	
Nov 03	Division 1	H	WEST HAM UNITED	0-0	
Nov 10	Division 1	A	Arsenal	1-1	Birch
Nov 17	Division 1	H	SOUTHAMPTON	2-2	Withe, Six
Nov 24	Division 1	A	QPR	0-2	
Dec 01	Division 1	H	SUNDERLAND	1-0	Rideout
Dec 08	Division 1	A	Luton Town	0-1	
Dec 15	Division 1	H	LIVERPOOL	0-0	
Dec 22	Division 1	H	NEWCASTLE UNITED	4-0	Evans (pen), Rideout (3)
Dec 26	Division 1	A	Sheffield Wednesday	1-1	Rideout
Dec 29	Division 1	A	Nottingham Forest	2-3	Gibson, Rideout
Jan 01	Division 1	H	WEST BROMWICH ALBION	3-1	Gibson, Birch, Rideout
Jan 05	FA Cup R3	A	Liverpool	0-3	
Jan 19	Division 1	A	Coventry City	3-0	Walters (2), Rideout
Feb 02	Division 1	H	IPSWICH TOWN	2-1	Cowans, Gibson
Feb 23	Division 1	A	West Ham United	2-1	Walters, Ormsby
Mar 02	Division 1	H	LEICESTER CITY	0-1	
Mar 09	Division 1	A	Norwich City	2-2	Evans (2, pens)
Mar 13	Division 1	H	ARSENAL	0-0	

Season 1984/85 *Continued*

Mar 16	Division 1	H	EVERTON	1-1	Evans (pen)
Mar 23	Division 1	A	Manchester United	0-4	
Mar 27	Division 1	H	STOKE CITY	2-0	Berry (og), Six
Mar 30	Division 1	A	Tottenham Hotspur	2-0	Rideout, Walters
Apr 06	Division 1	H	SHEFFIELD WEDNESDAY	3-0	Rideout, Ormsby, Evans (pen)
Apr 08	Division 1	A	West Bromwich Albion	0-1	
Apr 16	Division 1	A	Chelsea	1-3	Walters
Apr 20	Division 1	A	Southampton	0-2	
Apr 24	Division 1	H	WATFORD	1-1	Walters
Apr 27	Division 1	H	QPR	5-2	Rideout (2), Withe (2), Walters
May 04	Division 1	A	Sunderland	4-0	Gibson, Walters, McMahon, Withe
May 06	Division 1	H	LUTON TOWN	0-1	
May 11	Division 1	A	Liverpool	1-2	Birch

Top Scorers League and Cup

Paul Rideout 15
Peter Withe 12
Mark Walters 10
Allan Evans / Colin Gibson 6

Season 1985/86

Aug 17	Division 1	A	Manchester United	0-4	
Aug 21	Division 1	H	LIVERPOOL	2-2	Shaw, Walters
Aug 24	Division 1	H	QPR	1-2	Walters
Aug 27	Division 1	A	Southampton	0-0	
Aug 31	Division 1	H	LUTON TOWN	3-1	Walters, Hodge, Norton
Sep 04	Division 1	A	West Bromwich Albion	3-0	Evans (pen), Daley, Walters
Sep 07	Division 1	A	Birmingham City	0-0	
Sep 14	Division 1	H	COVENTRY CITY	1-1	Hodge
Sep 21	Division 1	A	Ipswich Town	3-0	Walters, Hodge, Birch
Sep 25	League Cup R2	A	Exeter City	4-1	Stainrod (4)
Sep 28	Division 1	H	EVERTON	0-0	
Oct 05	Division 1	A	Arsenal	2-3	Stainrod, Walters
Oct 09	League Cup R2	H	EXETER CITY	8-1	Gray (2), Stainrod, Ormsby (2), Williams (2), Birch
Oct 12	Division 1	H	NOTTINGHAM FOREST	1-2	Gibson
Oct 19	Division 1	A	West Ham United	1-4	Stainrod
Oct 26	Division 1	H	NEWCASTLE UNITED	1-2	Gray
Oct 30	League Cup R3	A	Leeds United	3-0	Walters, Stainrod (2)
Nov 02	Division 1	H	OXFORD UNITED	2-0	Evans (pen), Stainrod
Nov 09	Division 1	A	Watford	1-1	Gray
Nov 16	Division 1	H	SHEFFIELD WEDNESDAY	1-1	Gibson
Nov 20	League Cup R4	H	WEST BROMWICH ALBION	2-2	Evans (pen), Stainrod
Nov 23	Division 1	A	Chelsea	1-2	Gray
Nov 27	League Cup R4r	A	West Bromwich Albion	2-1	Hodge, Walters
Nov 30	Division 1	H	TOTTENHAM HOTSPUR	1-2	Walters
Dec 07	Division 1	A	Liverpool	0-3	
Dec 14	Division 1	H	MANCHESTER UNITED	1-3	Hodge
Dec 17	Division 1	A	QPR	1-0	Birch
Dec 26	Division 1	A	Leicester City	1-3	Walters
Dec 28	Division 1	H	WEST BROMWICH ALBION	1-1	Kerr
Jan 01	Division 1	H	MANCHESTER CITY	0-1	
Jan 04	FA Cup R3	A	Portsmouth	2-2	Kerr, Birch
Jan 11	Division 1	A	Coventry City	3-3	Stainrod, Gray, Elliott
Jan 13	FA Cup R3r	H	PORTSMOUTH	3-2	Evans (pen), Stainrod 2

Season 1985/86 *Continued*

Jan 18	Division 1	A	Luton Town	0-2	
Jan 22	League Cup R5	H	ARSENAL	1-1	Glover
Jan 25	FA Cup R4	H	MILLWALL	1-1	Hodge
Jan 29	FA Cup R4r	A	Millwall	0-1	
Feb 01	Division 1	H	SOUTHAMPTON	0-0	
Feb 04	League Cup R5r	A	Arsenal	2-1	Birch, Evans
Mar 01	Division 1	A	Everton	0-2	
Mar 04	League Cup SF	H	OXFORD UNITED	2-2	Birch, Stainrod
Mar 08	Division 1	H	ARSENAL	1-4	Walters
Mar 12	League Cup SF	A	Oxford United	1-2	Walters
Mar 15	Division 1	A	Nottingham Forest	1-1	Walters
Mar 19	Division 1	H	WEST HAM UNITED	2-1	Hodge (2)
Mar 22	Division 1	H	BIRMINGHAM CITY	0-3	
Mar 29	Division 1	A	Manchester City	2-2	Hodge, Stainrod
Mar 31	Division 1	H	LEICESTER CITY	1-0	Stainrod
Apr 05	Division 1	A	Oxford United	1-1	Stainrod
Apr 09	Division 1	A	Newcastle United	2-2	Daley, Hunt
Apr 12	Division 1	H	WATFORD	4-1	Dorigo, Evans (pen), Gray, Stainrod
Apr 16	Division 1	H	IPSWICH TOWN	1-0	Hodge
Apr 19	Division 1	A	Sheffield Wednesday	0-2	
Apr 26	Division 1	H	CHELSEA	3-1	Norton, Hunt, Stainrod
May 03	Division 1	A	Tottenham Hotspur	2-4	Stainrod, Elliott

Top Scorers League and Cup

Simon Stainrod 21

Mark Walters 13

Steve Hodge 10

Andy Gray 7

Season 1986/87

Aug 23	Division 1	H	TOTTENHAM HOTSPUR	0-3	
Aug 26	Division 1	A	Wimbledon	2-3	Evans (pen), Thompson
Aug 30	Division 1	A	QPR	0-1	
Sep 03	Division 1	H	LUTON TOWN	2-1	Kerr (2)
Sep 06	Division 1	H	OXFORD UNITED	1-2	Stainrod (pen)
Sep 13	Division 1	A	Nottingham Forest	0-6	

Manager: Ron Wylie caretaker

| Sep 20 | Division 1 | H | NORWICH CITY | 1-4 | Stainrod |

Manager: Billy McNeill

Sep 24	League Cup R2	A	Reading	1-1	Hodge
Sep 27	Division 1	A	Liverpool	3-3	Hodge, Thompson, Evans (pen)
Oct 04	Division 1	A	Coventry City	1-0	Thompson
Oct 08	League Cup R2	H	READING	4-1	Hodge, Gray (2), Walters
Oct 11	Division 1	H	SOUTHAMPTON	3-1	Elliott (2), Evans (pen)
Oct 18	Division 1	A	Watford	2-4	Walters, Stainrod
Oct 25	Division 1	H	NEWCASTLE UNITED	2-0	Hodge (2)
Oct 29	League Cup R3	A	Derby County	1-1	Daley
Nov 01	Division 1	H	LEICESTER CITY	2-0	Stainrod (2)
Nov 04	League Cup R3r	H	DERBY COUNTY	2-1	Birch, Thompson
Nov 08	Division 1	A	Manchester City	1-3	Daley
Nov 12	Full Members' Cup R2	H	DERBY COUNTY	4-1	Shaw (2), Evans, Daley
Nov 15	Division 1	H	CHELSEA	0-0	
Nov 18	League Cup R4	A	Southampton	1-2	Evans (pen)
Nov 22	Division 1	A	West Ham United	1-1	Thompson
Nov 29	Division 1	H	ARSENAL	0-4	
Dec 02	Full Members' Cup R3	A	Ipswich Town	0-1	
Dec 06	Division 1	A	Sheffield Wednesday	1-2	Evans (pen)
Dec 13	Division 1	H	MANCHESTER UTD	3-3	Hodge, Thompson, Evans (pen)
Dec 20	Division 1	A	Oxford United	2-2	Thompson, Walters
Dec 26	Division 1	H	CHARLTON ATHLETIC	2-0	Birch, Daley
Dec 27	Division 1	A	Chelsea	1-4	Elliott
Jan 01	Division 1	A	Everton	0-3	
Jan 03	Division 1	H	NOTTINGHAM FOREST	0-0	

Season 1986/87 *Continued*

Jan 10	FA Cup R3	H	CHELSEA	2-2	Cooper, Hunt
Jan 21	FA Cup R3r	A	Chelsea	1-2	Hunt
Jan 24	Division 1	A	Tottenham Hotspur	0-3	
Feb 07	Division 1	H	QPR	0-1	
Feb 14	Division 1	A	Luton Town	1-2	Evans (pen)
Feb 21	Division 1	H	LIVERPOOL	2-2	Lawrenson (og), Elliott
Feb 28	Division 1	A	Norwich City	1-1	Elliott
Mar 04	Division 1	H	WIMBLEDON	0-0	
Mar 07	Division 1	A	Newcastle United	1-2	Daley
Mar 21	Division 1	A	Southampton	0-5	
Mar 25	Division 1	H	WATFORD	1-1	Hunt
Mar 28	Division 1	H	COVENTRY CITY	1-0	Birch
Apr 04	Division 1	H	MANCHESTER CITY	0-0	
Apr 11	Division 1	A	Leicester City	1-1	Walters
Apr 18	Division 1	H	EVERTON	0-1	
Apr 20	Division 1	A	Charlton Athletic	0-3	
Apr 25	Division 1	H	WEST HAM UNITED	4-0	Hunt, Aspinall (2), Stainrod
May 02	Division 1	A	Arsenal	1-2	Aspinall
May 04	Division 1	H	SHEFFIELD WEDNESDAY	1-2	Robinson

Manager: Frank Upton caretaker

| May 09 | Division 1 | A | Manchester United | 1-3 | Birch |

Top Scorers League and Cup

| Allan Evans 8 |
| Garry Thompson 7 |
| Simon Stainrod 6 |
| Paul Elliott 5 |

Season 1987/88

Aug 15	Division 2	A	Ipswich Town	1-1	O'Donnell (og)
Aug 22	Division 2	H	BIRMINGHAM CITY	0-2	
Aug 29	Division 2	A	Hull City	1-2	Aspinall (pen)
Aug 31	Division 2	H	MANCHESTER CITY	1-1	Gage
Sep 05	Division 2	A	Leicester City	2-0	Walters, Lillis
Sep 08	Division 2	H	MIDDLESBROUGH	0-1	
Sep 12	Division 2	H	BARNSLEY	0-0	
Sep 16	Division 2	A	West Bromwich Albion	2-0	Aspinall (2)
Sep 19	Division 2	A	Huddersfield Town	0-1	S. Hunt
Sep 23	League Cup R2	A	Middlesbrough	1-0	Aspinall
Sep 26	Division 2	H	SHEFFIELD UNITED	1-1	Gage
Sep 30	Division 2	H	BLACKBURN ROVERS	1-1	Aspinall
Oct 03	Division 2	A	Plymouth Argyle	3-1	Walters (2), Lillis
Oct 07	League Cup R2	H	MIDDLESBROUGH	1-0	Birch
Oct 10	Division 2	A	Leeds United	3-1	Rennie (og), Aspinall (2)
Oct 17	Division 2	H	AFC BOURNEMOUTH	1-1	Walters
Oct 21	Division 2	H	CRYSTAL PALACE	4-1	Walters (3, 1 pen,) S. Hunt
Oct 24	Division 2	A	Stoke City	0-0	
Oct 28	League Cup R3	H	TOTTENHAM HOTSPUR	2-1	McInally, Aspinall
Oct 31	Division 2	H	READING	2-1	Blair, Lillis
Nov 03	Division 2	A	Shrewsbury Town	2-1	Keown, Aspinall
Nov 07	Division 2	H	MILLWALL	1-2	Keown
Nov 11	Full Members' Cup R1	H	BRADFORD CITY	0-5	
Nov 14	Division 2	A	Oldham Athletic	1-0	McInally
Nov 18	League Cup R4	H	SHEFFIELD WEDNESDAY	1-2	Thompson
Nov 28	Division 2	A	Bradford City	4-2	S. Gray (2), Birch, Thompson
Dec 05	Division 2	H	SWINDON TOWN	2-1	Thompson (2)
Dec 12	Division 2	A	Birmingham City	2-1	Thompson (2)
Dec 18	Division 2	H	WEST BROMWICH ALBION	0-0	
Dec 26	Division 2	A	Sheffield United	1-1	Thompson
Dec 28	Division 2	H	HUDDERSFIELD TOWN	1-1	Birch
Jan 01	Division 2	H	HULL CITY	5-0	S. Gray, Aspinall (2), A. Gray, McInally
Jan 02	Division 2	A	Barnsley	3-1	Aspinall, Birch, McInally

Season 1987/88 *Continued*

Jan 09	FA Cup R3	A	Leeds United	2-1	McInally, A. Gray
Jan 16	Division 2	H	IPSWICH TOWN	1-0	Keown
Jan 23	Division 2	A	Manchester City	2-0	Daley, Thompson
Jan 31	FA Cup R4	H	LIVERPOOL	0-2	
Feb 06	Division 2	H	LEICESTER CITY	2-1	Lillis, Evans
Feb 14	Division 2	A	Middlesbrough	1-2	Daley
Feb 20	Division 2	A	Blackburn Rovers	2-3	Platt, Thompson
Feb 27	Division 2	H	PLYMOUTH ARGYLE	5-2	S. Gray (pen), Platt, Birch (2), Thompson
Mar 05	Division 2	A	AFC Bournemouth	2-1	Daley, Platt
Mar 12	Division 2	H	LEEDS UNITED	1-2	McInally
Mar 19	Division 2	A	Reading	2-0	Birch, Thompson
Mar 26	Division 2	H	STOKE CITY	0-1	
Apr 02	Division 2	A	Millwall	1-2	Thompson
Apr 04	Division 2	H	OLDHAM ATHLETIC	1-2	S. Gray
Apr 09	Division 2	A	Crystal Palace	1-1	Platt
Apr 23	Division 2	H	SHREWSBURY TOWN	1-0	Aspinall
May 02	Division 2	H	BRADFORD CITY	1-0	Platt
May 07	Division 2	A	Swindon Town	0-0	

Top Scorers League and Cup

Warren Aspinall 13
Garry Thompson 12
Mark Walters / Paul Birch 7

Aston Villa: Seasons 1968–90

Season	Manager	Division	Pos	FA Cup	League Cup	Europe
1968/69	T. Docherty	Second	18/22	5th Rnd	2nd Rnd	N/A
1969/70	T. Docherty	Second	21/22	R 3rd Rnd	2nd Rnd	N/A
1970/71	V. Crowe	Third	4/24	1st Rnd	FINAL	N/A
1971/72	V. Crowe	Third	1/24 P	1st Rnd	4th Rnd	N/A
1972/73	V. Crowe	Second	3/22	3rd Rnd	3rd Rnd	N/A

From the following season three teams were promoted!

Season	Manager	Division	Pos	FA Cup	League Cup	Europe
1973/74	V. Crowe	Second	14/22	5th Rnd	2nd Rnd	N/A
1974/75	R. Saunders	Second	2/22 P	5th Rnd	WINNERS	N/A
1975/76	R. Saunders	First	16/22	3rd Rnd	3rd Rnd	UEFA 1st Rnd

Lost 5-1 on agg. to Antwerp 4-1, 0-1

Season	Manager	Division	Pos	FA Cup	League Cup	Europe
1976/77	R. Saunders	First	4/22	Quarters	WINNERS	N/A

6pts behind champions Liverpool; highest scorers, 14+ Liverpool;

lost 2-1 at eventual winners Man Utd in FA Cup

Season	Manager	Division	Pos	FA Cup	League Cup	Europe
1977/78	R. Saunders	First	8/22	3rd Rnd	4th Rnd	UEFA Quarters

Lost 4-3 on agg. to Barcelona in UEFA Cup 2-2, 2-1

Season	Manager	Division	Pos	FA Cup	League Cup	Europe
1978/79	R. Saunders	First	8/22	3rd Rnd	4th Rnd	N/A
1979/80	R. Saunders	First	7/22	Quarters	3rd Rnd	N/A
1980/81	R. Saunders	First	1/22	3rd Rnd	3rd Rnd	N/A

Lost 2-1 at Div. 2 Cambridge in League Cup in September; Lost to Ipswich in the FA Cup

Season	Manager	Division	Pos	FA Cup	League Cup	Europe
1981/82	R. Saunders	First	11/22	5th Rnd	Quarters	EURO Winners

Lost 1-0 at home to WBA in League Cup; Lost 1-0 at Tottenham in FA Cup

1982/83	T. Barton	First	6/22	Quarters	2nd Rnd	EURO Quarters

3pts off second Watford, 14pts off Liverpool; Lost 2-0 at Arsenal in FA Cup

1983/84	T. Barton	First	10/22	3rd Rnd	Semis	UEFA 2nd Rnd

3pts off sixth Arsenal, 20pts off Liverpool 1st

1984/85	G. Turner	First	10/22	3rd Rnd	3rd Rnd	N/A

8pts behind ninth Forest

1985/86	G. Turner	First	16/22	4th Rnd	Semis	N/A

3pts above relegation half the points of champions Liverpool - 88pts

1986/87	Turner/McNeill	First	22/22 R	3rd Rnd	4th Rnd	N/A

8pts off safety, McNeill's Man City finished second-bottom

1987/88	G. Taylor	Second	2/23 P	4th Rnd	4th Rnd	N/A

1pt above fifth-placed Blackburn

1988/89	G. Taylor	First	17/20	4th Rnd	Quarters	N/A

1pt above drop zone; 2pts above second-bottom West Ham

1989/90	G. Taylor	First	2/20	Quarters	3rd Rnd	N/A

9pts behind Liverpool but 7 pts ahead of Tottenham

Acknowledgements

THIS BOOK COULD NEVER HAVE BEEN WRITTEN WITHOUT THE generous time and contributions of the following interviewees, some more than others, such as the Holte End's own Andy Gray for his terrifically candid interview and his foreword that helped to set the scene to this book.

Ron Saunders and Sir Doug Ellis are undoubtedly the two most important protagonists throughout this era in Aston Villa's history and I am delighted to have been able to secure their stories from behind the scenes through the years. I give special thanks to the Saunders family who were particularly helpful and honest at a difficult time for the family. I hope readers will agree their transparency and memories reveal a fascinating passage through his time with the club but especially around the time leading up to his mysterious exit out of Villa Park.

I am grateful, too, for the time offered by Sir Doug Ellis and his personal assistant Marion. They recognized the importance of my endeavour to detail this key generation in Aston Villa's history like never before, and kindly invited me round Mr Ellis's house for my interview; there were many emails also that Marion with the help of Mr Ellis always responded to.

The feedback of former Club Secretaries Alan Bennett and Steve Stride has also been very much appreciated as, collectively, those two gentlemen witnessed every event to occur inside Aston Villa Football Club from 1969 to 2007.

I would like to thank the family of the late Tony Barton, whose part in this story is significant. Due to his premature death I relied on his son Chris and his wife Rose to shed much light on his time with Villa, which they did and more.

They were kind enough to allow me into their home and pass on family secrets from Tony's years with Villa.

I also want to thank my publisher deCoubertin – especially James, Simon and Megan – for their interest and faith in this story and for their ongoing support throughout the journey.

Huge thanks also goes out to the following interviewees, who were mostly former players, managers and officials: Charlie Aitken, Warren Aspinall, Ron Atkinson, John Barnwell, Chris Barton, Rose Barton, Alan Bennett, Dave Bennett, Andy Blair, Noel Blake, Tony Book, Des Bremner, Tony 'Bomber' Brown, Keith Burkinshaw, Harry Burrows, Terry Butcher, Willie Carr, Frank Carrodus, Wayne Clarke, Gordon Cowans, Jim Cumbes, Mervyn Day, John Deehan, Terry Donovan, Tony Dorigo, Paul Elliott, Sir Doug Ellis, Allan Evans, Jake Findlay, Maurice Freil, Colin Gibson, John Gidman, Andy Gray, Ray Graydon, Harry Gregg, Pat Heard, Steve Hodge, Steve Hunt, the late Harry Kartz, Martin Keown, Mark Lawrenson, Gordon Lee, Brian Little, Don Masson, John McGovern, Steve McMahon, Ken McNaught, Gordon Milne, Tony Morley, Dennis Mortimer, Terry Neill, Chris Nicholl, Mike Pejic, Leighton Phillips, David Pleat, John Richards, Jimmy Rimmer, Neil Rioch, Alastair Robertson, Ron Saunders, Ronnie Saunders Jr., Gary Shaw, Alan Smith ex-Leicester & Arsenal, Alan Smith ex-Villa Director, Graeme Souness, Nigel Spink, Steve Stride, Dave Stringer, Kenny Swain, Garry Thompson, Phil Thompson, Graham Turner, Peter White, the late Ray Wilkins, Gary Williams, Mike Wiseman, Peter Withe, Stephen Withe, Willie Young. Apologies if I missed anyone.

For a boy who stood on the Holte End for years and then later became friendly with some of these guys, I feel privileged to have written this book and I hope readers recognise the authenticity. There is no bias intended, what happened has happened and it is up to the readers to interpret this bizarre period in Villa's history as they prefer.

References

THE FOLLOWING SOURCES WERE USED FOR EITHER RESEARCH purposes or minimal quotation. I must single out The English National Football Archive website www.enfa.co.uk above all for being an invaluable information source helping me to check on all kinds of things, whether team selections, scores, scorers and more. Thank you Tony at ENFA for your assistance.

Aston Villa: Friendlies, Tours & Testimonials,
by Bryan Sheppard, YORE PUBLICATIONS, 2012

Billy McNeil: The Autobiography: Hail Cesar,
HEADLINE BOOK PUBLISHING, 2004

Budgie: The Autobiography of Goalkeeping Legend John Burridge,
JOHN BLAKE PUBLISHING LTD., 2013

Deadly Doug: Behind The Scenes at Aston Villa FC – Doug Ellis,
JOHN BLAKE PUBLISHING LTD., 2005

The Doc: My Story, by Tommy Docherty,
HEADLINE, 2007

The English National Football Archive ENFA
WEBSITE WWW.ENFA.CO.UK

Gray Matters: Andy Gray, The Autobiography,
PAN MACMILLAN, 2004

Ron Saunders' Aston Villa Scrapbook,
SOUVENIR PRESS LTD, 1981

The Scotsman newspaper,
for a brief quote with Alex Cropley, 2012

Settling the Bill, Memories of Bill Dugdale,
ENDEAVOUR LONDON LTD., 2011

Stride Inside the Villa – Steve Stride,
SPORTS PROJECTS, 1997

Wikipedia *various references*

Index

deCoubertin
B O O K S

www.decoubertin.co.uk